Changing People Changing Dogs

positive solutions for difficult dogs

Dee Ganley CPDT, CABC, CDBC

Edited by Christina Bond

Revised Edition edited by Debra Theriault

First published in 2006 by

Learning About Dogs Limited
PO Box 13, Chipping Campden, Glos, GL55 6WX, UK

Revised Edition published in April, 2008 by

DeesDogs
PO BOX 19, East Andover, New Hampshire, USA 03231

Cover photo: by Kevin Ganley.

Dee working with Tucker, Abby (Mini Poodle waiting her turn), Rufus (learning to wait for his turn) and Dazzle (lying down patiently).

CONTENTS

DEDICATION

To each and every one of the two and four-footed friends who have crossed my path and taught me so much, I dedicate this book. I know I am a better person - more just, more open minded, kinder, and certainly happier - because of the friendships I've had with all of you.

I can't wait to see what tomorrow brings.

SPECIAL THANKS

To my husband, Kevin, and daughter, Kim, for your continuing support and encouragement over the years and for allowing me the freedom to spend so much time helping others and their wonderful dogs. Thank you both.

To my good friend, Nancy Lyon, for all your help proofreading my written thoughts and for your continued support and guidance. The endless talks we've had about who dogs are and how we can help others develop their relationships with their dogs are treasures today and always.

Thanks to Shirley and Skye, whom I pictured in my mind while writing this book. You two were my inspiration from afar. Continue your journey together always.

Thank you, Tomie, for the kind words; it has been my pleasure to work with you and Bronté. Continued success on your journey together.

Christina, thank you for your thoughts and your tireless efforts editing the first edition of this book. I believe we are two kindred spirits who love dogs from deep within.

Debra what can I say ... the revision never would have happened if you hadn't taken the time and huge effort. The book looks fantastic with all the new pictures and editing. You are the best ...Thank You

"Thank You" seems so trivial compared to what so many have contributed in helping me bring "Changing People Changing Dogs" to others.

~Dee

Foreward by Carolyn Clark

I had heard of Dee Ganley for years before I actually met her at a workshop and had the privilege of working with her wonderful miniature poodle. Reading her articles, seeing her class set up, visiting the training center in New Hampshire, observing her at seminars, I know Dee understands and "reads" dogs. She understands and "reads" people too. When I heard she was writing a book I was delighted. This manual has been worth the wait! Dee's compassion, care and respect for both dogs and people are clear throughout. Her knowledge and experience shine through.

In the course of her career as a teacher of dog classes, training director at an animal shelter and consultant for owners of re-homed dogs, Dee has refined gentle, simple, effective techniques and methods. Helping owners change their perspectives and behavior is the first step in helping dogs change behavior. This book is an excellent guide.

Technically, "Changing People Changing Dogs" is well laid out, well illustrated and clearly written. It is easy to read.   Dog behavior, Learning Theory, Tools and Techniques are described clearly. The chapter of case studies explains the previous information in a practical way.

A good third of the book is an appendix giving step by step detailed and clearly explained instructions for numerous exercises. Two of the self-control exercises that I use with clients almost daily are the Settle: Relaxed Down on Lead, and the "Find It Game".

Thank you Dee!

Owners, Trainers, Class Instructors and Pet Behavior Counselors will all find something useful in this excellent manual.

Carolyn Clark, M.A.
Director
Centre for Applied Canine Behavior
Carolark: Teaching Families and Pets

MEET DEE GANLEY

I am one of those people who find joy and solace being with dogs. I am happiest in their company and proud to have their trust. I have experienced the deeply civilized "conversations" that flow between well trained dogs and their handlers. I know that I am a happier and better person because of the relationhips I have shared with my dogs.

The training and behavioral work I do with the public and shelter community is about how to achieve two goals: Getting behavior we want and getting rid of behavior we don't want, humanely and while having fun! I teach using positive reinforcement and I place a very strong emphasis on managing a dog's environment for safety.

"Loving" our dogs does not create trustworthy companions. Commitment by a dog to his people is the result of humane training and diligent management. It happens when we wholly accept the responsibility to lead, but not to dominate. Humane leadership allows the dog's capacity to think and feel to be used for learning rather than defense and avoidance.

Over the years, the dogs and people I have helped have returned the favor one hundred fold. They have taught me that learning and teaching is about "calm attentiveness". Fixing problems starts with paying attention - quietly, openly and always positively. Learning this, I have become much more relaxed, calm and decisive in my interactions with dogs. I have learned that you get attention when you give attention. Working effectively with dogs means communication starts with calm, attentive observation. Wonderfully, this way of listening with your eyes and your heart as well as your ears becomes a way of life and spills over into everything.

For 25 years I taught training classes and advised individuals on how to create positive partnerships with their dogs. In the mid-1990's I began sharing positive reinforcement training with the deeply committed people working in the shelter world. From 1998-2004 I was the Training and Behavior Manager for the Upper Valley Humane Society in Enfield, New Hampshire. My single most important goal was to create a shelter and training program that taught the dogs self-control skills. I worked with the staff, volunteers and the public, helping them use positive reinforcement to change rude and unruly dogs into agreeable family members. Shelter dogs have shown me that self-control skills are at the heart of a succesful adoption. For these dogs, self-control literally meant the difference between life and death.

Today, I am back in private practice, which now includes traveling to many wonderful places helping shelters, rescues, or folks who want to learn my practical, humane techniques to help our dogs and ourselves become friends and partners for life.

Certainly much of what I share with you in this book comes from many fine authors I have read and trainers I have known. I am deeply grateful for their insights. Most of all, it is the dogs who who helped me write this book. They have shown me their astonishing capacity to change when we are wise enough to reinforce them for trying.

Dee Ganley CPDT, CABC, CDBC

AUDIENCE AND PURPOSE

Changing aggressive, fearful, destructive and rude behavior means changing the dog's emotional view of the world around him. This is the challenge we will explore in this book.

This book is for those of you who want to make changes in the lives of your dogs, or help your clients' dogs by finding ways to live in peace and harmony - together.

In the recent history of animal training, the science of operant conditioning has been applied to dog training by some visionary people - Karen Pryor, Gary Wilkes, Bob and Marian Bailey, Donna Duford, Pia Silvani, Kay Laurence and of course many others. These people have shown us we can foster the best in dogs and the handler by using positive reinforcement, good management and timeouts, rather than punishment. Science supports our feeling that training need not include compulsion or physical punishment to be successful and fun.

You have already figured out that there is no "good dog" switch, or you wouldn't be reading this book right now. But positive reinforcement and good management are the next best tools! They really work. Training positively is a lot of fun and it fosters the kind of humane relationship we all want with our dogs. Changing behavior may also mean changing the dog's emotional view of the world he lives in. So, in addition to positive reinforcement training, we'll add classical conditioning and desensitization techniques. And you'll always have your eye on how to manage the dog's environment for success. You'll work hard to be sure you don't put your dog in a place where he can make a mistake.

Positive reinforcement training gives us amazing training opportunities once you start thinking creatively. Training this way gets you to notice your dog's behavior, which gets you thinking of all sorts of things you can teach your dog. One busy trainer taught the family dog (a high-energy type who desperately needed a job to do) to run around the house picking up dirty clothing and deposit it in the laundry room hamper. This elegant solution solved the problem of a dog who was going crazy with boredom, in a house where keeping up with the kids' tendency to drop things all over was driving their mother crazy with frustration.

In Changing People Changing Dogs you'll learn practical ways to effectively combine positive reinforcement training with classical conditioning and desensitisation. Through good management and proper reinforcement, you will increase the behaviors you want and extinguish behaviors you do not want. You will learn to lead but not to dominate.

Specifically, this book will help dog handlers and trainers to:

◆ Learn to identify the triggers of reactive behavior, which vary for different dogs.

◆ Learn counterconditioning, to desensitize dogs to scary stimulus.

◆ Learn positive reinforcement strategies to teach new, acceptable behaviors that will replace unacceptable behaviors.

The exercises (see Appendix A) in this book are designed to help the dog learn self-control. A dog with self-control can watch the world without reacting. Self-control is the only path to good choices. These exercises use positive reinforcement, a training approach based on the science of classical and operant conditioning. (Classical and operant conditioning are a set of scientific principles that explain what motivates an animal to change his behavior.)

Training dogs to live successfully with people always includes behavior modification. The more fearful or aggressive a dog is, the more likely you will have to make a serious investment of time, effort and commitment. Extraordinary progress is often possible as people and dogs change, learn and grow together. Certainly your efforts can improve your dog's chance for a calmer, happier life. What will astonish you is how this process can change you profoundly as well.

This program includes the following components:

OWNER/HANDLER EDUCATION

◆ Observation skills

◆ Canine communication

MANAGEMENT

◆ Managing the dog's environment and lifestyle

◆ Planning for success

REWARD-BASED LEARNING

◆ A relationship of reinforcement from the handler to increase desirable behavior and decrease undesirable behavior

CHANGING THE DOG'S RESPONSE TO SCARY STIMULUS

◆ Self-control

◆ Relaxation through touch, massage and specific exercises

◆ Counterconditioning

If you are reading this book as the owner of a dog who needs help learning how to live a calmer, less fearful life, then let me assure you that these exercises have all been used successfully by folks just like you. If possible, find a positive reinforcement trainer to help you because an additional objective and experienced guide and cheerleader on your side is always useful.

If you are a dog trainer/behavior consultant hired to help an owner work with their difficult dog, you must have qualifications and expertise in evaluating, managing and modifying a wide range of challenging canine behaviors. There is no substitute for the experience that comes with handling hundreds of dogs - like the pilot who must have a minimum of "flight hours". Consider finding a local shelter and start working with the shelter dogs. Become an attentive observer and they will teach you much!

For the trainer/behavior consultant, during the initial consultation process you will take a detailed history of the dog's behavior problems. You will also observe the dog's behavior and the interaction of the dog with family members. You will work with the family to set goals and then implement a plan to modify the dog's behavior.

To help build and strengthen relationships between the human and canine members of a household, you must emphasize prevention of behavior problems. You will need to create an atmosphere where all members of the household can learn and practice positive reinforcement techniques.

You will then follow up when needed by telephone or e-mail to monitor the dog's progress. Depending on the family's needs, you may offer ongoing support for training and behavior modification.

Throughout this book the person initiating the training,
management and rehabilitation will be referred to as
the "handler" who may or may not also
be the owner of the dog.

1 Communication

Listening is the better part of communication. Listening to a dog means calm attentive observation of that dog's body - both the parts and the whole. You will need to learn how to observe the microsecond to microsecond changes in your dog's body postures and learn to use these observations to interpret what your dog is feeling and what he intends to do about these feelings.

This chapter describes how to observe and learn to interpret canine body postures. To know how to change behavior you have to be PROACTIVE not reactive. That means you will have to understand what your dog is feeling and saying to you in the only way he can - with his body.

CANINE COMMUNICATION

As we know, dogs are social animals. Although most dogs enjoy social contact with their own species, they often have most of their social interaction with people. Dogs learn to comprehend and understand human body language but come hardwired with a complex dog-to-dog body language. This should be no surprise, yet we are often slow to learn what they are saying.

To enable them to live in social groups, dogs have developed complex communication skills. These skills allow dogs to interact safely and work cooperatively. Dogs use body postures to assert themselves or to defuse difficult or conflicting situations thereby avoiding the risk of injury to themselves and others. Unfortunately dogs raised with little or no exposure to other dogs often lack the basic dog-to-dog communication skills that help them avoid overt aggression with other dogs. Canine communication skills are learned through appropriate interaction with other dogs skilled in play and other activities particularly during critical puppy development periods. This is known as socialization. Where socialization is inadequate or inappropriate, a puppy can grow up without the ability to recognize and respond appropriately using canine communication signals.

Science has only recently become aware of canine communication signals. Marc Bekoff, an ethologist at the University of Colorado, was able to show after a decade of painstaking observation and analysis that canine play is actually a complex social interaction in which the participants constantly signal their intentions and check to make sure their behavior is being correctly interpreted. Dogs that exhibit inappropriate behavior, for example, by signaling play then delivering a harsh bite tend to be ostracized. For a social animal, being ostracized is highly aversive, therefore socially inappropriate behavior is unlikely to be repeated.

Communication comes through all five senses. The importance of each of the five senses varies in different species.

People prefer to communicate with verbal language (what we say and hear). Communication through language consists of content, volume, tone and emphasis. People can also communicate visually through body language, such as gestures of face, hands, shoulders and posture, to varying degrees. People can even communicate through scent; we are often only aware of the obvious smells but some of the more subtle odors affect our responses at a primal level.

Dogs communicate primarily through body language and also through other senses such as scent, touch and vocal communication. Dogs use scent in association with and in the absence of visual contact. They often use the tongue to communicate through touch. Although the importance of vocal communication for dogs is minimal, they do use vocalization to express loneliness (howl), to alert the group (bark) or to express fear or pain (yelp).

RECOGNIZING SIGNALS

When working with dogs, understanding canine communication is essential. Misunderstanding often arises between people and dogs when a social signal is misinterpreted. To people, a smile (showing the teeth, contraction of specific facial muscles that cause the corners of the mouth to turn upward and the eyes to crinkle) is interpreted as happiness. Humans can distinguish a smile from a grimace or angry expression. To dogs, a "smile" or showing of the teeth is an appeasement gesture when made in conjunction with lowered posture and wriggling. When in conjunction with other body language, such as raised posture and stiffness, showing the teeth can be a warning.

To live together, interact safely and work cooperatively, both humans and dogs need to learn to communicate with each other. Dogs learn to observe and understand that a human smile means something different than a canine smile. People need to observe and learn that a canine smile can mean either a warning or appeasement but that it is not particularly an expression of happiness as it is with our fellow humans.

Canine communication can be learned by watching dogs interact with a range of different dogs in many different situations as well as by watching lone dogs react to a range of different stimuli such as other animals or new environments. We can only interpret what canine communication signals mean by observing and analyzing subsequent behavior.

For example, if a dog stands in a particular way when hearing a sound, we can interpret the "way" he stands by observing the subsequent behavior. If the dog runs away from the sound, we can interpret his position when he showed his alertness to the sound as fearfulness. If he runs towards the sound, we could interpret the alertness to the sound as confidence or security. The "way" a dog stands, sits or moves is a complex collection of small postures of different body parts. A single body part does not provide enough information to interpret the dog's emotion. Each body part - ears, eyes, mouth, tail, top line (outline of the back) and balance - can indicate different emotions depending on the position of other body parts. This collection provides the whole picture.

A waving tail can indicate a dog responding with contentment or an unsure dog. However, the waving tail must be viewed in context with the whole dog: Is the dog tense? Is the dog leaning backward or forward? Are the ears pinned back or relaxed? Is the dog up on his toes?

Learning canine communication can be a lifelong process. If you want to really understand dogs, every opportunity to practice must be taken - dog watching can be fascinating!

Dogs use appeasement behavior, also known as calming signals to defuse stressful situations. Calming signals reduce the arousal level of other dogs. Calming signals out of context can be a clue to behavioral problems. To build your understanding of calming signals and how they are used, observe the dog's behaviors and make note of the results of those behaviors on other dogs.

Calming signals include:

▶ Turning the head away or averting the eyes.

▶ Turning completely away.

▶ Sniffing at the ground.

- ▶ Quick (often lizard-like) licking of the lips.

- ▶ Freezing in place.

- ▶ Moving excruciatingly slowly.

- ▶ Sitting or laying down.

- ▶ Play-bow position.

- ▶ Yawning.

People can learn to employ human versions of calming signals (such a shame we don't have tails!). Practice with a range of dogs in safe situations and discover if you can change a dog's behavior by using calming signals when the dog is stressed.

OBSERVATION

Dogs generally bite only as a last resort to protect themselves and their resources. Frequently they bite because we failed to observe earlier warning signs or because we punished them for growling. Growling is a dog's attempt to tell us how they feel about what we are doing. Dogs punished for growling may learn to suppress a very important means of communication.

Aggression is a dog's natural weapon against what he perceives as a threat. Helping a dog overcome fears (of other dogs, people, thunder, etc.) requires the ability to read the early signs of distress and defuse the situation. Through attentive observation, you can learn to "read" your dog and be ready to reinforce acceptable reactions and circumvent unacceptable reactions. So, if your dog growls, instead of punishing him, step back and think about how you can change how he feels about what is happening around him. If you punish a dog for growling instead of finding a way to redirect his attention and understand his feelings, he might just bite you! In this case, you forced the dog to act aggressively because you took away his ability to growl and communicate his distress.

Most dogs respond to canine communication signals. It is our responsibility to learn their language and help them become accustomed to the body language of humans. There are a number of canine rules of etiquette that cause grave misunderstandings between humans and dogs. Often when we are trying to say one thing, our dogs may interpret it as something else entirely. Some things that are polite behavior for humans are rude and threatening to dogs. When working with troubled dogs, it is often wise to avoid giving physical signals that a dog might misinterpret.

EYE CONTACT

For humans, it is considered polite to make direct eye contact when speaking to each other. For dogs, direct eye contact is confrontational. A fearful dog may feel threatened if you look him in the eye. If a dog feels threatened, he may feel compelled to respond to the threat. For a shy dog, eye contact may cause retreat. For a dog that believes aggression is his only option, eye contact might cause a confrontation. If you remove the eye contact, you remove the threat and the dog may not feel compelled to take action.

PERSONAL SPACE

Another misunderstood signal is patting dogs on the head or even worse, invading the dog's space by hugging him or pounding on his ribcage. Accepting petting and hugging is unnatural for the canine species. Dogs need to learn gradually about petting and hugging through positive associations.

Depending on the dog's history, petting and hugging may cause the dog either to move away or move into the contact. Dogs display obvious responses to physical contact unless they have been so corrected that they stifle their responses. Dogs with stifled responses can present a higher risk because the result can be an explosive response with no perceptible warning.

Children love to hug dogs like a stuffed toy. This can be dangerous for children, so parents must remind children that dogs find this to be rude and dog owners should protect their dog against inappropriate actions of children. Ask the child to think about how he feels when Uncle Harry comes to visit, squeezes his cheeks and hugs him for too long. He doesn't like it and most dogs don't either.

A dog can perceive reaching out your hand to introduce yourself as invasive and aggressive. Instead, stand upright, eyes averted and let the dog come to you. Keep your hand to your side. Standing sideways to the dog is a calming signal that allows the dog to approach you when he feels comfortable doing so.

When one dog wants to dominate another dog, he puts his head and neck over the neck or back of the other dog. When we bend over to greet a dog, the dog's natural response is to back away. When approaching a dog, stand upright and relaxed. If you have to get lower to pat a dog, bend at the knees keeping your body straight.

Do not lean over a dog when you have called him to you. Doing so will push the dog away from you, rather than encouraging him to come close to sit. Some dogs find being leaned over to be aversive and may percieve it as punishment for coming when called.

STRESS

Stress is dynamic. It changes from moment to moment and with each new situation. Levels of stress can vary dramatically from dog to dog and situation to situation. Not all stress is counterproductive however. Small amounts of stress can enhance awareness and performance.

Dogs that require behavior modification generally display stress to some degree. Identifying signs of stress will provide a means to measure progress. Identify what is triggering the stress and solutions to alleviate it.

The context is an important clue to whether the behavior is stress related or due to another stimulus. Stress signals can be indicative of other concerns such as a medical problem. Stress signals can also be learned behavior or a breed-specific trait. Familiarize yourself with the normal body carriage of the breed with which you are working, as well as the learning history of the particular dog.

The dog's body will tell you what he is feeling. When a dog is stressed, he will go through a series of easily observable behaviors. The first signs of stress can be as subtle as increased respiration or tension around the eyes. As stress progresses, the dog may try to avoid the situation (by looking away, or turning his back). If that doesn't work, then he may try to escape (by running or dodging). If he can't escape, he might just freeze. If you are paying attention, you can relieve the pressure by moving away so that he won't have to growl, bark or bite.

Dogs that react aggressively may have learned that subtle signals don't work, so they react with overt aggression. Such dogs are often called unpredictable. If the dog had been carefully observed, subtle changes in behavior would have revealed that he was under pressure and feeling stressed.

MILD STRESS - Body postures showing mild stress typically include:

▶ Lip licking.

▶ Shaking. You may see a full body shake when the dog is not wet.

▶ Yawning. Full body stretch with or without a yawn. Yawning is one of the most common signs of stress. Stress-related yawns will be more intense than "sleepy" yawns and accompanied with a squeak. The dog may be in an excited, as opposed to relaxed, state.

▶ Drooling. Drooling in the absence of a mouth injury or in anticipation of food usually indicates stress.

▶ Stretching. Stretching is a way to relax the muscles that tense from stress. This type of stretching is not related to sleeping or from staying in one position for a long period of time.

▶ Sweaty paws. Dogs can get sweaty paws when stressed in the same manner that people get sweaty palms. This reaction is often visible on hardwood floors or on metal examination or grooming tables.

▶ Mouthiness. This may range from gentle mouthing to snapping or biting.

MODERATE STRESS - Body postures showing moderate stress typically include:

▶ Wrinkled brows.

▶ Enlarged facial blood vessels.

▶ Dilated pupils.

▶ Rapid shallow or deep forceful panting. Panting with deep respirations and a relaxed tongue is normal for dogs that have been exercising or are hot. If panting is out of context (not due to exercise or heat) the dog may be stressed. When a stressed dog pants, the lips will be pulled back in a wide grimmace, causing furrows in the skin under the eyes and on the forehead. The tongue may be tense.

▶ Whining. Whining can be a result of anxiety or excitability.

EXTREME STRESS

Body postures showing extreme stress typically include:

▶ "Whale eye" (when the white of the eye is visible).

▶ Tail tucked.

▶ Ears plastered back.

▶ Body trembling or shivering. Many dogs will shiver when under stress. If the dog is not cold, consider stress as a cause. Shivering can also indicate high levels of anticipation (good stress). For example, the dog may shiver with excitement before going for a walk.

▶ Crouching or low body carriage. Dogs that move low to the ground are often exhibiting stress.

▶ Arching the back.

▶ Stiffness. Tension can create stiff gait and tail movement.

▶ Shrinking away from being touched.

▶ Excessive panting and drooling.

RESULTS OF STRESS

Stress can lead to a myriad of physical and behavioral issues, including:

▶ Excessive grooming. A dog that constantly licks himself may be showing signs of stress. Common sites for excessively licking are paws, legs, flanks and genital areas.

▶ Excessive sleeping. Every dog has a different energy level, so excessive sleeping may be difficult to recognize. This can be a sign of serotonin depletion and other chemical imbalances due to chronic stress.

▶ Excessive thirst. Increased drinking without a medical or exercise-related cause. This could be a sign of redirected frustration or an obsessive disorder.

▶ Increased frequency of urination or defecation. A stressed body will try to force fluids out of the system. Some "house training" issues are stress related. Inappropriate spontaneous voiding is an indicator of extreme stress. For example, dogs in a training class may need to "go pee" more often than is normal. This could be an indicator of a continuous low level of stress throughout the class.

▶ Lack of focus or attention. If the dog fails to respond to established cues, he may be distracted by a stimulus (such as a squirrel) or he may be stressed. When stressed, the dog is not ignoring the cue; he simply cannot respond. He may hear perfectly well, but his mind is unable to process the information.

▶ Confusion. Strange, abnormal or confused behavior can be the result of stress. Exercise caution when interpreting this behavior. It can also indicate a medical problem like a seizure or diabetic emergency.

▶ Hyperactivity. Stress may trigger a defense mechanism that can look frantic. Often this is interpreted as the dog defying the owner or "fooling around". The dog will eventually shut down when his system is depleted of adrenaline and other stress-related chemicals.

▶ Immune System Disorder. Stress lowers the immune system response to diseases and allergies.

▶ Self-mutilation. Tail chewing, paw licking and chewing or sucking on the flank to the point of causing open sores or wounds may be signs of stress. These behaviors may also have medical origins, such as allergic reactions.

▶ Vomiting and/or diarrhea. The digestive system is often the first system to react to stress. Dogs that normally take food, may refuse food when stressed. Their stomach has "shut down" and they simply cannot digest food.

RESPONSE TO STRESS

When under stress, a dog may respond by one or more of the following:

▶ Freeze - The dog may stand still, either not moving or moving in a slow and deliberate manner. A freeze can be a precursor to an attack, so heed this signal.

▶ Escape or Avoidance - The dog may turn away, shut down or run and dodge from the handler. If the dog is restrained, he may lunge to the end of the lead in an attempt to escape.

▶ Fight - The dog may growl or show his teeth and then air snap. This may escalate to a grab at the clothing or to an inhibited bite. If that didn't work, there may be a hard bite or multiple bites. Some dogs, in some instances, may skip the precursors and go straight to a hard bite.

If one action fails to relieve the stressful situation, the dog may try a different action.

UNDERSTANDING AGGRESSION

Aggression is a normal survival mechanism for all animals.

Aggression can be defined as threats, postures or harmful actions directed toward dogs, people or other animals. Often, aggression is used to warn another animal or person to move away.

Early signs of aggression include:

▶ Dog appears conflicted about something or someone's approach.

▶ Hackles in piloerection. (Raised hair along the back.)

- ▶ Head dropping. Is this the normal stance for this breed? What is this dog communicating to you?

- ▶ Increased respiration.

- ▶ Tense body posture.

- ▶ Clacking of the mouth or teeth.

These early signs may be very subtle. Aggressive displays using these subtle signals are a normal part of dog-to-dog communication.

More advanced signs of aggression include:

- ▶ Hard eye contact.

- ▶ Stiff body posture.

- ▶ Showing the teeth.

- ▶ Stiff stance.

- ▶ Threat barking.

- ▶ Crouched threat stance.

- ▶ Growling.

- ▶ Jumping up and muzzle-bumping. (Jumping up at you and nipping at your chin, face, arms, stomach, as though saying "I'm aroused. I may blow. I'm warning you that where I'm 'bumping' you is where I'll probably bite you, if I bite.")

- ▶ Lunging, snapping, biting.

Any dog can bite, it just depends on the circumstances. Make a list of arousal triggers as an exercise in observation. The list of triggers may include:

Aggressive display by people	Babies crying
Charged by dog or humans	Confronted in small space
Bones and toys around on the floor	Being grabbed at
Chasing bicycles	Being restrained
Garden tools	Lawn equipment
Children running and screaming	Flapping coats or hats
People shouting, running, jogging	The list goes on ...

UNDERSTANDING PREDATORY BEHAVIOR

Predation is a survival mechanism. Canines evolved using predatory behavior to survive. As a result, dogs are hardwired to chase things that move. Humans need to understand what triggers predatory behavior and how to avoid the problems it can cause in modern society.

The predatory sequence is eye - stalk - chase - grab/bite - shake - dissect/consume. In some breeds, specific behaviors in the predatory sequence have been strengthened, while others have been weakened. For example, Border Collies have a strong eye - stalk - chase response to movement selectively bred for herding sheep. Jack Russell terriers have strong chase - grab/bite - shake behaviors, selectively bred for rodent catching.

Stopping the predatory sequence early disrupts the chain. For example, distracting a border collie so that it loses eye contact with the moving object will disrupt the subsequent stalk - chase responses. The farther into the chain, the more difficult it is to stop the sequence.

Watch the dog. Is he seeing, scenting or hearing something to chase? Is he beginning to stalk? Is his body alert, anticipatory? What happens when he hears joggers or skateboarders?

If you know a particular dog's communication signals, you can deduce what the dog will do next, and you can intervene. Distract the dog before he practices unwanted behavior. Give him a high-value treat or a great game of retrieve or tug. Chasing is really fun for the dog, so your reward for his attention should be especially wonderful. Get between him and the distraction and make the food or game you have to offer a better distraction.

Control the dog's environment so you give him an opportunity to learn the behavior you want him to practice. If you aren't better than the distraction (the jogger, biker, or dog across the street) then don't put your dog in a situation where those distractions happen. Be prepared.

RISK ANALYSIS

Is this dog going to bite? To answer this, analyze the situation and the dog using the ABC's of aggression:

ANTECEDENT (the emotional response that precedes the behavior): Determine what occurred before the behavior. If the dog has bitten, what provoked or triggered it?

BEHAVIOR (the behavior in question): Dogs generally give clear signals to avoid aggression. Did the dog attempt to defuse the situation? For example, did the dog take a step away from the person or lower its head but the human kept approaching?

CONSEQUENCE (the reinforcement that drives the behavior): The consequence is everything that happens following the event. Research what the owner or handler did. What did they say or do to the dog after the behavior occurred?

Dogs in neutral territory are less likely to show aggression so it is difficult to assess the risk of aggression by observing the dog in a neutral situation. When working with aggressive dogs, neutral territory can improve safety.

When assessing the risks, use the dog's behavior profile and your investigative abilities. It is not the particular breed of dog, it is the individual dog. Observe the dog and the dog's environment, including the dog's family. Identifying the dog's triggers will be your mission during history taking and observations. Make sure the client understands the degree of risk to the dog's family or the general public.

While breed is one factor that contributes to a dog's temperament, breed alone cannot be used to predict whether a dog may pose a danger to the community. A study conducted by a group of veterinarians, medical doctors, and psychology and public health experts, published in the Journal of the American Veterinary Medical Association (VetMed Today: Special Report, September 2000), detailed dog bite related fatalities in the United States from 1979 through 1998. The report reveals that at least twenty-five different breeds or crossbreeds of dogs caused human fatalities during the study period. Breeds cited ranged from the oft-maligned pit bulls and Rottweilers to the legendary "forever loyal" St. Bernard. When assessing risk it is the individual dog, not the breed of dog that should be considered.

A dog's tendency to bite at any given time is a product of several factors, including but not limited to:

▶ Early socialization of the dog to people, other animals and the environment. Lack of early socialization can predispose a dog to fearful aggression.

▶ Strength of foundation skills prior to training other behaviors. For example, training an unstable dog (under-socialized, lacking basic obedience, fearful or overly assertive) fighting behaviors, such as schutzhund or ring sport, can increase the dog's tendency to bite when under stress.

▶ Quality of care, socialization and supervision by the dog's human family. Dogs need constant practice of social skills. A dog kept chained outside may not maintain the social skills necessary to reduce the risk of biting.

▶ Genetic makeup, including breed and strains or lines within a breed.

▶ Whether the dog is trained. Statistics show that a basic obedience class decreases the risk of dog aggression.

▶ Behavior of other animals and people in the dog's environment. Behaviors such as fast or sudden movement, high-pitched noises or staring can trigger a dog's aggressive or predatory responses.

▶ Whether the dog is spayed or neutered.

Sound obedience training based in positive reinforcement can provide the dog with acceptable default behaviors to perform when under stress.

If it is normal for dogs to communicate using aggressive signals, how do you identify an inappropriate response? What is appropriate for dogs among dogs can often be considered inappropriate in human society. For example, through habituation and counter conditioning, dogs can be taught that a human bending over and patting them on the head is not a situation to be feared.

Ideally, dogs can be taught to accept the human-oriented world of modern society. If not, it is the owner's responsibility to manage and protect the dog from situations the dog finds stressful.

Alert with interest and calm.

Ears are erect and alert. Soft 'long distance' eye, back is relaxed and balanced.

Anxious posture.

Weight is held low within the frame. Ears folded back. Anxious eye with white showing and low tail carriage. Hackles raised.

Appeasement.

Border Collie holds body low and soft and licks at the other dog's face.

▲   *A submissive roll and a warning posture.The warning dog is stiff legged, erect tail, pilo erection over the shoulders, ears pinned back but upright, lips drawn back revealing teeth and tongue, hard eye. Rolled dog has soft joints and exposes vulnerability.*

▲

Guarding a bone. Hard eye with whites showing, full teeth displayed, but lips not drawn back. Ears held backwards. Tense and ready for movement.

Invitation to play from the dog on the right.

Dog on the left is not too sure that she wants to play.

◄

A cautious greeting.

Dog on left is sniffing noses with the cat politely in greeting. Dog on right is not sure about what the cat might be or do. Note extended neck on the terrier. Cat is very confident and social. ▶

Here are some examples of what responses are appropriate and inappropriate in modern society:

Situation:

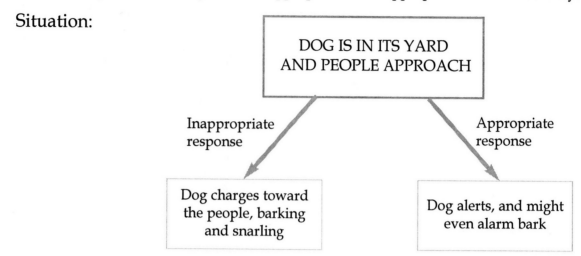

Situation:

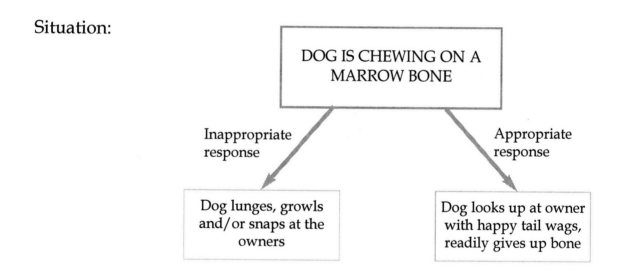

2   Learning

In order to change a dog's behavior you must first understand how the dog learns. This chapter defines the basic terminology used in modern dog training practice including the concepts used in learning theory.

Dogs do what works. If aggressing gets a dog what he wants (such as your attention or space between him and a scary thing) he will do more of it. Reinforce behaviors you want and you will get more of those behaviors over time. If you inadvertently reinforce behaviors you don't want, or if those behaviors are self-reinforced or reinforced by the environment, their occurrence will increase.

Note: When working with a fearful or reactive dog, be aware of the dog's stress levels and any stimuli that may trigger the dog's anxiety or fear. Don't hide the dog away from life in a pen, down in the basement, or tied in the back yard. Take an active role in teaching the dog how to cope with life through careful management and positive reinforcement of desirable behaviors.

THE BASICS OF LEARNING

Behavior is changed when it is reinforced. If you reinforce positively, the behavior will strengthen. If you reinforce negatively, the behavior may be lessened but you also risk avoidance, fear and unpredictable learning.

LEARNING IN A NUTSHELL

1. Train new behaviors in a zero distraction environment. Using a reward marker, (such as a clicker or a special happy word) pair reinforcement with the desirable behavior. Reinforcement is something that has value to the dog. It might be food, play, toys or activities.

2. If successful, gradually increase the duration of the desired behavior.

3. Begin to introduce distance (gradually distancing yourself from the dog) if appropriate for the exercise.

4. In a familiar environment, begin to introduce mild distractions, at a level where the dog is comfortable but aware. When introducing distractions, reduce duration and distance at first and then gradually work the dog back to longer times and distances.

5. Set the dog up to successfully perform the behavior and to be reinforced. Let the dog's comfort level dictate the progress. Be prepared to step back a level at any time to ensure the dog's success.

6. When the behavior is reliable, add the cue.

REINFORCE DESIRABLE BEHAVIOR

Dogs learn through practice or rehearsal. A behavior that is rewarded is more likely to occur again. Be patient. Start with the dog "where he is" and reward any tiny hint of the behaviors you want. Gradually, as the dog begins to repeat the rewarded behaviors, you will be able to fine tune fun tricks or useful behaviors as you increase the criteria. What are rewardable behaviors for a reactive dog? Watch the dog! Look for moments when he shows relaxed body language and a calm demeanor. Mark and treat any calm and non-reactive behaviors. Reinforce behaviors as small as calming signals like shaking off, yawning, lip licking or sniffing the ground. Enthusiastically reinforce eye contact such as the "Watch Me" game. Anticipate situations that trigger problem behaviors and get in front of the event by reinforcing an alternate behavior before the reactive behavior can begin. Alternate behaviors could be looking at you or calming signals such as turning away. Convince the dog that the cookie jar opens whenever scary things appear and that good things are offered for calm behavior.

MARK THE BEHAVIOR

A reward marker, such as a clicker or the word "yes" can be used to mark the exact moment the desirable behavior occurred. A marker is used to improve our communication with the dog. When using a marker, it is first paired (associated) with a reward such as a food treat. When the handler marks the behavior, the dog immediately gets a food treat. The dog begins to learn that the click means a food treat. The reward marker can then be used at the precise moment the dog performs the desired or 'target' behavior. The dog learns which behavior has earned the food. The benefit of using a marker is timing; out of 10 different behaviors that may have occurred at any given time, the dog knows precisely which behavior earned the reward when a reward marker is used.

A marker is particularly useful when working with reactive dogs. Over-reactive dogs are often low in self confidence and do not understand how to behave appropriately. Set the dog up so he is certain to respond with the appropriate behavior, then mark the behavior to communicate success: "Good decision!" Very quickly the dog begins to understand what to do, and the pressure is released, giving him more opportunity for success in a stressful situation. The most common markers used in dog training are clickers, a word such as "yes" or a mouth-cluck sound. The clicker is usually first choice since it is the most consistent. If a dog is noise sensitive, you can use a soft voice or a muffled clicker. To muffle the clicker, hold it in your pocket while clicking or layer tape on the metal clicker-tongue.

A clicker can be used by different people and remain a consistent marker. But a clicker can be inconvenient, because at times the handler may not have it in hand. Associate or pair a marker for those times when you don't have your clicker with food (use a word or cluck sound) and be as consistent as possible when you use it. The marker will mark the moment the dog achieves the goal you have set and promises the dog a great reward. You can, of course, use a clicker but you may be doing a lot of opportunistic training and it is helpful to have a word or sound like "Yes!" or "Good!" handy. The marker means your dog has earned a reward. It is not, in and of itself, the reward. You should always follow the marker with a reward, such as treats, praise or play.

"Charge" your marker by saying it or clicking and immediately giving the dog a treat. Make sure the marker comes first and the treat comes second. Repeat this 10 times over three separate sessions (minimum) so your dog begins to associate the marker with treats. Whichever marker you use, a clicker, word or other sound, it is always followed with a treat, praise or play.

I never use the clicker or "yes" marker when the dog is aggressing, upset or fearful. It is my personal opinion and practice to avoid use of the clicker or reward marker if the dog is in any of these emotional states out of concern that the dog might attach their emotions to the CLICK or reward marker. This is not technical, but in my experience working with thousands of dogs, I have found that fearful or aggressive dogs learn and improve faster using classical conditioning, counter conditioning or good desensitization techniques. Most of my pet dog owner clients are not highly skilled with a clicker so I also worry about timing or that clicking at the wrong moment might reinforce an undesireable response.

ADD THE CUE

A cue, or conditioned stimulus, is a predictor that a specific behavior (if offered immediately after that cue) will be reinforced. Due to "first order learning" (meaning, that an association that is learned first for a novel stimulus, is remembered best), cues have a strong association when they are attached to finished behaviors. Add the cue only when:

1. The dog offers the behavior regularly, on a variable reinforcement schedule (when the dog is reinforced for the behavior only some of the time).

2. The behavior is perfected, just as the handler wants it.

3. The behavior occurs 95% of the time within 5 seconds of the dog finishing the reward for the previous occurrence or performance of the behavior.

To add a cue:

1. As the dog is in the process of performing the behavior, say the cue. Mark and reinforce the behavior. Repeat 10 times.

2. Just before the behavior occurs, say the cue once and wait for the behavior. If the behavior occurs within 5 seconds, mark and reinforce it, then repeat 30 to 50 times over several training sessions. It takes 30-50 repetitions of the cue before the dog learns to associate the cue with the behavior.

If the behavior does not occur within 5 seconds, reposition yourself and the dog to reset the trial, and say the cue again. Click or mark and treat for any part of the right behavior. If the behavior does not occur within 5 seconds of the cue, it is too early to add the cue. Go back to shaping or practicing the behavior by reinforcing it when it occurs. (*See: Shaping on page 27*)

To build a reliable response:

1. Strengthen the behavior through repetition of cue-behavior-reinforcement until it is so strong, no warm-up (such as luring or rewarding of a less-than-perfect version of the behavior) is required.

2. Put the behavior on a variable reinforcement schedule, gradually thinning out the reinforcements (1 behavior for a treat, then 2, then 1, then 3, then 5, then 1, then 3, then 7, etc.).

3. Ask for different cued behaviors and only reward the right behavior for the right cue, so the dog learns to differentiate among cues. Don't reinforce the behavior unless it has been cued.

4. Gradually add distractions. When adding distractions, reinforce any attempt to perform the behavior until the dog's skill level returns.

If a behavior reliably occurs in response to a specific cue, and not to other cues, in a variety of situations, the behavior is under stimulus control. Discrimination and generalization, taken together, result in stimulus control. If the dog can discriminate between the "roll over" and "sit" cues by performing the behavior learned for each, the dog is able to discriminate the cue. If the dog is able to perform the behavior on cue in different locations, when the cue is presented by people with different reinforcements, the dog has generalized the cued behavior.

STRENGTHEN BEHAVIORS USING THE FOUR D'S

Almost any task or behavior can be divided into several different criteria or dimensions: distance, duration, distraction and difficulty. Failure to train a behavior, or failure of a behavior under pressure, often finds its roots in having raised multiple criteria simultaneously. Each dimension should be given special training time. Taking the time to focus on each one ensures a strong foundation.

Distance. Gradually increase distance. For example, start by standing next to the dog when teaching sit-stay. Over time, gradually increase the distance, but keep it variable. Stand 2 feet away, then 5 feet, then 3 feet, then 7 feet, then 5 feet, etc.

Duration. When you first begin to teach a behavior, ask for very little duration. Gradually increase duration of the behavior over many training sessions. For example, start with 10 second sit-stays. Gradually increase the duration, but keep it variable. Practice 20 second sit-stays, then 40 second, then 30 second, then 60 second, then 50 second, etc.. Using your "keep going" marker ("goood") helps increase duration.

Distractions. Start with distractions that are low in intensity. For example, once the dog is fluent in a behavior in the house, begin practicing the behavior in the yard. If the behavior is loose leash walking, walk in the backyard around a lawn chair or a stationary lawnmower to start with. Once the dog is working well with these minor distractions, turn the lawnmower on and work the dog around it. After a week or so of practice, heel around the lawnmower while it is moving or while another person is in the yard.

Gradually, over time, begin to add neighborhood children playing, yelling, screaming and just being kids. Next, take the dog a little farther away, such as two houses down the block. Make it more difficult in terms of distraction but never so difficult the dog cannot succeed. Each time you move to a new location, lower the criteria a bit. For example, reward a shorter sit-stay. This will help the dog succeed and the dog will begin to generalize the behavior.

Difficulty. Difficulty is adding two D's at the same time. For example, increasing the distance and the duration of a sit-stay, simultaneously.

Stephen Rafe developed the Four D's [tm] concept in 1985 and began teaching it in Starfire's behavior-training courses at that time. The concept first appeared for mass distribution in 1987 when it was published in Stephen's book, "Training Your Dog for Birdwork"

TRAINING TECHNIQUE

USING THE PREMACK PRINCIPLE

Both people and dogs can learn self-control behaviors by linking a less desired activity with a more desired activity. This rule is called the Premack Principle and here are some examples:

> "Clean up your room and then I will take you shopping."

> "As soon as you finish your homework, you may go play outside."

> "Eat your vegetables and then you can have dessert."

> "Wait politely at the door and then you can go out to sniff and play."

> "Keep four paws on the floor and I will bend down and pat you."

To use the Premack Principle, link fun activities to self-control behaviors:

◆ Watch your dog and notice what he likes to do.

◆ Use this activity as a reward for what you want him to do.

For example, if your dog loves to chase the ball when you throw it, show the dog a ball and ask for a sit. The moment he begins to sit for an instant, throw the ball. The ball toss becomes the reward for the sit. Once the dog consistently sits for a ball-throw, begin to use the reward ball-fetch to teach "sit and stay" by moving from an instant of sitting before throwing the ball to minutes before throwing the ball.

The Premack Principle works particularly well for active dogs. If your dog is a free spirit and wants to run like crazy, use Premack to your advantage. Ask the dog to heel for a few minutes, then say "free!" and release your dog to run free. This will build a very strong reward association for your dog; if you always make running "free" contingent upon heeling behavior (walking calmly at your side), your dog will look forward to heelwork because he will begin to anticipate running "free" as a good reason to heel.

FADING THE LURE

Fading a food lure can be difficult. The fading process is usually not emphasized in training and the dog's response to cues, once the lure is faded, can be less than expected.

If you lure, stick to the rule of three:

◆ Have a plan of how you will fade the lure.

◆ Lure with food three times, then immediately begin to fade the lure.

If a food lure is used to teach a dog to sit, then steps for how the food will be faded from the picture must be included in the plan. Lure only three times, then begin fading the lure. For example, hold an invisible cookie in your luring hand and, when the dog sits, reward with a treat from your other hand. This way you help your dog learn that treats are magic and he cannot predict where they might come from next.

If your dog only offers the behavior when you are holding food, the presence of the food has become part of the cue for the behavior. To avoid this, don't teach new behaviors while visibly holding food in your hand. Use small pieces of moist food that are easily hidden in the palm of your hand. Quickly get the food away from your body to various hiding places around your house and other training areas.

SHAPING BY SUCCESSIVE APPROXIMATIONS

Shaping by successive approximations, or "shaping" can be used to teach a dog any new behavior, simple or complex, from tricks to obedience skills. With shaping, skills are broken down into tiny, progressive steps, called "target behaviors". The dog perfects each target behavior before moving onto a slightly more difficult target behavior (known as "raising the criteria"). This way, each target behavior is a strong foundation for the next, more difficult, target behavior.

Shaping is a hands-off process with minimal interference from the handler. The dog offers various behaviors voluntarily, without any prompting from the handler. No force or coercion is ever used because the dog is motivated to earn a reward.

When the dog offers the target behavior, the handler marks that behavior with a click and reinforces with a treat. The dog learns to offer behaviors until he is clicked and to repeat the reinforced behavior to continue earning rewards. Gradually, the simple behavior is honed into a more complex behavior, by raising the criteria gradually, over many training sessions. When criteria is raised, the click is withheld while the handler waits for the dog to perform the slightly more difficult target behavior. By breaking behavior down into simple steps and training each step to perfection, complex behaviors can be trained. As an added benefit, a dog trained through shaping learns to learn and becomes motivated to try to figure out what earns a reward. The dog becomes a thinking partner.

For more information on shaping, read "Don't Shoot the Dog" by Karen Pryor, Sunshine Books.

TARGETING

Touching a dog while he is learning a new behavior can distract and mislead him. Teaching a dog to target different body parts (nose, front paw, back paw, shoulder, hip) gives the handler a hands-off means of directing the dog's movements. The more the dog is allowed to participate as an active partner, the more actively the dog's brain will work to resolve the problem of "how do I earn that treat?".

For a step-by-step process to teach the dog targeting of various body parts, see Kay Laurence's book "Dances with Dogs", available through www.learningaboutdogs.com.

For uses of targeting to teach heelwork, agility, and other skills, view Gary Wilkes' video "On Target", available through Dogwise.com

SYSTEMATIC DESENSITIZATION AND COUNTER CONDITIONING

To change how the reactive dog feels about certain events in the world, combine the principles of systematic desensitization and counter conditioning with positive reinforcement. Both shy dogs and aggressive dogs are over stimulated by certain events in their environment. We call them "reactive" dogs. The shy dog withdraws and avoids any action that might trigger "bad/scary/dangerous" things. While the pushy/growling/aggressive dog also thinks the stimulus is "bad/scary/dangerous" but tries to solve the threat by making it go away. Training skills to replace reactive behavior is a powerful way to change how a dog feels about what he currently fears. When working with a reactive dog, be mindful of the dog's stress levels and of any stimulus which may trigger the dog's anxieties or fearfulness. Always begin with the dog "where he is" and reward any good behaviors.

Systematic desensitization is controlled, gradual exposure to a stimulus over time to produce habituation. If the stimulus has no consequence, the dog ceases to respond to it. For example, if a dog fears traffic noise, and is exposed to a period of low-level traffic noise, the dog may begin to ignore the traffic noise (at that level). If the noise level is gradually increased, and the dog is allowed to become desensitized to that level before it is increased to the next level, the dog can be taught to ignore very loud traffic noise.

Counter conditioning is the use of classical conditioning to change a stimulus that provokes a particular emotion into a stimulus that provokes an opposing emotion. For example, something that evokes fear or aggression can be counter conditioned to evoke an expectation of pleasure. The dog fears traffic noise, and is exposed to traffic at a distance. The handler gives the dog yummy treats each time a car passes. The dog may begin to associate traffic noise with the yummy treat and therefore begin to look forward to traffic noise. The distance from the traffic noise is gradually decreased and the dog is allowed to become counter conditioned to each distance before it is decreased further. Over time, the dog can be taught that very loud traffic noise leads to something nice. Changing the emotional association changes the behavioral response.

Desensitization and counter conditioning take patience, planning and repetition. A conditioning against fear or aggression can take months or even years. Each time fearful or aggressive behavior is practiced, it reverses hours of systematic desensitization or counter conditioning. Therefore, management during and between training sessions is critical. Management requires setting up the dog's environment to ensure fear or aggression is not triggered in day-to-day life. Remember the point system (*See Measuring Success page 83*). Because it can change an emotional response, systematic desensitization and counter conditioning are powerful tools. To keep the conditioning strong, brief refresher sessions should be practiced throughout the dog's life.

THINK POSITIVE!

Shy or over-reactive dogs lack confidence. It is particularly important to continuously reinforce good behavior with these dogs. Positive reinforcement of desirable behaviors should become the dog's lifestyle. Lots of quick easy "default" behaviors such as sit, down, give a paw, roll over, etc., mean lots of proof to the reactive dog that they are safe and can succeed.

AVOID FLOODING

Flooding is prolonged exposure to a stimulus at high level in order to cause extinction of response to that stimulus. For example, if a dog is mildly anxious of traffic noise, exposure to a high level of traffic noise can at first increase, and then reduce, the fear response.

Counter conditioning and systematic desensitization take time, patience and planning, so flooding is sometimes attempted as a "quick fix" instead. Unfortunately, the net result of flooding can be increased sensitization leading to increased reactivity (or even generalized fear to similar stimuli) rather than extinction of response. Flooding may also result in learned helplessness.

AVOID PUNISHMENT

Punishment in the form of positive punishment (*See Terminology, page 25*) works to decrease behavior by causing avoidance. Punishment can therefore exacerbate fear and aggression. Punishment should be avoided in training programs, particularly with reactive, fearful or aggressive dogs. Positive reinforcement, and occasional negative punishment (such as a timeout), are the most appropriate means of teaching and learning. Positive reinforcement builds confidence and trust. Timeouts, applied appropriately, maintain boundaries by teaching the dog what behaviors are not rewarding.

USE TIMEOUT PROPERLY

Dogs do what works. Inappropriate behavior can be extinguished by making sure it doesn't work- by avoiding any and all reinforcement for that behavior.

Timeout can be used to cause the dog to lose what he attempted to gain by performing inappropriate behavior. For example, he may be jumping up for attention. A timeout would remove attention, thereby avoiding reinforcement of jumping up.

The following method should be used for timeout:

1. Mark the incorrect behavior (for example, with the word "timeout") at the moment it occurs.

2. Immediately but gently escort the dog to the timeout area (a crate or quiet room), and leave the dog there for 1 to 3 minutes (never longer).

3. When the dog is let out, practice and reinforce alternate behaviors to replace the inappropriate behavior.

For timeouts when you are out and about:

1. Use the cue ("timeout") to mark the incorrect behavior.

2. Immediately turn your back.

3. Don't allow the dog to interact with anything for several seconds. (If the environment is distracting, put the dog on lead.)

4. On the third offense during an outing, put the dog in the crate or car, or leave the site to avoid practicing the inappropriate behavior. Better yet, set the dog up so he cannot make that mistake again.

Because timeout does not teach the dog appropriate behavior, it should be used sparingly. Ideally, the handler should set the dog up so he cannot practice inappropriate behavior.

TERMINOLOGY

An understanding of learning theory is essential for the dog training professional. Learning theory provides access to the range of science-based techniques and strategies that can be applied to solve practical problems. Following is an overview of learning theory terminology.

Behavior: Any single action an animal or organism can perform. This can be a frown, bark, paw wave or growl.

Behavior Chain: A collection of behaviors that when performed in succession creates a multi-faceted behavior. The retrieve is a behavior chain of the following components: trot out to article, pick up article, turn toward handler, trot to front of handler, sit, place article in handler's hand.

Cue or Stimulus: A signal that reliably results in the dog performing a particular behavior. For example, the word "sit" or a hand signal are cues to sit, "here" or a whistle the cues to "come". Cues can also be environmental so the appearance of another dog can be a cue to "watch me".

Unconditioned Stimulus: An unconditioned stimulus always produces an unconditioned response. Example: the smell of food (unconditioned stimulus) produces salivating (unconditioned response).

Conditioned Stimulus: Anything that has become associated with an unconditioned stimulus and now produces the response. Examples: the bell in Pavlov's experiment was rung before food was presented and became associated with food. The bell became a conditioned stimulus for salivating. Most dogs wear a collar with tags that jingle as the dog moves around. This sound can become a conditioned stimulus to responses associated with another dog.

Unconditioned Response: The natural reflex reaction to an event. For example, drooling is an unconditioned response to the presence of food. Tension or submission is the unconditioned response to growling from another dog.

Conditioned Response: A response to a conditioned stimulus. Also *Conditioned Emotional Response (CER)*. For example, if the dog has learned to associate the collar jingle with an approaching dog, the collar jingle can cause the dog to go on "alert". Becoming alert is a conditioned response. The process in this is classical conditioning.

Reward: Anything that the dog perceives as rewarding at that time. What is rewarding for one dog may not be rewarding for another. What is rewarding in the dog's home may not be rewarding out on the street. Examples: yummy treats, roast beef, turkey, cheese, toys and balls for playing, freedom to check out the environment, freedom to play with another dog.

Reinforcement (R):   Anything that makes the learner more likely to repeat a behavior, i.e., the behavior becomes stronger. Examples: food, toys or going for a walk. A reinforcer must be something the animal actually wants, not something we think he or she wants.

Punishment (P): Anything that makes the learner less likely to repeat a behavior, i.e., the behavior becomes weaker. Example: a physical punishment or the withdrawal of attention. If a dog barks and you spray water in his face and the dog stops barking, you have applied punishment.

Positive Reinforcement (R+): Something good (such as food, play, praise) happens after the behavior. Example: presenting a treat to the dog after the dog sits, reinforces the sit. The dog will sit more eagerly next time, expecting the treat. This is also referred to as Positive Teaching.

Negative Reinforcement (R-): Something bad (such as pain or pressure) ends or is taken away. For example, pressing on the dog's lower back to elicit a sit. When the dog sits, the pressure is released and the dog experiences relief. The feeling of relief reinforces the sit.

Positive Punishment (P+): Something bad starts or is presented (threatened). Example: the dog jumps up and gets a knee in the chest or the person begins to raise a knee as a threat.

Negative Punishment (P-): Something good ends or is taken away. Example: the toy goes back into the pocket when the dog grabs at it roughly.

Classical Conditioning: Associating an unconditioned stimulus with a conditioned stimulus. For example, in clicker training the clicker has a classically conditioned association with a food reward. Classical conditioning is a powerful tool because it operates on involuntary, often emotion-based, responses. Because it is so powerful, classical conditioning can be used to help the dog overcome fear and aggression, such as through counter conditioning. (See counter conditioning below).

Operant Conditioning: An analytical response to cause and effect. Operant conditioning involves thinking and reasoning to associate a behavior to its consequences. The consequence of a behavior can be positive or negative reinforcement, or positive or negative punishment. An animal with free choice, who has learned which behavior results in which consequence, is most likely to choose to perform behaviors with the most reinforcing and the least punishing consequences. For example, if a handler has reinforced the dog with food each time the dog sits, but has always ignored the dog for jumping up, the dog may be more likely to sit than to jump up. Classical conditioning and operant conditioning work together because classical associations are made during operant conditioning. Because classical conditioning is so strongly linked to emotive responses, it can override operant conditioned responses. For example, noises associated with fearful events can evoke fear that causes the dog to temporarily refuse to perform operant conditioned responses, such as sit.

Primary Reinforcer: A consequence of behavior that is rewarding in itself. Examples: eating food that has been offered or stolen, the adrenaline rush of chasing cats, or the pleasure of being stroked and petted.

Secondary Reinforcer (or bridging stimulus): A marker, such as a unique sound, that is associated with a reward but is not inherently rewarding in itself. For example, a word or the clicker is associated with a primary reinforcer through classical conditioning.

Habituation: The weakening of a response due to a repeated stimulus. Habituation occurs at a primal level within the nervous system. Habituation is different from fatigue. For example, you buy a new alarm clock that makes a chirping bird sound. The first time the alarm goes off, the dog startles awake from a sound sleep, his ears go up and he cocks his head at the bird sound. After a week or so, the alarm clock is successfully waking you up but your dog snores peacefully on.

Flooding: Prolonged exposure to a stimulus at high level to quickly habituate the dog to that stimulus without gradually increasing the stimulus. For example, if a dog is mildly anxious about traffic noise, exposure to a high level of traffic noise from a safe environment (such as the owner's arms, sitting in a car, at the roadside) can at first increase, and then reduce, the fear response. However, the net result of flooding can be increased sensitization rather than desensitization, particularly with shy or over-reactive dogs. Learned helplessness may result. "Flooding is also called 'response blocking' because the animal wants to run away and the trainer is blocking that response." (Lore Haug DVM, letter to author, July 2, 2007). "Flooding involves prolonged exposure at a level that provokes the response so that the animal eventually gives up. This is exactly the opposite of the approach taken in desensitization. It is far more stressful than any of the other therapy strategies and, used inappropriately, could damage the animal. The most common side effect is enhanced fear. This technique should be used only by those with extensive experience and as a last resort" (Merck). (*See Learned Helplessness page 27*).

Desensitization (or Systematic Desensitization): Controlled, gradual exposure to a stimulus over time, to produce habituation. The stimulus has no consequence, therefore the dog ceases to respond to it. For example, if a dog fears traffic noise and is exposed to a period of low-level traffic noise, the dog may begin to ignore the traffic noise (at that level). If the noise level is gradually increased and the dog is allowed to become desensitized to that level before it is increased to the next level, the dog can be taught to ignore very loud traffic noise.

Counter Conditioning: Changing a stimulus that evokes an emotion into a stimulus that evokes an opposing emotion. For example, changing something that evokes fear (such as an unfamiliar person approaching) into something that evokes expectation of pleasure (such as receiving a yummy treat). Counter conditioning aims to change the dog's emotions, which will in turn change the dog's reactions to a specific stimulus. (*See Classical Conditioning page 25.*)

Learned Helplessness: The weakening of the escape response due to continuous exposure to an unavoidable aversive stimulus. Example: a dog shocked repeatedly with an electric collar may lie down, shaking and not move. Learned helplessness is often the result of flooding. Learned helplessness can also occur when a dog is never permitted to try new behaviors without modeling or luring or verbal direction occurring first - the dog does not learn to problem-solve on his own. The dog learns that if he waits - the trainer will solve the problem by telling or showing him what to do next.

Shaping: Rewarding behaviors that closely approximate the desired response. Over time, behaviors must be closer and closer to the desired behavior to be rewarded until eventually only the desired behavior is rewarded.

Extinction: The weakening of a response to a stimulus due to absence of a reinforcer. Example: a dog has been rewarded with talk and petting when jumping up on people. To extinguish the behavior, the dog is ignored when it jumps up. Reinforcing an alternative behavior such as sitting will accelerate the process of extinction. Extinction will not work for behaviors that are self-reinforcing.

Spontaneous Recovery: The return of a previously extinguished response after a lengthy period of time has passed between the last exposure to the stimulus and the one that re-elicits the response. For example, your neighbor's dog is afraid of Halloween masks and has a terrible time each year around October 31st (he gets fearful and snaps at people). By showing up at the neighbor's house twice a day wearing a mask for three weeks, the dog becomes used to masks and no longer responds fearfully. Your neighbor thanks you! The next Halloween you show up at your neighbor's house wearing a Yoda mask and his dog experiences spontaneous recovery and bites you on the butt.

Extinction Burst: While extinction results in the eventual decrease of a behavior, in the short term a dog might experience what is called an "Extinction Burst". If an animal has a history of reinforcement for a particular behavior and that particular behavior is no longer being rewarded, a dog might persist in trying to get the behavior to produce a reward. In an extinction burst, dogs may perform the behavior repeatedly and in a frantic manner. As long as the behavior does not produce a reward, it will diminish, but sometimes it appears that an unwanted behavior is getting worse before it diminishes. Example: a dog has been rewarded for begging at the dinner table by an occasional tidbit of people food. The begging at the table has been reinforced. If, to extinguish the behavior everybody stops feeding the dog from the table in an effort to extinguish the begging, the dog may beg with more energy and intensity before the begging behavior extinguishes.

The Premack Principle: Behavioral psychologist David Premack's discovery that you can increase the frequency of any low probability behavior by making it contingent upon a high probability behavior. *(See page 20.)*

"To deny an animal's emotions is to distance yourself from him as a feeling being."

Suzanne Clothier ~ Author of
"Bones Would Rain From The Sky"

3 Assessment

This chapter describes the process of assessing the dog, client, lifestyle, and relationship. If you are seeking a behavior consultation for your dog, this chapter can help you know what to expect.

WHY EVALUATE?

Your job as a behavior consultant is to take a history, observe the dog's behavior, and then apply your knowledge to behavioral analysis.

Unfortunately, what handlers report to the behavior consultant is often skewed. For example, the handler may not want to admit all the dog's odd habits, especially if they feel they may have played a part in the dog's problems. In many cases, the handler anthropomorphizes the dog's behavior, mistakenly believing that the dog has the ability to understand the nuances of human language or that the dog can reason in the same way a human does. Therefore, behavior consultants cannot simply rely on the handler's account of the dog's behavior. A behavior consultant must develop good investigative skills to gather relevant information and solve the issues presented. Your job is to evaluate the existence and cause of unwanted behavior to the best of your ability.

COMMON BEHAVIORAL SCENARIOS

Aggression can be created. In training classes, we see many people and dogs. Handlers rarely have issues with young puppies. As time goes on many of these people call for advice and help because now their nice puppy is causing problems in social settings. Following are some examples:

EXAMPLE CASE 1

Dog's Specifics: Black Labrador, 3 years of age, female, spayed

Problem: Charging over the invisible fence and fighting with other dogs.

History: As a puppy in class, the dog was more on the serious side and just wanted to chase her ball. She did not really want to play with other puppies. The handler was advised that putting her behind an invisible fence system could cause problems but did so anyway. Every time another dog passed by and she moved to the fence, she was "corrected" with the electric shock collar. The dog-fighting behavior began 2 years ago and increased over time. Now she is charging through the fence and is classified by the town as a "Dangerous Dog" in the community.

EXAMPLE CASE 2

Dog's Specifics: Golden Retriever, 18 months old, male

Problem: Bit a child.

History: As a young pup, Chance was dressed up and dragged around the home and neighborhood by the family children. The parents felt that this would be a good experience for the dog and the children. Chance began growling and biting at the kids whenever they reached for him, so the father began to grab the dog to make it submit. While resting on his dog bed, Chance bit a child who walked past his sleeping spot.

THE PROCESS OF BEHAVIOR MODIFICATION

These steps should be followed when working with a client who has a reactive dog:

1. Assess the dog.

2. Assess the handler.

3. Teach the handler new skills to help the handler become pro-active in the relationship and to teach the dog new skills so the dog is less reactive.

Some dogs and handlers will be able to jump ahead quickly to the skill training, while others will need to build a reinforcing relationship before behavioral modification training can begin.

When serious emotional behavior issues are presented, it is my opinion that the use of a clicker for skills training is less effective than the use of a verbal reward marker. Clickers can increase arousal and stress for some dogs. In my experience the use of a verbal reward marker is a safer choice.

1. ASSESS THE DOG

PRELIMINARY WORK

Have the client complete a Behavior Profile *(see Appendix C Forms, page 187)* before your scheduled meeting. Send it by email or mail it to them. Ask them to send it back to you before the consultation. If appropriate, suggest management changes that the handler can implement immediately to improve safety for the dog, the family and the general public.

Before beginning behavioral training, have the client consult a veterinarian to rule out any medical problems that may be contributing to or causing the aggressive behavior.

BEHAVIORAL ASSESSMENT

The first face-to-face meeting usually takes about 90 minutes. It is best for this meeting to take place in a neutral location, not the client's home. In a familiar environment, like his own home the dog might be inclined to guard his resources from you, the stranger, or he may be allowed to rehearse undesirable behaviors.

I use a large room (5' x 18' or 2m x 3m) with vinyl flooring and windows. Bring special food treats that are smelly, moist and chopped into tiny pieces. Cheese or cooked meat is ideal. Have balls and toys available. No other dogs or people (other than the client, his family, and possibly a student you may be mentoring in behavioral assessment) should be in the room.

The dog should be on lead. If the dog is not stiff or reactive and it is safe to do so, ask the handler to drop the lead to allow the dog freedom to walk around. Watch the dog while talking with the handler: assess how both dog and person are feeling. Be calm and non-threatening. Keep extra special yummy treats in your hand and have a stash close by, out of the dog's reach.

If you are sitting, sit with a relaxed posture. Move in a slow and relaxed manner, never suddenly or quickly. Toss treats to the ground to help the dog relax and move around the new environment. The dog may notice you have something and come over to investigate. If he is calm, quietly ask him to sit. Keep interactions with the dog to a minimum at this point in the assessment. Allow the dog to settle enough to show you who he is. Look for the answers to the following questions:

- ▶ What is the dog's arousal level?

- ▶ Is he over reactive?

- ▶ How worried is he about being in a new area?

- ▶ Will he take food? Dogs that refuse food can be over their stress threshold.

- ▶ How is he feeling about you?

Watch the dog's body language. Look for calming signals. Assess the following:

- ▶ Does the dog startle easily?

- ▶ Can he handle the new room?

- ▶ Can you move around without scaring him?

- ▶ Is he feeling comfortable with you now that he knows you have treats or a ball or a toy?

Finding something that the dog will work for is critical to changing how he feels about the stimulus that now makes him reactive. If the dog takes a long time to settle in the environment, or if he lacks interest in the reinforcers you have to offer, he will be a greater challenge to recondition. For some dogs, toy play, including retrieve, chase or tug, can be a valuable reinforcer. Find out what the dog values by watching and interacting with him.

As you observe the dog, verbalize for the client your interpretation of how the dog is feeling by what the dog is doing based on your observations of his body language. Point out how he is reacting to different things in his environment, such as the sounds, sights, and smells in the room. Encourage the handler to watch and interpret the dog's body language with you opening up lines of communication.

2. ASSESS THE HANDLER

The handler's body language plays a significant role in the dog's reaction to his environment. Watch the handler's response to the environment. Is the handler relaxed or nervous? How long does it take the handler to relax? Frequently, the handler feels a need to talk about what has been happening. Take the time and use your listening skills. Reaffirm what the handler is saying, to show you understand. The handler needs to feel comfortable before you begin making suggestions for behavior modification.

Once the dog is relaxed, ask the handler to show you what the dog knows. The handler may use food or other reinforcers. If your movement scares or provokes the dog, stay still and relaxed while the handler works with the dog.

Watch for the following:

▶ Does the dog orient to, and give attention to, the handler? Or is the dog disinterested in what the handler is doing?

▶ How does the dog and handler act toward each other? Are they comfortable with each other? Or does either show uncomfortable body language in response to the other? How patient are they with each other?

▶ Does the dog need food to respond to the handler? Will the handler use food?

Remember how they entered the training area. Was the dog leading or was he following?

This is an assessment of the human/dog bond and their relationship. If the handler is receptive and interested in learning, talk to him/her about:

▶ How a person can build a bond with their dog and how easily it can be broken. In particular, how punishment or misuse of dominance theory damages a dog's trust and confidence in his relationship with his handler.

▶ How to observe the dog and let the dog's body language be a guide to how the dog is feeling.

▶ How dogs learn and how reinforcement affects learning.

▶ How to focus on even the smallest "good" or correct behaviors and develop these behaviors in small, successful increments, so the dog begins to choose to offer good behaviors.

▶ Redirecting an undesirable behavior to a desirable behavior.

Emphasize that the handler should not put unrealistic demands on the dog. Learning will be slow and incremental. The handler must train new behaviors the way they would like to learn: with support, respect and reward for achievement. Reflect this approach as you teach the handler new skills by letting the handler know when he/she has tried hard, got it right, or done a really good job.

Educate the handler on these 4 points:

1. That their dog can be away from them (left home alone) and still be a confident and happy dog. For example, crate the dog for short periods of time when they are home to make crating a normal part of daily life rather than a cue that the dog will be left alone.

2. Have quiet times with the dog. Touch, massage and be close to the dog.

3. Train and guide the dog throughout his life. Positive reinforcement training is a form of play for dogs. When owners see how much the dog enjoys learning using positive reinforcement they will enjoy it too.

4. Don't be angry when the dog is just being a dog. Learn from these amazing animals and realize the dog IS a different species. Observe the dog's canine uniqueness and allow yourself to be enthralled, riveted and amazed by it.

Be prepared to spend about 45 minutes watching, reinforcing and talking before the "real work" begins. If the dog and handler respond to increasing reinforcement for good behavior, they are ready for some behavioral modification exercises. Send them home with some desensitizing and self-control homework. *(See Exercises, Appendix A page 21 & 80.)*

PHARMACEUTICAL INTERVENTION

If the handler works to change the dog's behavior, medication can often be avoided. However, if the dog does not respond significantly, or if predictable triggers cannot be identified (idiopathic behaviors), behavior modification techniques should be developed to work in concert with pharmaceutical intervention.

3. CHANGING PEOPLE

Changing people will require teaching them new ideas and skills so they can change their behavior, thereby changing the dog's behavior. A large part of a behaviorist's job is teaching.

"EDITH" is a methodology used in teaching. EDITH helps the learner organize his thoughts so he can learn effectively. EDITH consists of a series of steps. The model of EDITH, outlined below, is an effective teaching guideline. EDITH encompasses <u>listening</u>, <u>watching</u> and <u>doing</u> to maximize your student's learning

E XPLAIN

- ▶ Tell the students what you are about to show them, without the distraction of having them do it.

- ▶ Explain what to do.

- ▶ Explain how to do it.

- ▶ Explain the real-life relevance of it.

D EMONSTRATE

- ▶ Show the students exactly what you told them.

- ▶ Demonstrate more than once.

- ▶ Demonstrate with a different orientation (angle) to give them a better view.

- ▶ Explain as you demonstrate; repeat yourself.

INSTRUCT

▶ Give detailed step by step instructions as the students do the exercise.

▶ Tell them what to do.

▶ Tell them when to do it.

▶ Tell them when to stop.

TRAIN

▶ Allow the student to work on the exercises independently.

▶ "Going solo" motivates a student and increases the liklihood of practice.

HELP

▶ Use your observation skills to help those experiencing difficulty.

▶ Assess the students' progress.

▶ Assist where needed.

▶ Praise to build confidence and to reinforce the behavior.

The remainder of this book is dedicated to showing you how you can go about changing people and changing dogs. The journey will include strategies, techniques, exercises and case studies.

When talking to your students, bear in mind the following points:

Specific Instructions
Explain to your students *exactly* what you would like them to do. For example:
Suppose you want to teach the "sit" behavior by luring. Instead of saying, "Take the treat and lure your dog into a sit," you might say something like this:
"With your dog facing you, hold the leash in your left hand. With your right hand, take a treat, and move it slowly towards the dog until your hand is over his head. Now, move the treat a bit higher and away from you."
Remember to speak clearly, slowly and confidently.

Phrasing
Make suggestions, not corrections. Be very clear and detailed in your instructions.
Use common, everyday terminology. If you use training terminology, be sure to define it.
Be positive in your choice of words. Avoid negative language (don't, not, never).

Small Increments
Break each exercise into small increments. By doing so, you will set achievable goals for your students. Each tiny goal achieved becomes another success for your students.

Relevancy
Explain why you are teaching each exercise and its use in day-to-day living. (Ex: "A sit stay can be used when you have visitors so your dog won't slip out the door." or "The 'leave it' behavior can be a lifesaver if you drop a bottle of Tylenol.) By making the exercises important in your student's mind, they will be more likely to train. An increase in training sessions will lead to greater success on their part.

When demonstrating a new skill, make sure all can see what you are doing.
Try and be upbeat and keep the mood light and cheery. Laugh and be lighthearted if things don't go as planned.

Special thanks to Sue Sternberg who created EDITH based on Glen Johnson's EDICT (Explain, Demonstrate, Instruct, Correct, Train) of teaching. Visit her website http://www.suesternberg.com

Johnson, Glen, Tracking Dog: Theory & Methods, 1977

"Tell me and I'll forget.

Show me and I'll remember.

Involve me and I'll understand."

~Chinese Proverb

4 Training Resources and Equipment

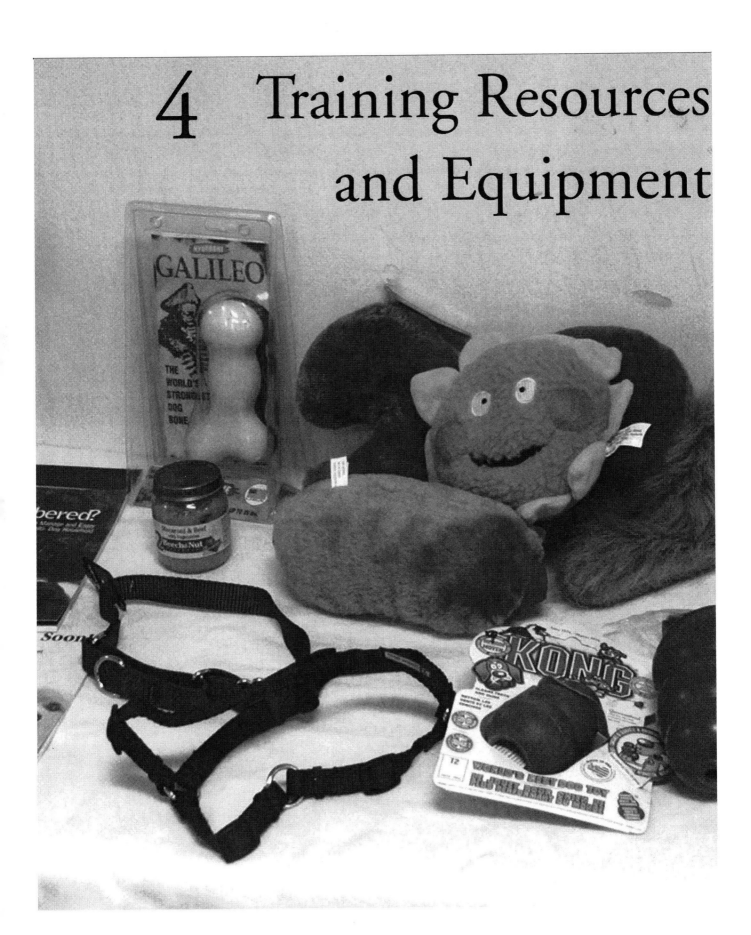

Tools do not teach dogs. Consistent reward-based training teaches dogs. However, using the right tools correctly can greatly facilitate success in teaching and learning.

This chapter describes the tools available, which tools are recommended and which are not, and the correct use of the recommended tools for positive reinforcement training techniques.

RESTRAINT AND CONTROL EQUIPMENT

Collars and harnesses are used for restraint and control. The effect of different restraint equipment on a dog varies depending on the equipment and the dog. Some equipment is recommended, and others should be avoided (particularly for over-reactive dogs). Any type of restraint and control equipment can cause injury if fitted improperly or misused.

Below is a table that provides the advantages and disadvantages of different types of restraint equipment. (Tools with ♦ are those I recommend.)

	Advantages	Disadvantages
Flat Buckle Collar ♦	Can be used for ID tags. Does not tighten to constrict around the dog's neck.	Minor risk of getting caught on an object if left on while the dog is unattended.
Halter ♦ (Halti, Snoot Loop, Gentle Leader, New Trix halter) 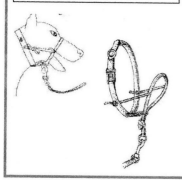	Does not choke, restrict the airway, or put pressure on the trachea or spine. Can have a calming affect on some dogs. The handler can control the dog's head without strength, and achieve good results with minimal training. Useful for reactive dogs, since the dog's head (the sharp end with the teeth) can be controlled.	Non-traditional appearance, so public may assume that the dog is aggressive and wearing a muzzle. If fitted improperly, can rub fur off the dog's nose and irritate the eye area. If the handler jerks on the leash, neck injury can result. Desensitization to halter is required. Some dogs may become anxious or stressed when wearing the head collar, so the dog should be conditioned to the halter before use. *See "Conditioning to a Halter" page 128*
♦Front Ring Harness Sense-ation or EasyWalk Harness 	Leash attaches to the chest strap. When the dog attempts to pull, pressure on the leash causes him to turn. Avoids the opposition reflex (a major reason dogs pull). Easy to put on. Can be left on during off leash activities (while the dog is supervised).	Some dogs can back out of the harness. The dog can chew the harness off if left unattended.

The Sense-ation harness

"Moe" owned by Mary Taylor

Martingale collars, with chain and fabric versions.

	Advantages	Disadvantages
Martingale Collar	If fitted properly, there is a limit to the amount of choking, therefore less harmful to the windpipe than a choke collar. Sometimes called 'Greyhound Collars" they are often recommended for narrow-headed dogs like Greyhounds and Whippets who can easily back out of buckle collars.	If fitted too snugly, the martingale collar acts like a slip collar; if the dog pulls, it can put unlimited pressure on the trachea. There is risk of the fabric loop or loose ring getting hooked on foreign objects, causing the collar to tighten and strangle the dog.
Prong Collar or Pinch Collar 	Does not put pressure on the trachea. Pinching action can be modified by inverting the prongs. Effective for strong, pain insensitive dogs and weak owners.	Risk of injury: Should never be left on unattended dog. Can become loose, causing collar to fall apart. Non-traditional appearance. Painful corrections can result in fearful or aggressive behaviors in sensitive dogs. The general public may assume a dog wearing a prong collar is aggressive. Difficult for an arthritic person to put a prong collar on the dog.
Choke Collar or Choke Chain 	Can be recycled as a leash attachment to discourage dogs who like to bite and mouth their leashes.	Unlimited constriction. Risk of pain, injury or even death by choking if pulled too tightly or if the 'live' ring becomes caught on something and the dog panics. If used improperly and fitted the wrong way, these collars will constrict but not release.

	Advantages	Disadvantages
Electronic Shock Collar or (E-Collar)		Must be charged for use. Works by causing fear due to pain. Use of pain, such as shocks delivered by E-Collar, can elicit fearful and aggressive responses. Results of a recent study show that, even when used "properly", an E-Collar undermines the dog-handler relationship and poisons cues by associating the handler, the cues and the training area with painful experiences. [1]

[1] "Training Dogs with Help of the Shock Collar: Short and Long Term Behavioral Effects", Matthijs B.H. Schilder and Joanne A.M. van der Borg, Applied Animal Behavior Science 85 (2004) 319-334

Any restraint and control device can cause injury if used improperly. For example, if a handler hauls or yanks hard on a dog's neck, injury is possible with any collar. The electronic, choke, prong and (to a lesser extent) martingale collar are typically used in punishment based training. Punishment-based restraint and control devices can cause painful and aversive experiences for the dog and therefore I do not recommend them, particularly for over-reactive dogs. For safe restraint and control of the dog, proper use of a flat collar, Sense-ation harness or halter is recommended.

BARK COLLARS

Below is a table that provides the advantages and disadvantages of different types of bark collars. (Collars with ♦ are those I recommend.)

	Advantages	Disadvantages
Citronella Collar ♦ 	Has an 88% effective result from study by Tufts University.	Need to refill the citronella often. No on/off switch, so battery needs to be removed when not in use. Less effective on longhair dogs, since the dog's hair can obstruct the spray. Being sprayed in the face with citronella is aversive to the dog. Can be stressful and may cause a negative association with the area of use (such as the dog's crate). The dog learns he is not punished for barking when the collar is off. Punishment does not teach a dog what to do, so reinforcement for quiet behavior is necessary for punishment to be effective. Can activate from other dog's barking or similar noises.

	Advantages	Disadvantages
Electronic Bark Collar 	Only 50% effective, according to a study by Tufts University.	Need to remove the battery when not in use. The dog learns he is not punished for barking when the collar is off. Punishment does not teach a dog what to do, so reinforcement for quiet behavior is necessary for punishment to be effective.

The best solution for barking is to set up the dog's environment so he is not inclined to bark, and reinforce quiet. Don't allow a crated dog to see or hear activities that cause him to bark, such as other dogs running. Provide exercise before confinement to set the dog up for a Kong chew session or a nap.

EYE COVERINGS

Trish King of the Marin County Humane Society, Novato, California, developed the Hoody or Calming Cap. Eye coverings have been used to calm hawks, horses and wild animals for years. The Calming Cap uses the same principle and is used to calm reactive dogs. It is extremely helpful to desensitize against movement such as car chasing, joggers, cyclists and car sickness or fear whilst travelling, noise phobias and reactivity towards other dogs.

"River" owned by Jill Davis

INSTRUCTIONS FOR USE

IMPORTANT: Introduce the cap slowly to the animal. Some dogs are very accepting of the Calming Cap and others need more time.
◆ Desensitise the dog to any sounds from the Velcro fastener. To do this, begin at a distance, opening and closing the Velcro strip while gradually bringing the Calming Cap closer to the dog. Each time you move closer you should treat the dog for a positive response to the noise. If you notice a fearful or stressful response take a step back to where the dog was comfortable with the noise and start again.

◆ Allow the dog to sniff and investigate the Calming Cap. Treat for each positive interaction. *Note: Do not place the cap on the dog's head yet.*

◆ Allow the Calming Cap to sit or lay across the dogs muzzle and treat.

◆ Allow the Calming Cap to sit or lay across the dogs face and eyes and treat.

◆ Allow the Calming Cap to sit or lay or across the dogs face, eyes and head and treat.

◆ When you can successfully complete the above steps with the dog feeling comfortable move onto placing the Calming Cap onto the head.

◆Leave Calming Cap on for longer and longer until you can guarantee that dog will not try to remove.

◆Place your fingers through the elastic end of the Calming Cap while holding a treat in same hand and gently slide Calming Cap onto the muzzle, give treat and remove it.

◆Repeat for as many times as it takes for the animal to feel comfortable.

◆Once the dog is comfortable slip the Calming Cap up and over the eyes. Treat and remove the Calming Cap.

◆Increase the time the Calming Cap is left on always treating.

◆ Once you can leave the Calming Cap on the dog comfortably for several minutes slip the Velcro fastener (located at the top back of the Calming Cap) under the collar, back over and fasten to Calming Cap, do the same with the velcro under the muzzle.

◆By now the dog should feel comfortable and relaxed wearing the Calming Cap. At this point allow the dog to chew on a bone or a stuffed Kong so the dog is comfortable to it being on for a while then do the same in the car.

◆If you need to walk the dog with the Calming Cap in place then make sure he is used to this in the safe area of your home first making sure the dog doesn't bump into anything.

◆Make sure another dog doesn't ever rush or approach your dog unexpectedly. Control dog to dog meetings with lots of cookies and space for both dogs or you can do more harm than good.

DOG APPEASING PHEREMONE (DAP ™)

DAP is a synthetic formulation of the pheremone releasd by a nursing bitch. It comes in a spray, a diffuser similar to plug in air fresheners and is also available in a collar dispenser. DAP is said to create a relaxed sense of well being and is successful in reducing stress for some dogs. Useful for some cases of noise phobia and separation anxiety.

LEASHES

A leash is a tool for safety and control. As a tool for safety, a leash prevents the dog from getting into a dangerous situation, such as in the path of road traffic. As a tool for control, a leash prevents the dog from performing inappropriate behavior; it is part of setting up the dog's environment for success.

Dogs learn best by choice, not coercion or physical manipulation. To teach the dog, the handler should set up the environment so the dog is unlikely to perform (therefore practice and be inadvertently reinforced for) inappropriate behavior, but likely to perform the desired behavior. The handler then repeatedly reinforces the desired behavior, and the dog becomes more likely to repeat that behavior than any inappropriate behavior.

Learning is strongest when the dog is allowed to choose and rehearse rewardable behavior. Choice behavior creates and strengthens neural connections in the dog's brain, allowing the dog to learn analytical and mechanical skills. To allow choice behavior, a leash should not be used as a training tool to teach the dog what to do, but rather a tool to prevent the dog from performing inappropriate behavior .

Different types of leashes can be used to fulfill various safety and control needs.

TRADITIONAL "WALKING" LEASH

Walking leashes are made of leather, nylon, fabric or metal chain. Metal chain is uncomfortable to hold, so is not recommended. Leather takes time to dry when wet, but is comfortable to hold. Nylon or fabric leashes are comfortable to hold, and both can be easily washed.

Leashes come in various lengths, from 2 to 6 feet. A walking leash should be long enough so that, while your dog strolls next to you, the leash flows comfortably from your hand down to the dog's chest, then up to the dog's collar, halter or Sen-sation harness.

EXTENDING LEASH

An extending leash is a plastic handle with a thin nylon cord rolled up inside. The cord extends as it is pulled, and automatically retracts when released. The cord comes in different lengths. Common lengths are 10 feet and 26 feet. To act as a normal leash, the cord can be locked to a specific length by pressing a button on the handle, so it does not extend or retract.

Extending leashes have a mild but constant pull (the dog can never provide a "loose leash"). Therefore, they should only be used with a traditional harness or flat collar. Because there is a constant pull, the dog can feel whether the extending leash is on or off. An extending leash is not particularly useful for training an off-leash recall, since the dog may learn to come only when he feels the pull (therefore knows he's on leash).

Joggers sometimes use extending leashes because there is never slack in the leash to trip over and the leash can be attached to a belt with a quick-release snap (this is not recommended for large dogs).

There are safety issues with extending leashes. The handle of an extending leash can easily pop out of the handler's grip if jerked by the dog. The cord can burn skin if it is held while the dog is running, so handlers should avoid grabbing the line to stop the dog. Other loose dogs can run through the extending leash because the line is nearly invisible.

Extending leashes should only be used in safe, open areas. Never use an extending leash near traffic or where the dog needs to be under close control.

DRAG LINE AND TAG LINE

Training a reliable recall is important, particularly with a maturing puppy or adolescent dog. A drag line (also known as a "long line") can be used to teach the dog to stay with the handler, even if the handler is not directly interacting with the dog. The drag line allows the handler to practice off leash training while keeping the dog safe in an unfenced area. It is a useful tool for keeping the dog safe while he develops a relationship with the handler. To make a drag line, buy a snap-release clip and 1/4" (50mm) nylon rope between 20' - 100' (6m - 30m) in length (whatever length suits the handler's needs for the particular dog's size and speed). If the rope is nylon, use a match or open flame to melt the ends so they won't unravel. Wrap brightly colored plastic tape about 10 feet from one end, then tie the snap release clip to the other end. The tape marks the approach of the loose end so that the handler can step on it easily as it drags along the ground.

A drag line should be used until the dog believes that returning to the handler when called is better than all other choices. Keep the dog on a drag line during all outdoor training, play and exercise sessions. Always use the drag line when you have the dog off leash, unless you are 100% certain that the dog will come when called in that particular environment.

If the dog is able to give you his attention in familiar areas, such as parks where you frequently train or around home, he may not be able to give you the same attention in new places. Use a drag line in new or highly distracting places, until you are certain the dog will come when called.

SAFE DRAG LINE USE

1. Before turning the dog loose, clip a drag line to his flat buckle collar or harness.

2. Let line drag on ground.

3. Let the dog wander and explore. Stay close enough to step on the end of the drag line if the dog is preparing to get into trouble.

4. If the dog is distracted and you are unable to get his attention by calling or luring him, calmly step on end of drag line and wait silently for his attention. The very instant the dog gives you his attention, click and treat. When the dog gets to you, jackpot him with a toy, play and praise.

If the dog doesn't give you his attention, try one of the following:

◆   Run backward to help attract him to you.

◆   Throw yourself to the ground and, when the dog comes to investigate, reward and play.

◆   Make yourself more appealing than normal by having someone else stand on the drag line while you run and hide.

If the dog still doesn't give you his attention, you are working in an area with too much distraction for the dog to handle at his current level of training. Practice attention games in less distracting locations.

TAG LINE

When the drag line becomes shortened to the point it no longer drags, it is called a tag line. A tag line is a short rope, between 1 and 3 feet (.3 - 1m) in length, that can be used to safely get hold of the dog. Grabbing a tag line is safer than grabbing the collar.

Use a 3 foot (1m) tag line that can be stepped on to prevent jumping.

Rules for Drag and Tag Line Safety

◆   Don't ever use the drag line as a leash.

◆   Don't ever use the drag line to pull the dog to you.

◆   Don't leave a drag line or tag line on a dog unattended.

FOOD TREATS

When using food treats for training, make sure you begin with a hungry dog. Use nutritious training treats as all or part of the dog's meal.

Overweight dogs are prone to the same illnesses as overweight people, so don't allow the dog to become overweight. In general, with a dog in good weight:

◆   You can feel the dog's ribs easily when you lightly run your fingers across his ribcage.

◆   When viewed from above, his body has an hourglass shape.

◆   When viewed from the side, his undercarriage has a dramatic rise from his ribcage to his abdomen (his abdomen is about half the width of his ribcage).

The most effective food treats are moist, smelly and diced into tiny cubes (about ¼ inch square). The smaller the treats, the quicker they can be swallowed and the more times a behavior can be rewarded before the dog becomes satiated or satisfies his daily caloric intake. Moist treats are more palatable: They slide down the dog's throat easily and are generally smellier, so they maintain the dog's interest longer.

Training treats can be a large proportion of a dog's daily caloric intake, so should be nutritious. Avoid packaged treats containing corn gluten, various sugars, manufactured flavors and colorings. Use home-cooked foods or high quality moist dog foods such as Rollover or Natural Balance (this type of dog food comes sausage-shaped, packaged in plastic, and is easy to dice).

For convenience, treats can be chopped, split into training session portions and frozen in plastic Ziploc freezer bags.

Vary the types of food used to maintain the dog's interest (at least 3 types of training treat per training session). The following food, diced into cubes, work well as training treats.

Cheese. String cheese works great and is easy to tear into pieces

Freeze dried liver

Baked gizzard or heart

Cooked steak, pork or other meat

Baked skinless, boneless chicken

Sausage. (Avoid spiced sausage. Don't over-use hot dogs or frankfurters since these contain a large amount of salt. Use chicken or turkey hotdogs for less fat.)

Rollover or Natural Balance (or similar sausage-shaped moist dog food).

Raw diet (may be messy; wash hands after use to avoid bacterial illness).

Carrots (for dogs on a low calorie diet).

Rice cake (for dogs with sensitive stomachs).

Zukes Mini Naturals, Zukes Hip Action Treats, or other packaged treats prepared without artificial preservatives or coloring.

Some foods can be toxic to dogs.

Do NOT feed your dog any of the following foods:

grapes	raisins	macadamia nuts
garlic	onions	chocolate

Veterinarians occasionally discover additional foods that can be toxic to dogs. For the latest, see the ASPCA (Association for the Prevention of Cruelty to Animals) website: http://www.aspca.org, menu item "Pet Care".

ENVIRONMENTAL ENRICHMENT

An environment rich in activities and novel items provides a dog with a means of burning off excess mental and physical energy and encourages him to interact and learn. Many types of toys are available to enrich the dog's environment.

USE TOYS FOR SOCIALIZATION AND TRAINING

Games with toys can be used to enhance the handler's relationship with the dog and teach the dog social skills. *(For dogs that lack toy motivation, see "Teaching Toy Motivation" page 189)*

◆ **VARIETY**

Rotate the dog's toys weekly by keeping four or five toys easily accessible and putting the rest out of reach. Provide toys that offer a variety of uses: One toy to carry, one to "kill", one to roll and one to chew.

◆ **INTERACTION**

Use toys as a means to interact with the dog. For example, play hide-and-seek by hiding the toy and letting the dog find it. A "found" toy is more attractive than a toy blatantly introduced. Interactive play such as hide-and-seek, fetch or tug can expel pent-up mental and physical energy in a limited amount of time and space. This greatly reduces stress due to confinement, isolation or boredom. For young, high-energy dogs, interactive play offers an opportunity for socialization and helps them learn appropriate behavior with people and other animals.

◆ REINFORCEMENT

Initiate play when the dog is generally at his most active, and the dog will find play motivating. A play-motivated dog is a joy to train. Use play to consistently reinforce appropriate behavior. For example, the dog sits and the ball is thrown. Never force a tired dog to play, since this can be punishing to the dog.

CHOOSE SAFE TOYS

There are many dog toys on the market for chewing and play. Although there is no guarantee for the dog's safety with any specific toy, here are some useful guidelines to help keep the dog safe:

◆ Dog-proof the dog's environment. As with children, dogs are curious, so are often attracted to novel (possibly dangerous) situations. Dogs have the potential to ingest normally innocuous items, such as string, ribbon, rubber bands, children's toys, pantyhose or pea gravel. Remove potentially dangerous items from the dog's access.

◆ Never play fetch with sticks. Sticks, especially for the exuberant dog, can puncture a dog's chest and lungs or become lodged in a dog's throat, requiring emergency veterinary surgery and possibly causing death.

◆ Match the toy to the dog. Toys should be appropriate to the dog's size, chewing strength and activity level. Balls and other toys that are too small can be swallowed or become lodged in the dog's throat. Small rawhide chews, such as the pencil-sized twisted rawhide sticks, are dangerous for medium or large dogs. Small rawhides can be swallowed whole by medium or large dogs. This can block the dog's airway or intestine. Larger toys like hooves, pig's ears and big rawhide bones may be given, but chewing should always be supervised. For strong chewers, hard toys such as Kongs or Nylabones are safer, and last longer, than soft toys.

◆ Check the toy materials. Fabric toys should be machine washable. Check labels for child safety. Fabric toys labeled safe for children under three don't contain dangerous fillings, such as nutshells and polystyrene beads. However, even "safe" stuffing is not digestible. Fabric toys are not indestructible, but some are sturdier than others. Avoid toys with yarn, false eyes or other parts that can be chewed off. Take note of any toy that contains a "squeaker" buried in its center. The dog may feel that he must seek-and-destroy the source of the squeak. He may ingest the plastic squeaker parts, which could block his intestine. Discard damaged toys.

◆ Supervise. Most toys are not meant to be left with the dog while unattended, due to choking hazard. Discard damaged toys before bits can be chewed off. Swap the chew toy for a yummy food treat before it becomes small enough to become a choking hazard.

TOYS FOR CHEWING

Chewing is a natural dog behavior that burns physical and mental energy. Chewing is pacifying to a dog. Use chewable toys as an opportunity to play exchange games and to proof the dog against resource guarding. For example, have the dog play fetch with a rawhide chew chip several times before he begins to chew it. Chewable toys that are edible should be used in moderation since they become part of the daily calorie intake. Check the ingredients to be sure edible chew toys are a nutritious part of the dog's diet.

BONES

Raw bones are a nutritious chew toy. Only use heavy bones, such as cow knuckle bones. Never feed cooked bones or bones small enough to be swallowed. When a bone becomes small enough to be a choking hazard, trade it for a treat and discard it. Wash hands after handling raw bones or meat.

RAWHIDE CHEWS

Rawhide chews give the dog chewing exercise and help keep the teeth clean. They come in many shapes and sizes. Choose a size appropriate to the dog. They also come in different types, including chips, pressed and knotted. Beware flavored bones, since the coloring may stain carpet. Purchase rawhide that has been manufactured (not just packaged) in the U.S.A. or U.K.. Places such as Brazil/Mexico or the Far East do not have stringent manufacturing regulations, so toxins and bacteria may be present in rawhide products manufactured there. Don't leave a dog unattended with a rawhide chew, since choking is a possibility.

KONGS

Kongs are a brilliant invention. A stuffed Knong can keep a dog busy and quiet for a good 10 or 20 minutes. Kongs and similar hard-wearing stuffable toys can be filled with food again and again, lasting many years. Only by chewing and licking the Kong diligently can the dog access the food. There are many foods that can be used to stuff a Kong. Here are a few (check with your vet to be sure these foods are safe for your dog):

Peanut butter	Cubed cheese
Cottage cheese	Tripe
Liver	Chicken
Canned dog food	Dog kibble

Kong Stuffing (sold at pet stores in squeeze-top cans)

Cheese Whiz (soft cheese in a squeeze-top can)

Feel free to mix-and-match several different foods in the same Kong. Keep a few Kongs made up in the freezer for a handy snack.

FOOD DISPENSING TOYS

There are a number of interactive treat dispensing toys on the market. The toys release pieces of kibble or treats when the dog moves them around using his nose or paws. Trying to get the kibble keeps a dog entertained.

The downside to the hard plastic food dispensing toys are that they make a racket on wood or tile floors and some designs easily get stuck in corners of the room or next to furniture. When one of these toys gets stuck, it no longer delivers treats. Some dogs give up before they figure out how to get the cube moving again.

NYLABONE

Very hard rubber or plastic toys, such as Nylabones are available in a variety of hardness, shapes, sizes and flavors. This type of chew toy can be long-lasting. Puppy Nylabones are soft, so don't give them to puppies or dogs that are strong chewers. The longest lasting Nylabones are the hardest ones.

Some dogs enjoy Nylabones immediately, and others need to be enticed. Develop the dog's interest by tossing the Nylabone around, alternating fetch with keep-away games. Once the dog learns the Nylabone is nice to chew, he will be more likely to accept the next Nylabone offered.

To avoid choking hazard, purchase a hard enough and large enough Nylabone for the chewing strength and size of the dog. Discard the Nylabone when the rounded ends have been chewed off.

TOYS FOR PLAY

SQUEAKY TOYS

Squeaky toys come in many varieties, from plastic or rubber to stuffed fabric toys. Many of the latest fabric squeaky toys are made of fairly durable materials, and some float for water-fetch games.

Some squeaky toys are tougher than others. Make sure the size and durability of the toy is appropriate to the size of the dog to avoid a choking hazard. For dogs that enjoy carrying, the toy should be small enough to pick up. For dogs that want to shake or "kill", the toy should be the size of "prey" for that size dog (mouse, rabbit or duck size).

Fabric toys are useful because they can retain familiar scent, therefore can pacify a shy dog. However, fabric toys are not appropriate for all dogs. Strong chewers and dogs that like to dissect can dismember a fabric toy in seconds.

If the dog has a tendency to dissect toys, don't leave him unattended with squeaky toys. The dog may pull out and swallow the squeaker, or may chew off and swallow bits of the toy. For strong chewers, use hard-rubber toys such as Kongs or Nylabones.

TUG TOYS

Tug is a great outlet for dogs, and helps build motivation and teamwork skills. *(See Tug Games page 190 and Teaching Toy Motivation page 189)*

A tug toy should be long enough so that both you and the dog can hold it, with comfortable distance between your hand and the dog's mouth.

Tug toys should be tough enough so that they are durable, but soft enough that they don't hurt the dog's mouth. Some dogs are tough tuggers, others are shy tuggers, so choose a tug toy appropriate to the dog (tough tugs for tough tuggers, soft tugs for shy tuggers). Avoid using rope that is thin or hard, since this can injure the dog's mouth. Thick, soft rope or fabric (such as a dishtowel or old T-shirt) is best.

A terrific source of affordable, durable and soft handmade tug toys is the Canadian company "Crash Test Toys" at http://www.axxent.ca/~crasher/. Tugs from Crash Test Toys have a nylon strap in the center, so last a long time, with a braided fur fabric cover, so they are soft on the dog's mouth.

CHASE TOYS

A horse lunge whip is a great energy burning toy for prey driven dogs, particularly for handlers unable to run due to physical limitations. Purchase a horse lunge whip and attach a fuzzy piece of material onto the end. Jiggle it around like a mouse moving to entice the dog to pounce on it. Begin moving it in larger circles. Most dogs love to chase the toy at the end of the whip. It's a great energy burner that will tire the dog quickly. A fun toy known as the 'Chase-it" is commercially available.

FETCH TOYS (AND EXERCISE)

Playing fetch is an inexpensive and enjoyable exercise. (*See Retrieve Exercises page 178.*) Fetch toys include Frisbees, rubber bumpers and balls, among others. Frisbees are available in different materials, from hard plastic to soft rubber to tough fabric. Rubber or fabric Frisbees are easier on the dog's teeth than hard plastic Frisbees. Rubber bumpers are durable and they float, so they can be used for water fetch games. Balls are available in many materials. Avoid foam and soft rubber balls since small parts can be chewed off and swallowed. Hard rubber or tennis balls are safer.

Make sure the size of the ball is appropriate for the size of the dog. Standard sized tennis balls (those used for tennis) are fine for most dogs. Don't use tennis balls that are soft or broken, or balls that are too small for the size of the dog's mouth, because these can become lodged in the dog's throat when caught. Chewing on tennis balls can cause the dog's teeth to wear down, so tennis balls should not be left with the dog unattended.

When using a standard tennis ball, a Chuck-it or similar "throwing arm" can be used to get speed and distance which can help the dog learn to run faster and farther, giving him more exercise.

A fast and furious game of ball fetching is great fitness training. However, speed produces strength not stamina. To keep the dog fit, follow these pointers:

◆ The dog should have a warm up before heavy exercise, and a cool down afterward.

◆ Watch for a thickened red tongue during ball fetch or other heavy exercise. Any tint of blue means the dog needs a short rest to get the oxygen back into his blood.

◆ Balance ball-fetch and other speed-based exercise with stamina-based exercise, such as walking or trotting.

◆ Keep the dog's muscles toned and balanced through limbering exercises.

CRATES

A crate should be large enough that the dog can stand with his head up in a natural position, turn around easily, and curl up or stretch out while lying down. This generally means a minimum of six inches longer than the dog's length from chest to tail and six inches taller than the dog's shoulder height. Larger is better, particularly for long periods of confinement (more than an hour).

BEDDING

The dog's bed should be a place where the dog can feel relaxed and secure. Bedding should be comfortable and washable. Dog beds sold in stores have various stuffing, including cedar shavings (which smell nice and repel fleas), poly foam and memory foam (nice for older dogs, since it shapes itself to the dog's body, avoiding pressure points). Many dog beds have an outer cover that can be machine washed.

CRATE MANAGEMENT

Careful crate management is important, particularly for herding or guarding breeds, or for an over-reactive dog. A dog in a crate may feel vulnerable, particularly an over-reactive dog. Avoid crate-guarding reactivity by placing the dog's crate as far from foot traffic, and other stressors, as possible. Never place the dog's crate next to an access way where other dogs or people pass by. When attending an event (such as a competition) be aware of the noise levels in the area and set up the crate in an area away from noise, even if it means you have to walk farther to get to the arena.

When using a crate in an area of high activity, such as a dog training class or agility competition, face the crate door away from the activity and cover the back and sides of the crate with a sheet. This allows ventilation but does not allow the dog to see the activities. A dog allowed to watch and become aroused by fast-movement activities may learn to stare and target: Behaviors that can later lead to chasing or dog aggression. Always provide access to water. Small water dishes and water bottles are available specifically for use in crates.

A dog should associate his crate with safety and relaxation. Teach the dog that his crate is a place for rest by removing arousing stimuli and providing a Kong or bone for him to chew. (*See Crate Conditioning page 136.*)

	Advantages	Disadvantages
Fabric Mesh Crates 	Lightweight. Folds easily for travel.	Not cheap. Ventilation not as good as with wire mesh crates. Can be washed, but takes time to dry. Dog can destroy the crate and possibly escape by chewing the fabric. Some dogs can escape in a matter of minutes.
Wire Mesh Crates	Fairly inexpensive. Excellent ventilation. Fold up easily for travel. Durable. Fully washable.	Heavy to carry. Sometimes welding needs to be done to repair them. Unless they are covered, wire crates do not provide much privacy to the dog.
Plastic Crates	Inexpensive. Durable. Some manufacturers follow airline standards, so may be acceptable on airline. Fully washable.	Heavy to carry. Poor ventilation; not recommended for hot weather. Does not fold up (split in half for storing or travel).

CLICKERS

There are many different clickers on the market, several of which are fairly new. Different clickers have different advantages. The handler can use a variety of clickers to train a dog, as long as each clicker has been charged (the dog has learned a strong association between the clicker noise and a treat). *(See "Learning", Chapter 2, "Mark the Behavior" page 17.)*

◆   Traditional Clicker. A traditional clicker is a tiny plastic box with a metal tongue that clicks when pressed and released using the thumb. Traditional clickers can be loud. If the dog is sound sensitive, the handler should quiet the clicker by layering tape on the metal tongue. The layers can gradually be removed as the dog begins to associate the sound with food treats. Alternatively, the clicker can be pressed only when in the handler's pocket (which will buffer the noise).

◆   i-Click. The i-Click can be worked using the thumb, mouth, or foot. The i-Click emits a quieter sound than the traditional clicker, so is useful for sound-sensitive dogs. However, the i-Click is not useful for noisy environments, such as training classes.

◆   Clicker+. The Clicker+ is similar to the i-Click, but it is electronic. The Clicker+ provides multiple sounds and volume control. However, there is a very slight delay in the Clicker+ sound that does not occur in a Traditional clicker or i-Click. Also, there is no off/on switch, so the battery must be removed when not in use.

◆   Treat and Train. Now called the "Manners Minder" and marketed by Premier Products, the Manners Minder is a mechanical device that delivers a tone and drops a piece of kibble or treat into a bowl by remote control. The Manners Minder is good for certain applications, such as distance work, weaning food off the handler's body and crate conditioning. The Manners Minder has some limitations. For example, moist food cannot be used and occasionally kibble fails to drop, or more than one kibble is dropped. As with the Clicker+, there is a very slight delay between the button press and the sound of the tone (the marker). The Manners Minder is particularly useful for remote applications, such as reinforcing a dog for quiet while he is in his crate or for staying on his mat. Agility trainers find them useful for training contacts. For timing and control of treat location (such as tossing the treat in different directions to generalize a behavior) the traditional clicker or i-Click is best.

I do not use clickers when working with dogs who are upset, aggressive or over-threshold. When there are serious emotional issues involved, I prefer to use a verbal reward marker. Clickers are amazing and wonderful tools for teaching new behaviors to mentally healthy dogs.

TREAT BAGS

There are many types of treat bags on the market, so choose one that's comfortable for you. Types of treat bags include:

▶ Waist pouches.

▶ Shoulder pouches.

▶ Carpenter's pouches. Very inexpensive cotton pouches sold at hardware stores for holding nails and other hardware work great as treat bags.

▶ Multi-pocketed training vests.

Treat pouches can have Velcro or pop-hinge openings to avoid spillage and allow easy access to the treats. The old fashioned jacket pocket is another good idea for carrying treats. Practical tip: Keep the treat bag or pocket clean by containing the treats in a plastic Ziploc bag, inside the treat bag.

Some training should be done without food on the handler. For example, place small bowls of food around the training area, where the dog cannot reach them. Cue a behavior, mark the behavior, then praise the dog while you walk to a bowl to get a treat for him.

OTHER EQUIPMENT

A lifelike stuffed dog can be very useful for working with dogs who have problems with other dogs. Many toy stores sell life-sized dogs of various breeds. Look for one with a natural posture.

Pictured here is Dee's co-worker Fred. Fred wears a bandana that has been worn by a real dog for scent, a collar and leash. Fred's open mouth, lolling tongue and tipped-over tail show a relaxed posture.

OBSTACLE COURSE EQUIPMENT

Plastic cones, poles and other safe pieces of equipment can be used to provide an obstacle course, such as a set of cavalettis, for the dog to navigate. In navigating an obstacle course, the dog must concentrate on where his next step will be, and is reinforced for managing the course while ignoring any scary stimuli. This is particularly useful for desensitizing or counter conditioning over-reactive dogs.

For a detailed description of cavaletti course use, *see "Cavaletti Course" page 124.*

"Dogs are not our whole lives,
but they make our lives whole"

~Roger Caras

5 Strategies and Techniques

This chapter evaluates the strategies and techniques to be employed to move the dog and handler toward their goals.

Note: All training exercises referred to in this chapter will appear in bold type. These training exercises are fully described in alphabetical order in Appendix A. When you see any of these exercises refer to Appendix A to learn how to train the behaviors.

OVERVIEW OF EXERCISES

FOUNDATION AND RELATIONSHIP SKILLS

Active Attention ♦	Voluntary Look Back ♦
Body Block for Control ♦	Down ♦
Exchange Games ♦	Gotcha Game ♦
Grooming ♦	Loose Leash Walking ♦
Look Back ♦	Name Recognition ♦
Relaxed Down (shaped) ♦	Retrieve Games ♦
Settle-Step on the leash Relaxed Down ♦	Scent Games ♦
Sit, Sit for Greeting ♦	Stay Using the Body Block ♦
Taking Treats Politely ♦	Teaching Toy Motivation ♦
Wait ♦	

♦ *Suggested exercises to begin with, depending on the needs of the handler and dog.*

SELF-CONTROL SKILLS

Chill Out Game	Food Bowl Games
Leave It	Tug Games
Self Control with Distractions	Scent Games

BEHAVIOR MODIFICATION PROGRAMS

Waiting for Permission

Countering Lunging or Chasing

Cavaletti Course

Counter Condition Fear or Aggression

Redirecting vs. Desensitization

Nose-Target

Desensitizing Separation Anxiety

Head and Shoulder Desensitizing

Recall using Premack

Counter Conditioning Dog to Dog
Resource Guarding

CONDITIONING EXERCISES

Crate Conditioning

Gotcha Game

Quiet at the Door

Conditioning to a Halter or Muzzle

On-Off (Placement)

Preparing for the Vet visit

MANAGEMENT EXERCISES

Crate Conditioning

Leaving the House

Greeting Visitors at the Door

Creating a 'Safe Zone'

PROOFING BEHAVIORS USING THE 4 D'S

Down Stay

Leaving the House

Refresher Attention Games for a Week

Recall from Distraction

Side-by-Side Walking

Finding the Heel Position

Passive Attention

Recall Games

Recall using Premack

Waiting for Permission

BASIC CARE

When bringing a dog into your home, you are morally obligated to feed, protect and nurture him. The dog cannot naturally make "good" choices regarding human values like living with clean floors and furniture or not barking at strangers and so forth. The dog can be supervised for his own protection and taught to behave appropriately with animate and inanimate objects that matter to you. For the relationship to be playful, fun and mutually enjoyable, you must understand the difference between your needs and your dog's needs. You must anticipate and plan for these differences. Understanding provides the basis for a lifetime of friendship between you and your dog.

Set up for success! Prepare the house and yard for proper management so the dog won't become overly aroused and get into trouble.

▶ Have a crate where the dog can rest safely when you are unable to supervise him, such as at bedtime or when you are out. Use the crate for at least one hour a day during a time when you are at home to ensure it does not become a cue that you are leaving. The dog should not learn to view his crate as a prison, but as a safe and relaxing place for rest. (*See* **CRATE CONDITONING** *page* 136.)

▶ Set up doorway (baby) gates within your house for safety and management.

▶ Dog-proof the house by removing access to anything the dog should not eat or chew (toxic chemicals, dangling power cords, precious possessions, etc.).

▶ Fence outside areas with solid materials, to keep visual stimulation to a minimum. This will help prevent bad habits such as chasing passing pedestrians, bicyclists, etc..

Organize your schedule for:

▶ Feeding twice a day.

▶ Frequent trips outdoors for potty breaks with playtime after elimination.

▶ A minimum of 15 to 30 minutes twice a day of physical exercise for dogs over 5 months old depending on the breed of dog. Some breeds need more, some less. Use caution running with large breeds to avoid joint injury. (*See* **SCENT GAMES,** *page* 179, **SELF-CONTROL WITH DISTRACTION** *page* 180.)

▶ Daily training to teach new tricks and basic behavior, practice behaviors the dog has already learned, and play scent games. (*See* **TEACHING TOY MOTIVATION** *page* 189.)

▶ Veterinarian care. (*See* **PREPARING FOR THE VET** *page* 166.)

LEADERSHIP

In today's world of dog training, leadership is a controversial topic. Although most agree that the extreme domination-by-force approach to dog training should be dismissed, total rejection of any kind of pack behavior or leadership based in "dominance theory" ignores the genetic qualities of the canine species. The problem is in finding a middle ground that is safe and comfortable for the human-dog relationship.

There is something absolutely fundamental about this topic. I call it "relationship", to avoid the baggage of the other terms. Relationship, unlike domination, requires listening, respect and intuition.

When you take a leadership role in your relationship, dogs recognize it instantly. For example, when I take the leash of a boisterous dog in class the dog pauses almost immediately, looks at me and calms down. Unfortunately, this skill is a challenge to teach to others.

I have no personal experience with many of the problems my clients deal with. My dogs were raised with clear and consistent messages about what behavior is acceptable and what is not. I do not train them specifically for day to day life. It is just that I establish a relationship with them in which unwanted behavior never becomes an issue. It simply doesn't occur.

I started thinking "What am I doing that my clients are not doing? What makes the difference?" The answer is leadership. Leadership is communicated continuously in every day interactions, sometimes in tiny details. For me, acting as my dogs' leader is intuitive. It is a normal component of daily interaction. My dogs respond to what is communicated in my behavior and my body language.

A good human-dog relationship is like dancing. Sometimes the handler leads and other times the dog leads. When the handler needs a desired outcome, he leads. When the handler needs the dog's input, the dog leads. This is a respectful balance and allows teamwork between handler and dog.

Leadership is all about balance, poise, inner being and presence. In order to teach leadership to my clients, I need to translate some of the intangible qualities of leadership into practical, do-able, learnable behaviors or "rules".

People who establish appropriate leadership do not need to go through rank reduction programs or artificial, gimmicky rules that try to spell out leadership through force, punishment, or other practices that are destructive to their relationships with their dog. Misunderstandings about the meaning of leadership often result when the rules of leadership are over-simplified, or when people follow those rules blindly, without understanding the underlying principles of leadership and relationship.

For example, if a competitive obedience handler gives control and initiative over to their dog in every interaction, the handler might then wonder why the dog "never listens". The relationship lacks leadership, so the dog is taking control of the relationship and becoming the leader. The relationship would benefit from a few clear and consistent instructions or rules from the handler.

Years ago, the human dominated 100% of the relationship. For me this was uncomfortable. I didn't like bossing my dogs around. When the clicker came into my life, out went the dominance part of training. With new puppies we no longer maneuver the dogs around. Teaching good manners became wrapped up in teaching fancy tricks. Using the clicker, I taught agility and tracking to dogs that were categorized as difficult, who otherwise would have been euthanized.

A hands-off method, using a clicker, is brilliant for difficult dogs, except that the clicker may not help these dogs develop a tolerance for touching or handling. Along with clicker training for training new behaviors, it is important that a program for desensitization to touch and handling be incorporated to teach tolerance and build a new and better relationship. Shelter dogs that would not accept handling after weeks of training would eventually be euthanized for liability reasons. For owned dogs, a muzzle allows the dog to be conditioned to being handled safely for as long as necessary. When the dog begins to look forward to physical touch and massage and the owner can safely handle the dog, the muzzle can be excluded from handling sessions.

A dog on the furniture is not particularly a problem. However, problems can occur if the client allows the dog to be disruptive on the furniture. For example, the handler is sitting in a chair. The dog climbs up, pushes behind the handler and settles down comfortably while handler perches precariously on the edge of the seat. The handler is apparently oblivious to what has just happened, allowing the dog to practice behavior that is disruptive. In this case, the handler should be made aware of what happened, why it is a problem, and what to do about it.

There are several possible solutions for this issue. The handler can:

▶ Body-block by settling in comfortably and ignoring the dog's attempts to push in. The handler should not push the dog away, but should not concede an inch. He should assert the right to occupy the space and not allow the dog to obtain the reward of gaining the space.

▶ Use every opportunity to strengthen alternative behaviors. For example, rewarding the dog while on the floor or while on the furniture without being disruptive.

▶ Teach the dog to lie on a special mat by rewarding the dog for lying on the mat. The dog can be invited up onto the furniture as an occasional privilege.

▶ Allow the dog to get on the couch but practice asking him to get off without resentment, rewarding the dog for responding to the "off" cue.

All these approaches are non-confrontational and can be used simultaneously. This type of training teaches the dog boundaries while rewarding good behavior. This enhances the relationship between dog and handler.

The over-simplified and over-stated rule "*Don't allow your dog on the couch because it will create dominance aggression*" is incorrect. The correct rule is "*Be aware of the subtle interactions that occur in a relationship, with behavior as simple as sitting on the couch*". The simplified instruction for a beginner would be "*Teach your dog to lie on the mat*" and (if there don't appear to be any problems) "*Sometimes allow your dog on the couch as a privilege, but make sure he or she will get off when you ask. Revoke couch privileges if your dog shows signs of aggression.*"

These examples are about "establishing leadership" (or an appropriate relationship). This is different from introducing a program of rank reduction to a dog that has already established leadership and is showing aggression to maintain his position. If that is the case, attempts to establish leadership through confrontational techniques can provoke aggression, so should be avoided.

For example, performing a body-block technique with a dog that has already established his leadership and wants to maintain it can be very dangerous, while doing it with a naive dog can be very effective. Dogs are creatures of movement and body posture; they occupy territory and move through space. Dogs and people occupy space, the doorway is a narrowing of the space. Two into one is not a good mix. Something has to give.

A client of mine had a very active, outgoing Labrador/Golden Retriever cross pup about 16 weeks old. The puppy threw herself at life. This included barging through all doorways. Something had to give. In this case it was the owner's elderly mother. She got knocked off her feet and broke her arm as a result.

Obviously this was not a deliberate display of dominance on the part of the pup. The pup needed to learn that people occupy space, are worthy of notice and deserve spatial respect. She needed to learn to sit instead of jumping up, sit at the door, wait to be invited in and go around people instead of through them. These all become part of the house rules. (*See page 66 for a list of Lifestyle Tips and how to implement them.*)

Patricia McConnell devotes the entire second chapter of her wonderful book, *"The Other End of the Leash"*, to explaining how dogs read our body position and silhouette. She convincingly describes how we can use our body silhouette and position to effectively tell our dogs where we want their body to be in relation to us. She says that we need to learn how to "herd" our dogs. She calls this herding technique "body blocking".

Body blocking can be used to prevent the dog from moving into a specific space by occupying it yourself, or to encourage the dog to move into a specific space by repositioning your body. (*See **BODY BLOCK EXERCISE** page 123.*)

By acting consistently and fairly with dogs, you will take on a leadership role.

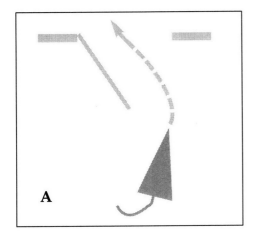

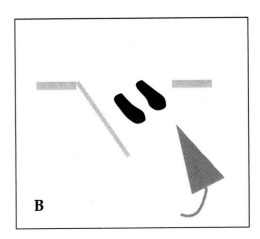

A - Dog has access through open door.

B - The dog is "blocked" in doorway by person.

C - The person opens the space and allows the dog through.

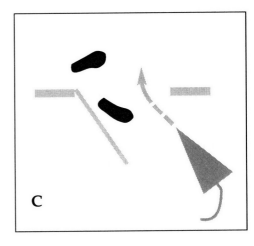

BONDING

The bond between you and your dog is determined by the depth of trust, respect and love that develops between you. Training with positive reinforcement supports this bond and can result in a dog who eagerly, happily and willingly responds with eye contact and his full physical and mental attention.

A dog's behavior is the result of his genetic history and his reinforcement history developed through interactions with you and through interactions with the environment.   The quality and consistency of a dog's behavior is directly related to the skillful use of reinforcements. Use reinforcements to reward behavior you want or to reward the dog for not doing something that you don't want him to do. Avoid inadvertently reinforcing inappropriate behavior. Dogs are learning all the time whether we want them to or not!

Reinforce not barking, calm greetings, sitting, attention, laying down, retrieving, playing with you and other skills and behaviors you would like to see in your dog. Do not reinforce (and discourage through management) barking, wildness, begging, whining, stealing and games of possession.

LIFESTYLE TIPS

Dogs can quickly learn to look to us for leadership. We don't need to use force, intimidation, or coercion. All we have to do is "pay" them for good behavior with what they need - food, shelter, enjoyment, exercise and loving social contact. Because we can provide all these resources for our wonderful friends, we have everything we need to help our dogs feel secure, guided, confident and content. The trick is learning how to "pay" only for good behavior.

Nagging or being over-bearing toward your dog isn't any fun and it certainly doesn't produce a harmonious loving relationship. More importantly, you don't need to use emotional (shouting) or physical (correcting) force to have a "good dog". Positive reinforcement training and good management will mean you won't need to worry about your dog taking over the world or your household. You can throw out your concerns about preventing doggy dominance by learning how to be a fair, attentive, positively reinforcing leader.

Here are some important pointers to help you create and maintain harmony and build leadership in your daily relationship with your dog.

FEED ON A SCHEDULE

Feed your dog on a schedule. Feeding time can be once or twice a day, depending on your own personal schedule and the dog's age or medical conditions. Avoid self-feeding or free feeding (don't leave a large amount of food always present in your dog's food bowl).

When you feed on a schedule, you know how much food your dog is eating and you see when your dog is off his food. Realizing when a dog is off his food may help determine if there is a medical condition brewing. If you are faced with an emergency medical situation involving your dog, it is very helpful to be able to tell your Veterinarian exactly when your dog ate last, especially if surgery is a possibility.

By feeding on a schedule, your dog will look to you for this valued resource. This makes you 'The Bearer of the Caribou" in his eyes. His attention is the most important part of your training program. If you provide the resources that your dog wants, you will have an eager and willing training partner.

NO FREE LUNCH (NFL)

Don't put your dog on welfare by letting him live on handouts. Don't turn him into a beggar. Instead, create jobs, such as obedience behaviors that will earn the attention, food or play he desires.

By allowing the dog to earn rewards, you are giving him some control over his environment, with boundaries. Allowing him to earn will help him develop a cooperative work ethic. If he earns the food and play he wants and deserves, he will become a friend, a partner, and a proud member of the family.

No Free Lunch (NFL) means the dog earns while he learns. This applies to more than just food. The dog needs to earn everything: pats, praise, food and toys are the dog's pay check for practicing socially appropriate behavior.

Notice and reward desirable behaviors. Keep a container of food, out of the dog's reach, in every room. As you go about your daily business, notice the dog's behaviors. Whenever he performs a behavior you like (for example, lying down out of the way, or sitting to be petted) mark that behavior and give him a treat. The dog will learn that some behaviors are more highly rewarded than others and therefore will repeat those behaviors.

If you want the dog to perform certain behaviors only when you cue them only reward those behaviors when they are cued. For example, if your dog drops the ball at your feet wanting to play, ignore the ball. If you cue the dog to play and he brings the ball to you, play ball with him. This gives the dog a clear signal that play is initiated and carried out only by you. Play must be your idea, not your dog's. If the dog nudges you for a pat, ignore him. If you cue him for a pat and he comes to you, pat and praise him. He only gets patted and rubbed when you decide the time is right.

Take the time and effort to initiate activities the dog enjoys, such as meals, going outside, play and attention. Have the dog complete a simple obedience behavior before allowing him to engage in activities he enjoys. For example, cue a sit before releasing him to go through the door. If needed use Body Blocking. *(See* **BODY BLOCKING EXERCISE** *page* 123.)

If you are consistent, the dog will learn that all good things come from cooperating and interacting with you. You will impress upon him that you make the decisions in the house because you control the pay check. The "tougher" the dog, the more necessary and effective an NFL program will be. Best of all, you will have created a loving and loyal partner without any form of coercion or punishment. Not all dogs require 100% "no free lunch", but most can benefit from being on the payroll at least part time.

MAKE TRAINING ENJOYABLE

Train and guide your dog through life. Learning is a part of life for all species and is ongoing throughout life. Positive reinforcement training is a form of play for dogs. When you see how much your dog enjoys it, you will enjoy it too.

TEACH ATTENTION

All learning begins with attention. Teach your dog that attention on you is very rewarding. (*See* **ACTIVE AND PASSIVE ATTENTION** *page* 121 & 165, **VOLUNTARY LOOK BACK** *page* 191, **REFRESH ATTENTION IN A WEEK** *page* 171.)

ASSOCIATE THE DOG'S NAME WITH GOOD THINGS

Learned associations are powerful. If your dog gets excited when you take the leash out, this response shows he has learned a positive association: leash means fun walk. Dogs can inadvertently learn hundreds of associations to sights, sounds, smells and other stimuli. For example, the dog biscuit container means yummy treats, the smell of bacon cooking means a snack, the sound of running water means a bath. As with all these associations, each time your dog hears his name, he is learning to associate that sound with the related event.

If you call the dog's name and then take no action, the dog will learn that his name is irrelevant. When he hears his name and nothing in particular happens he may subsequently ignore the sound of you calling his name. He is not being obstinate. He is doing what he learned, what you taught him.

For example, if you say *"Honey, Rover was so cute today! When Sam visited, Rover played so nicely! Even Carl liked Rover!"*, the dog (ignored for paying attention to his name three times because you weren't talking to him) will begin to ignore the sound of you saying "Rover".

If you call the dog's name and do something that the dog perceives to be aversive (such as crating the dog before you leave, clipping the dog's toenails, or interrupting the dog's off-leash play to put him on leash) the dog may associate his or her name with a punishing event. With a strong enough association (enough repetitions, or one really aversive event), the dog may subsequently refuse to come when called. He is doing what comes naturally to him: avoiding something aversive.

For example, if you say *"Rover, Shut Up!" "Get Down, Rover!" "Rover, NO!"*, you are teaching the dog that Rover - his name- is a reprimand or a punisher.

In traditional training, handlers use the dog's name to get its attention and then use the command to tell him what to do. Get his attention? What was he doing, worrying about the mortgage? When was the last time you entered the room and DIDN'T get a dog's attention?! This belief contradicts what we know about how dogs (and all animals) learn in regard to association. The only behavior cue you should prefix with the dog's name is "come", because coming to you should be among your dog's greatest joys. This is consistent with all the other positive things with which the dog's name is associated. Use your dog's name to get his attention. If you fail to get your dog's attention by speaking his name, do not repeat his name over and over --GO GET HIM. Use a long line if your dog has not yet learned to respond to his name.

A common myth is that, in a multiple dog household, the handler must use the dog's name before cuing behavior or the dogs won't know which one of them the handler is talking to. This is incorrect. How many times, in a family gathering, do you say your brother's name while speaking to him? If you are looking at a particular dog, he will know you are cuing him.

One of the most common desires of dog owners is to have the dog come when called. This is much easier and more reliably successful if you first remove any reason the dog might not come when called. If the dog's name has been poisoned by reprimands or aversive events, using the dog's name will give him a reason not to come when called. To reverse this, either use a different name (such as a nickname) or counter condition the dog's name to mean something wonderful.

For the dog to learn to associate his name with something good, don't use the dog's name unless you are going to offer something fun. Use the dog's name only when you are directly addressing him in a positive way, for example, when giving a meal, treats, massage, petting, walks and whatever he really likes. The dog will learn that, when you call his name, he will always get something wonderful when he comes to you. As a result, he will be more likely to come when called.

TEACH AN ACCEPTABLE GREETING

Guide your dog down the road of acceptable greetings. Help him realize that humans of any shape, size or age aren't going to reinforce him when he jumps on them or licks them. Dogs jump up to get something they want, such as attention or play. Don't ever react, no matter how cute the dog is. Substitute a desirable behavior for jumping, and reward that behavior. (*See* **SIT FOR GREETING** *page* 186, **GREETING VISITORS AT THE DOOR** *page* 153.)

TEACH SPATIAL AWARENESS

Teach your dog that moving out of the way, when need be is highly rewarding. Don't nag your dog to get off the couch or move out of your way. Make the result of moving out of the way a rewarding experience. (*See* **BODY BLOCK,** *pages* 123 & 186, **On/Off Placement,** *page* 164)

USE REWARD AND NO-REWARD

Focus on what your canine friend is doing correctly and encourage all good behavior by developing it in small successful increments. Redirect undesirable behavior into desirable behavior. Don't allow inappropriate play with other canines or people. If the dog has a tendency to body slam, hump, or use other physical force to get what he wants, reward appropriate behavior and use timeout to decrease inappropriate behavior.
(*For more information on using Timeout see Chapter 2, Learning, page* 23.)

Use a clicker or reward marker to mark appropriate play. This means a lot of clicking for everything that is "good play": looking at another dog, sniffing another dog, walking away from another dog, ignoring another dog, lip-licking or other calming signals near another dog, etc.

Use a no-reward mark like "OOPS" or "Too Bad!" (NRM) to let him know what he did that earned him the timeout. Adopt a "three strikes and you're out" policy. The first two body slams (or other inappropriate behavior) earn him timeouts. The third time, calmly place him back in his crate or away from the other dogs. Playtime is over.

Timeouts must be carried out neutrally. Use a neutral tone of voice for the NRM, with no talking other than the NRM. If he has a temper tantrum when placed in timeout, ignore him. Do not let him out until he is calm and quiet when your 'three strikes' policy is in effect.

You may notice an extinction burst (an increase in body slamming or other inappropriate behavior) at first, particularly right after timeouts. An extinction burst means the dog is ramping up for a behavior change. He's got dozens of appropriate choices he can make, so give him time to figure out which behaviors earn timeouts and which earn clicks.

PLAY ~ WITH YOU

Play with your dog. Dogs love interactive games like "fetch". So do most humans... although some people don't know this yet because they have never tried it. Teach your dog that giving up an object on cue is loads of fun because he gets it back again or gets a better object in exchange. Allow your dog to initiate playtime sometimes (unless you are using a "no free lunch" protocol). Initiating playtime does not mean your dog is going to take over your household; he is simply expressing his current desire to play. Allowing a dog to initiate and offer behaviors allows him to express himself, to be creative and to learn self-confidence. You can take your dog up on the offer to play only if you want to. This will teach the dog that he doesn't always get what he wants, but it doesn't hurt to ask. (*See* RETRIEVE GAMES *page* 178.)

BE FAIR

Don't put unrealistic demands on your dog. Teach new behaviors the way you would like to be taught. Be supportive and respectful. Let your dog know when he has done a great job or tried hard.

TEACH CONFIDENCE

Teach your dog that he can be away from you (left home alone) and still be a confident and happy dog. Be sure to crate him for short periods of time when you are home too. (*See* DESENSITIZING SEPARATION ANXIETY *page* 142.)

SUPERVISE

Always supervise young children and dogs when they are together. If something happens to a child when left unsupervised, it is not the fault of the dog or child, it is YOUR fault!

PROTECT

Many dogs are insecure or intolerant when approached by other dogs, particularly dogs with "rude" or unskillful canine communication signals. For example, dogs that rush other dogs using a straight-line approach rather than a rounded approach.

I recently worked with a dog that I was told had dog aggression issues. I had the "aggressive" dog, Rufus on leash in a secure area. After settling the "aggressive" dog, I let out my female Aussie, Dazzle, whom I trust not to provoke other dogs. Rufus was far from being actively aggressive. In fact, he was frightened. He tried to get as far away from her as possible.

I told Rufus he was okay and we moved off to another part of the yard. Dazzle stayed at a distance and I purposely kept myself between the two dogs. The "aggressive" dog was wide-eyed and nervous, expecting Dazzle to get in his face. Clearly, Rufus had experienced some very rude dogs who had been permitted to harass him until he couldn't take it any longer and snapped.

After a few moments, Rufus seemed to realize Dazzle wasn't going to pester him and he began to relax. Once he began to sniff around, I turned him loose but stayed near him. When Dazzle started to walk over to say "hi", he turned his head away (a signal to Dazzle that he wasn't going to challenge her). I reassured him and sent Dazzle further away. I wanted him to know I wouldn't let her intrude on his space when he showed good manners by giving ground.

A bit later, I walked both dogs to a friend's home to extend the training session. Rufus was willing to go with me but afraid to walk in brace position with Dazzle, even though she had been polite to him. I respected that this was too close for comfort for him and I let him walk on my right side.

When we got to my friend's home, Rufus enjoyed investigating the large yard and was not upset when Dazzle came near. My friend asked if I could put Rufus away in a crate for a few minutes so they could let their male dog out to play with Dazzle, as they were good doggie friends. As I led Rufus to an empty crate, my friend's dog began to bark. Instead of being aggressive, Rufus, the "aggressive" dog stopped suddenly. When I felt the leash tighten and looked at him, he was again wide-eyed and shaking, clearly asking me not to make him go near the barking dog. Could I make him get in the crate? Yes, but I saw no reason to do so when he was so clearly not aggressive, just nervous. I took him back to my house and he willingly trotted into a crate.

Later that night, he lay quietly in the crate while my male Aussie, Tucker, was loose in the room. Tucker is used to male dogs visiting and respects their privacy when crated.

Rufus only became aggressive when he was put in a position where he had no other choices. It's not a hard problem to fix.

A handler should not allow his dog to invade another dog's space or do rude things to other dogs (rush toward, sniff, stare at, bark at or race around) if it makes the other dog uncomfortable. None of us likes having to put up with rude children or adults. We resent having to tolerate someone being noisy or rowdy in our space. Why should it be any different for dogs?

Good manners make life more pleasant. Like us, there are things in life that our dogs have to learn to do that they'd rather not. But expecting our dogs to consistently tolerate rude behavior from other dogs and people is unfair. We need to reward tolerance and provide protection from rude behavior. Too often, dogs are expected to show a much higher level of tolerance than humans would.

A relationship of trust is built on cooperation, appreciation and having acknowledgment of the others' feelings. One way we demonstrate that we are our dog's leader is by protecting his space.

APPRECIATE

Don't be angry when your dog is acting like a dog. Learn from these amazing animals and realize dogs ARE a different species. Observe your dog's canine uniqueness and allow yourself to be enthralled, riveted and amazed by it.

BUILDING RELATIONSHIP THROUGH PLAY

Activities, such as games and sports, help develop a dog's self control and promote trust between the handler and the dog.

Most of our dogs don't grow up with other puppies. Once they leave the litter, their companions are their human families. When you adopt a puppy you become the how-to-play role model. When he jumps on you or bites your pant leg or bites and tugs the leash, your dog is trying to play with you. Play training is a way to teach your dog the games that you and he can play together safely.

Enjoy discovering these games. Have fun. Have an open mind and heart. Don't start with expectations about what your dog likes. Learn from your dog by using your "superior" intelligence to watch what interests your dog when playing by herself. Then make up games from what you have learned.

Once the dog is good at fetch, chase or scent games in the house, try playing in the back yard or during a walk.

A tired dog may find games aversive or punishing, so always stop playing before your dog is bored or tired.

Don't let a game of fetch turn into "chase me for it" or "tug of war". It's too easy for your dog to win these, so you no longer control the fun reward for the dog.

Play toys fall into two categories:

◆ Toys that are chased and retrieved. Balls, Kongs, or Frisbees are a few examples. Use a tennis racket to send the ball long distances. If your dog loves to use his nose, send the toy into thick woods and bushes to increase the challenge. Let the dog carry the toy back to the house when you are finished playing. If giving up the toy is hard, always exchange it for a high value food item.

◆ Toys that are tugged and shaken. Many dogs enjoy holding and tugging, often in rough play. Soft ropes, rubber hoses or knotted towels make very motivating rewards. Motivate your dog by making training the only time you play rough tug games with him. While you play tug, you can begin to teach the dog to accept firm touch by running one hand over his sides, neck and face. You can thump him, not hurtfully, but playfully, on the side of his body. This helps dogs learn to play fight safely. Watch your dog's response carefully when you play with him. Don't do anything that appears to threaten him. Play rough and then allow the dog to win by releasing the tug.

If your dog is too rough, is losing self control or is just plain hurting you, say "ouch" loudly and stop playing. When he backs off, start playing again. This is how dogs tell other dogs they have had enough. Incorporate rest periods into your play to keep the dog from becoming over-aroused. When you know your dog well, you will be able to manage the tempo of your play so it never gets out of hand.
(See Chapter 4 for a list of safe, fun dog toys, including home-made toys.)

In addition to toys, the environment holds many games dogs enjoy playing. For example, dogs love to sniff, so put scenting on cue. Many dogs enjoy swimming, running or chasing snowballs. There are thousands of things that you and your dog can find of interest.

INITIATING PLAY

Watch how dogs get other dogs to play. They tease each other. They play hard to get. They play keep away. You can't get good play without being interactive. You have to figure out how to get your dog to believe he has tricked you into giving him the toy. You must be willing, in the beginning, to let your dog push at you to get the toy.

Don't push the toy at the dog. A toy the dog can't quite get is MUCH more attractive than the toy you are trying to push into his mouth. Dogs want what you have. Appear to be having fun with the toy all by yourself. Let the dog "press" you to play, don't press the dog.

Have two, three or four balls of exactly the same type. Start by playing with the ball by yourself. Toss it, make excited noises, and generally have fun. As the dog comes to see what the toy is, make it possible for the dog to try for the toy, but make getting it from you a challenge. You should be fluid, bending away and then toward the dog, adjusting your movements to draw the dog into you. If your dog likes to chase, as he is trying to get the toy from you, throw it. Once the dog has the toy, produce another and play with that one. Convince the dog that the one you have is even better than the one he has. This will give you the beginning of a retrieve.

If the dog likes to tug, let him take hold of the toy as he presses you for it. Tug and pull and play; then let him take it from you and win. Produce another tug toy and play with it yourself, making high-pitched, excited noises and flipping the toy in and out of the dog's sight. The dog can't have the new toy until he drops the old one. Remember, no compulsion, just wily teasing on your part. The instant the toy is dropped, mark it with "yes" and give him the new toy.

Remember to always stop playing before the dog is bored or tired.

ENDING THE GAME

When you are finished playing, tell the dog "game over" by using a clear word cue and body language. Stand straight, trade the toy for food and put the toy away (or let the dog carry it back to the house). Look right at the dog and say in a firm convinced voice "we're finished". Then turn and walk away. Don't be drawn back into the game. Don't laugh and give in if your dog finds a funny argument to try to entice you back into playing. Consistency matters.

If you run out of toys and the dog won't release for a treat, slowly move one hand under the dog's chin and reach for his collar, while holding onto the toy with your other hand. Gently pull the dog up and toward you by his collar so he is on front tip toes. Relax the tension on the toy and wait. The dog can't tug, so he will let go. Immediately ask the dog to grab the toy, and repeat. As the dog releases the toy, you can start adding the word Release or Give. This is an old schutzhund trick.

OUTDOOR ACTIVITIES

All the best running, tugging and chasing games are played outdoors. Outdoors should be the place the dog knows he can have the most fun with you. If the dog isn't bouncing around, always looking to you for the next good game, then you need to work on building the relationship. If you haven't put energy into developing a great play relationship, the dog will believe the rest of the world is more fun than you are. If the dog would rather head into the woods than play with you, you need to raise his pay (play!).

Outdoors should mean two things to the dog: bathroom duties or playing/working with you. If you let your dog learn to self reinforce (crittering, chewing rocks, carrying sticks, swimming by himself, etc.) you've put the dog in charge of his own pay check.

Play games that your dog enjoys.

For example:

> ▶ Chasing thrown objects such as balls, Kongs (tm), or Frisbees (tm). If needed, play fetch with several toys so the dog returns to you to keep playing. Know what your dog enjoys and always plan to have what your dog wants.

> ▶ Tugging. For those dogs that love to hold on and pull, combine chasing with tugging. Throw the ball, then run away trailing the tug toy. When the dog grabs the tug toy, have a game of tug, then throw the ball and start again. Freshen the game by swapping the tug toy for a different toy and start the throw/tug game again.

> ▶ Scent games. Hide the toy and let the dog use his sniffing talents. Throwing the toy in areas of dense foliage combines chasing with scent work. Have the dog stay, hide the toy, return to the dog, and then release your dog to find the toy. This is a great way to teach self control. For a food-motivated dog, toss some dry kibble out in the yard for him to find.

Use your clicker or "yes" marker, and treats, to reinforce good choices while working and/or playing outside. Food reinforcement works particularly well for self control behaviors like:

> ▶ Watching, but not growling at, unfamiliar people or dogs.

> ▶ Watching, but not chasing, moving objects.

> ▶ Coming back immediately when recalled or asked to "leave it".

> ▶ Giving attention to you when a distraction is near.

LEASH HANDLING

Get a Handle on Your Leash Handling!

Goal

To manage leash tension so it remains soft and relaxed when the dog is in the correct position. Good leash handling communicates how to walk as friends – close enough and amiably enough to have a good conversation and not like a musher trying to slow down the sled dog team!

Your dog can be on either your left or right – that's up to you. All these directions are for the dog near your left knee with the leash in your right hand, but you can pick either side – just stick with it. If you'd rather have your dog next to your right knee, switch the hand you hold the leash with. A 6' foot leash is best, and the steps below are for a 6 foot leash.

1. Clip the leash to your dog's collar.
2. Place the loop end of the leash over your right thumb and allow the leash to remain slack.
3. To make the leash length flexible, "shorten" it by sliding your left hand about one foot down the leash to make a fold and bringing the folded leash up to your right thumb. Folded in two, one foot of length equals two feet of leash.
4. Transfer the folded part of the leash into your right hand so all four fingers grip the doubled leash in your right hand. Your 6' leash is now 4' long.
5. Bend your right arm and hold the leash near your body at about waist height.

Start walking. If your dog stays near your knee as you walk you will never need to make your leash longer. There should be no tension on your dog's neck from the leash.

If your dog starts to walk forward, release the 2 extra feet of leash in your right hand while still holding onto the end of the leash loop that is over your thumb. While your dog is walking forward, make an about turn and change your direction as the dog continues moving in the previous direction where he will soon realize you are going some place else. You don't say anything! When your dog catches back up to you, wordlessly collect the 2' extra leash loop back into your right hand - maintaining a loose, but re-shortened leash and keep walking. Praise and treat only when the dog is in position and walking with no tension on the leash. Your hand should never be on the leash close to the dog's collar. The hand closest to the dog is swinging freely at your side – NOT holding any part of the leash. Only your right hand is holding the leash

Tactics

If you are walking and your dog leaves position, release the leash till the dog gets to the end. Then change direction till he catches up. Smoothly shorten and lengthen the leash so that your dog never really feels you dragging on him except when he reaches the end and you change direction. It takes a little practice!

If you are standing with your dog on leash and the dog moves away, let him go to the end and gently but firmly guide him back to position with your left hand sliding down the leash to help him back to your side. Once he is in place, re-shorten the leash to the "next to me" position and praise, letting go of the lead with your left hand, which is closest to the dog.

Very quickly your dog will figure out that all he has to do to walk sociably without pressure on his collar is to stay by your side.

RELAXATION AND STRESS REDUCTION

Relaxation exercises can be used every day and also in extreme situations. Relaxation exercises include touch, massage, learned relaxation through performing specific behaviors and management of the environment to reduce stress.

RELAXED DOWN

By rewarding relaxation, you can teach your dog to control his own arousal level. There are several behaviors you can reward to encourage relaxation.

Focus on relaxation exercises and teaching the dog emotional control with operant conditioning (using the clicker). The classes I designed for the Upper Valley Humane Society are based on impulse control first and foremost, rather than the basic behaviors sit, down and come. Once a dog has impulse control, we work on an automatic sit as the handler walks toward the dog and a relaxed down when the handler stops to chat.

I have always included impulse and emotional control exercises in my classes and I am putting greater emphasis on this now. I recently started a pure "impulse and emotional control" class with some adult dogs. I am seeing good results, thanks to enthusiastic and dedicated owners. Some of these dogs are competitive obedience and agility dogs, but they lack impulse and emotional control. Impulse and emotional control exercises have also become an integral part of my puppy training classes.

It is interesting to compare similarities and differences in training "prey" vs. "predatory" species. The head lowering exercises that Alexandra Kurland does with horses for emotional control really got me thinking. Alexandra Kurland teaches horses to lower their heads right down to the ground on cue. Because horses only graze when they are totally relaxed with their surroundings, this position induces emotional calmness in otherwise stressed horses.

I wondered whether there was an equivalent position for dogs. What could I do with my dogs to trigger the same emotional control when they start to get "emotionally high"? When my dog is totally relaxed at home: he is in a down position on one hip, his head stretched out on the floor or between his paws and he has total muscle relaxation. This was going to be my end goal: A relaxed down.

A relaxed down position helps calm the dog, as long as he is feeling secure. This exercise is a must for the classes with reactive dogs.
(*See* **SHAPED RELAXED DOWN, EXERCISE** *page* 182.)

A relaxed down can be lured or shaped. I shaped this behavior by starting with the dog in the down position and clicked for any movement of the head toward the ground. I gradually raised my criteria until I was only clicking for the head on the ground. This took about 5 minutes. I then added variable duration, counting 3 seconds, then 5 seconds, then 4 seconds, then 10 seconds, etc.

Dogs have a tendency to lie down in the sphinx position, always ready to be released, ready for action. So I looked for a secondary behavior to reinforce while building duration. This was the dog shifting over on his hip. As the duration increased, the dog settled into a more relaxed position by going over onto his hip. After a few clicks, the dog would lie down, put his head on the floor and rotate onto his hip. So, I had reached my second goal.

As I progressed with duration, the dog settled into a relaxed down position, understanding that he wasn't going to be doing anything anytime soon. As he began to relax his entire body, I clicked. My criteria now included relaxed muscles.

If your dog gets up every time you click, stop clicking and calmly use the word "goood" and then reinforce. The word "goood" is my "you're doing well, keep going" signal. Draw the word out as you are saying it, so it has a soothing tone. When the dog understands the exercise, begin to add controlled distractions. If the distractions become too much for the dog, use the word "good" to calm the dog. Then reduce the distraction to help the dog to relax.

This position should be highly reinforced, whether cued or offered freely by the dog. Use a cue such as "relax". It sounds appealing in public and may naturally evoke a gentle tone of voice. By heavily reinforcing a relaxed down, it becomes default behavior. The dog will naturally offer default behavior whenever he is not quite sure what you want. For example, he may volunteer it in the kitchen, which is where treats are kept.

Train your dog that it pays to relax by reinforcing him when he sighs deeply, a sign of true relaxation.

When I tether my youngest dog while working with another dog, she will put herself into the relaxed down on her own. Instead of lying in a sphinx position, eagerly watching me work the other dog she is in a relaxed position, quiet and calm. I encourage this by reinforcing the behavior.

MASSAGE

Have quiet times with your dog. Touch, massage and be close to your dog. It will do you both a lot of good to realize how rewarding calmness is.
(*See* **RELAXATION AND STRESS REDUCTION** *page 74.*)

Performing massage on your canine friend can change how your dog feels about you, himself and the world. It can be relaxing for both of you.

You don't need to be a professionally trained masseuse. You just need to understand a few basics about where and how to touch. It is the time spent making quality physical and emotional contact that will make the difference. Massage is a quiet, relaxing way to bond with your dog.

Don't start if you are stressed, anxious, tired or running short on time. Set aside your personal concerns and worries; you want to completely involve yourself in this work. Make this a really pleasurable time for yourself as well as your dog. Set up the environment for success. Choose a comfortable and serene place, play soft music, and dim the lights.

Make sure you know how you want to touch your dog. There are excellent videos on canine massage and touch techniques that will help you feel more confident. (See the resource list in the appendix for excellent books and videos on canine massage/touch.) Your goal is to create a gentle, calm physical relationship between you and your dog, building a positive relaxed physical response to touching your dog.

How you begin your massage determines the potential positive results. Some dogs, just like some people, may not like being touched. They may tense up and feel invaded or threatened. Take time to develop trust between you and your dog. Speak softly and kindly to the dog as you approach and present your hands fully open. Don't move fast. Give the dog a chance to enjoy what you are going to do together.

If you need to help your dog stay in one place, give him something to chew on. Listen to the dog's breathing pattern as you start so you can tell when he begins to relax. Make sure your hands are warm. Feel how his body reacts to your touch: Does he tense, flinch, pull away or just stay rigid? Be very calm, slow, and gentle in your touch until you can feel him begin to relax.

Start on the muzzle and head first, then the back of the ears and head. Go slowly; let the dog tell you when you can leave the head. Gently bring your hand down his neck, then continue down his withers (top point of the shoulders). Don't lift your hands off one part of the body and put them down on another part. Instead lightly slide your hand to a new location so your dog knows where the next touch will happen. Don't make any surprises for your dog.

Be fully focused on how your dog is reacting. Massage teaches your hands and eyes how to "read" your dog. Learn to recognize his signs of apprehension, such as raising or turning his head toward you, or widening or dilating his eyes.

Massage gives you a chance to be sure your dog is not in a pain from disease or injury. Take note of where you are touching if your dog becomes tense and seems to want to move away. Note if his breathing is short and hard, if he is whimpering, or if he makes a short yelping sound. Pay attention to any sudden reactive jolts or tension as you touch him. If you sense pain, determine whether he may need medical attention.

Learn how your dog shows you he is relaxed. Are his eyes half closed, head held down, ears to the sides of his head? Is he making heavy sighs, sure signs of relaxation and enjoyment? If you monitor your dog's body language all the time you are touching him, you can adjust your massage techniques accordingly.

MANAGEMENT

There are several key elements in managing a dog:

▶ **Plan** ~ Every interaction is a teaching/learning opportunity. Prepare physical and emotional environments to set the dog up for success. Always have a plan and the tools available to manage your dog. For example, carry yummy treats with you at all times, so you can switch to counter conditioning mode if a scary thing appears in the environment.

▶ **Watch** ~ Keep your attention on the dog unless he is in a solid down or sit stay. Always watch and be ready to reinforce right choices and to interrupt inappropriate choices before they occur. Always notice and reinforce calm watchfulness.

▶ **Relate** ~ Use your relationship skills to build the dog's trust in you. Make yourself the source of all important reinforcement for the dog.

AVOID REHEARSAL OF INAPPROPRIATE BEHAVIOR

Dogs learn by rehearsing, or practicing, behavior. Manage the dog's environment by having a crate (covered, if necessary), a drag line and other tools available to keep the dog from practicing barking, lunging and other inappropriate behavior.

To provide some off-leash control, indoors or outdoors, attach a drag line to a flat collar or harness. As the dog begins to mature and focus more on you, the length of the drag line can gradually be shortened until finally it is nothing more than a tag line. Until the dog consistently and reliably listens and responds to cues like "wait", "come" and "leave it" while dragging a drag line, he is not ready to be off leash, particularly outdoors.

If your dog is barking at the window at strangers, step in front of him, facing him, and move him back. Say "leave it". (This cue should be trained ahead of time. (*See* **"LEAVE IT" EXERCISE** *page 159.*) When your dog turns to you, give him an alternative behavior and reinforce it. For example, play a fetch or tug game with him. If your dog wants to charge the door when someone comes over, set up the situation so that you know when the visitor is about to arrive. Put the dog on leash, step in front of the dog and move him away from the person. Say "leave it". Then toss the ball or biscuit to your guests and let them toss it for the dog. Within a few days, the dog will be bringing his ball to play with your guests!

PHYSICAL AND MENTAL EXERCISE

Make sure your dog is getting good aerobic exercise at least 2 times a day for 20 to 30 minutes at a time. Walking on leash is not aerobic exercise and is not enough for most dogs under the age of 4 years. Teach your dog how to play fetch, hide and seek, or tug. Enroll in private Agility or Freestyle (doggy dancing) lessons. Shaping exercises, such as Karen Pryor's "101 Things with a Box", will help exercise your dog's body and mind.

HANDLING LOOSE DOGS

Anticipate and have a plan of action for events out of your control. For example, loose dogs that might rush your dog when you're out for a walk. No single strategy will work with every dog. Police departments and postal services have tried many techniques with the same result: works approximately 70% of the time, no effect approximately 20% of the time, intensifies attack approximately 10% of the time. Have two or three strategies planned, practiced and available for use.

Tossing treats for the loose dogs headed in your direction is generally ineffective, because the dog is usually so caught up in charging mode that he won't notice treats. However, chucking a handful of treats at the loose dog's face might get his attention for a moment, buying you time.

Use that moment to step in front of your dog, keeping your dog on a short leash behind you. Lean forward toward the loose dog, using body blocking to counter each of the loose dog's moves. If the owner is not in sight, try to turn your back, with your dog behind you, to an obstacle, such as a tree, car or fence, so you don't need to worry about the loose dog circling around you.

When you block the loose dog he may stop and look at you making eye contact as if to say *"Get out of my way"* or *"Who are you?"*. If you get this reaction, command "sit" or "stop", then "go home". Use a low monotone voice (never high or frantic.) Stay calm so your dog does not become frightened by your response. Stand firm. Keep your body leaning forward even if your dog is barking and wiggling behind you. Forward body language will normally cause the other dog to leave. Often you won't have to say a word: strong body language says everything. As an extra precaution, you can carry citronella spray and/or a pepper spray, such as "Direct Stop" by Premier. You can find these sprays on websites, such as http://www.animalbehaviorsystems.com/. You can also use household air freshener spray or really cheap stinky hair spray but these may not be effective in cold climates because the contents can freeze, or on windy days because the spray may drift.

I have only had one dog in over 25 years not stop. My daughter and I were on a beach having a nice, quiet walk with our small dog and minding our own business. A medium-sized (50 lb) dog came at us. He was trying to bite my daughter and our little dog. He was so determined that I had to kick him twice in the head before he would back off. Once he realized I wasn't going to stop, he left us. After that walk, I always made sure I had one of my bigger dogs with us. I never saw that particular dog again, thank goodness. I'm sure he would not have tried to attack us if my German Shepherd or Doberman had been with us.

If you have problems with a loose dog, find out who owns the dog, if possible. Let them know what happened and, if there is a leash law, remind them of it. Then give them the name of your trainer and let them know they can work on their dog's issues. Reduce your risks of a repeat incident by avoiding that area if at all possible.

TRAINING PLAN

Successfully reconditioning a reactive dog requires analysis and planning. Your dog is learning all the time, whether or not you are training. To ensure the dog does not practice inappropriate behavior, carefully consider where you take the dog - always. Planning (where a scary stimulus will appear, at what distance, etc.) will allow you to control what your dog learns.

Teaching a dog a difficult task that requires a lot of self control, such as "don't jump on the guests", requires time and commitment. It is like teaching a child to read. For the child to be able to read books, you must first teach the letters of the alphabet, then the words, then phrases. After that, the child can read sentences, then eventually stories, then entire books. You have taught the child a basic set of skills that have opened a new world to him.

What we want the dog to learn is the equivalent of teaching a child to read. You start by teaching first the alphabet, then words, then sentences, then stories. Basic behaviors like "watch me" build the foundation of the vocabulary. The chain of behavior may begin with glancing at the handler, grow to sustained attention, to attention with distractions, and so on.

TRAINING DIARY

A training diary will help you plan your training, review your progress and modify your training plan as needed. Your training diary should include a big-picture outline of training steps to desensitize and recondition your dog. Each time you train, review your training plan before each training session. It will help you keep your perspective and allow you to be flexible if the plan isn't going right.

Before each training session, write out your goals for that session, where it should occur and what you'll need to make it successful. Think about how to raise the criteria in small enough increments to make learning as easy as possible for your dog. Always be prepared to move away from any stimulus that is too much for your dog. Be flexible and always set the dog up for success!

At the end of each training session, note your goals for the next session while "what happened" and "what was learned" are fresh in your mind.

The training plan should include an Exercise Grid listing the exercises completed each week.

Following is an example of a training plan.

Exercises in bold type are described in Appendix A.

Week 1	Week 2	Week 3	Week 4
Charge (load) clicker and/or word marker *See Chapter 2*	Beginning Recall, indoors **ATTENTION** **NAME RECOGNITION** **LOOK BACK**	Beginning Recall, backyard **RECALL USING PREMACK**	**RECALL FROM DISTRACTIONS**
ATTENTION **VOLUNTARY LOOK BACK**	Moving Attention **PASSIVE ATTENTION** **WAIT AT DOORWAYS**	Introduce variable reinforcement with tug, ball and treats *See Chapter 4.*	**WAIT OFF LEASH**
NAME RECOGNITION *See page 146*	Now start using the dog's name with light distraction	Go to a new location **WAIT FOR PERMISSION**	Down Stay with distractions distance
SHAPED RELAXED DOWN OR DOWN ON MAT	Continue shaping **RELAXED DOWN/MAT** in a new location	**RELAXED DOWN** with duration	Begin working with distractions
LOOSE LEASH WALKING	**LOOSE LEASH WALKING** with 4D's	More **LOOSE LEASH WALKING**	**FINDING HEEL POSITION**

GOOD HANDLER PROTOCOL

Never train if you are in a foul mood. Your dog will know and react badly. The training won't be enjoyable or productive for you or your dog.

Don't work using verbal cues until you are 100% certain your dog understands them. Otherwise, your dog will learn to ignore your verbal cues.

Always have a management plan that will cover the unexpected. Use a Gentle Leader or Sensation Harness, as well as a leash or drag line, if there is any possibility the dog will react to a stimulus by running toward it or away from it. Manage your dog for success.

Training occurs with every interaction you have with your dog so teach the behaviors you want your dog to practice. Sit for a leash to be attached, sit by the door while it opens, loose leash walking to the potty place, etc. Be prepared to reinforce ALL the time.

Never call your dog to you and then do something he might perceive as punishing such as cutting his nails or giving him a bath.

WHERE TO TRAIN

Always check your training location first without your dog. Make sure the location will allow you to move your dog quickly away from any stimulus that is too strong.

If you're going to a training facility, choose a time when few or no people are there. Be sure there are places where you can move away from other people or dogs. Don't set yourself up to be trapped. Ideally, you should be able to get behind a barrier so you can relieve some pressure on the dog without actually having to leave the building. You might turn a table on its side and put it in a corner so you can get behind it just in case someone comes into the building while you are working. Post a sign on the door asking people to knock or look in before entering the building. Plan and organize for success!

If you're going to a park to train, visit it many times before you show up with your dog so you can see when it is least busy. Don't train there when it is full of dogs, kids, and other scary things.

WHEN TO TRAIN

You can train in very short intervals when your dog is less reactive. In the beginning, plan enough time to allow your dog to habituate (get used) to the training area. Just getting your dog used to new places is going to be a huge part of your training program. If you allow enough time, you'll both enjoy the training session.

OBSERVATION

Work on your observation skills. Practice reading your dog's body language. This is how you will gather information about your dog's state of mind. His body will tell you what is starting to worry him so you can create distance before fear causes him to lose his ability to think. Success will depend on you being continuously observant.

REINFORCEMENT

Always be prepared with reinforcements that your dog really values. You need the best of the best when reconditioning reactive dogs. You can't change his emotional response to scary things if you aren't offering something so good he wants to get what you have more than he wants to react to what scares him. So have plenty of different kinds of good yummy treats and the dog's favorite toys with you.

Food and toys: positive reward based training depends on the dog working for reinforcement. Food or a high value toy can be used to reinforce attention and your dog's interest in what you want him to do. Small pieces of smelly food work well, such as hot dogs or cheese. For some dogs, the hope that you'll play fetch or tug works as well as, or better than food.
(*See "Training Resources and Equipment", Chapter 4.*)

Food is best used to train new behaviors and to reinforce non-moving or calm behaviors. Toys are the best reinforcement for moving or physically active behaviors especially those that require speed.

Voice: use sweet, eager praise. Use the voice to croon, intrigue and seduce. "*Yeeeessssss! Goood dog. Aren't you clever!*" Pair your voice praise with food reinforcement. Praise is a reinforcer, so only praise for actions you want repeated. Most of us talk to our dogs because it makes us feel good but dogs don't talk for pleasure. If you want words to matter to the dog, only use your 'special voice' when you want him to do something or when you are reinforcing him for doing something. If you chatter away for your own pleasure, the sound of your voice may become irrelevant and your dog might stop listening.

Learn to say your dog's name in a quiet, warm, and personal way. Use a conversational tone as you would talking to your best friends. This is the way the two of you are going to talk for years. Find a comfortable crooning style. Always smile when you speak your dog's name. Say his name with a voice and heart filled with respect, eagerness and enthusiasm; give to your dog what you want in return.

Facial Expressions: smile whenever your dog looks to you while you verbally praise and before you give food reinforcement. Make your face, voice and food a single, coordinated reward. As the relationship matures any one of these can be used as reinforcement. If the dog has aggressed in any way, you must allow your face and expression to change and be disappointed. Your approval is a strong indicator to the dog that all is going well. Use your smile and encouragement and disappointments as you would when communicating with a spouse, a friend or a family member. Have good conversations when all is well and limit or remove your talk and attention when you are out of sorts. Dogs understand our emotions better than we do some times. Remember that physical punishment doesn't promote learning. Always strive to communicate effectively with your four footed friends. (*See* **VOLUNTARY LOOK BACK,** *page* 191, *and* **ACTIVE ATTENTION** *page* 121, *and* **PASSIVE ATTENTION,** *page* 165.)

BODY SIGNALS:

1. Move backward or turn quickly to lure the dog to follow.

2. Use touch and verbal praise. While praising, pat the dog using a few short, firm pats. Separate cuddling from training; you may want to have the dog in your lap to stroke, but don't allow your need to cuddle your dog disrupt your consistency in training. Most dogs don't naturally like lengthy caressing. Because we humans like to caress, our dogs learn to enjoy it, but it is not a natural behavior for many dogs.

3. Keep your posture dog-friendly. Stand up straight while training. Don't bend over when asking for attention. You may squat down or bend briefly to pat and praise. At the beginning, pair physical petting and touching with food.

4. Use physical play to reinforce attention. Don't be afraid to roll on the floor and play with your dog but be matter of fact when playtime is finished. This way, the dog lerans that your are a playmate and friend, but that when you signal the end of play it is time to settle down.

USING FOOD REWARDS SAFELY

Although we use food rewards alongside other reinforcements, there is no need for the dog to learn to bite your fingers as he takes the food. This is an indication of a lack of self control. Mouth control (bite inhibition) should be learned by young puppies through interaction with other dogs. Lack of mouth control can be the result of failure to learn bite inhibition in the puppy months, or by careless food delivery.

Avoid careless food delivery by taking the treat between index finger and thumb and curling the other three fingers out of the way. Pop the treat directly into the dog's mouth by pressing down lightly on the dog's lower jaw right behind the front teeth as you release the treat. Immediately get your fingers out of the way; don't wait to feel the teeth clamping down. (*See* **TAKING TREATS POLITELY** *page* 188.)

Nervous dogs can begin to bite food rewards harder when they become aroused. This is a physiological response to stress. Use this hard-mouth response as an indication that you need to reduce the dog's stress by increasing distance from what he fears or by removing him from that environment and allowing him to calm down gradually.

CONTROLLING REINFORCEMENT

Teach your dog that the party is with you. Don't take him out and let him exercise himself or he may learn that he can find better reinforcement on his own than you have to offer. Reward him often for interacting with you.

If your dog does something inappropriate (for example, barking at you for attention), give him a timeout by ignoring him for 1 to 3 minutes. Get up and leave the room (if you know he can't get into any trouble). Don't talk to him if he comes over to say hello. Make sure he can't find his own rewards in the environment such as attention from other people or dogs or amusement in various objects in the room.

RAISING THE CRITERIA

Once your dog can handle a training area that used to cause problems, you can raise the criteria (raise the bar). Find a suitable dog (calm with non reactive body language) and handler who can help you begin to desensitize your dog to other dogs while training. You can do this one of two ways:

1. Have the helper and their dog already in the room or outdoor space where you plan to train. They should be calm and quiet. They are not doing any running or jumping, just waiting calmly in your training area. Walk into the training area with your dog. If your dog becomes over aroused, calmly take him outside and have the helper and their dog leave the room quietly. Enter again, without the helper and their dog in room. Keep alternating until you can walk in quietly with your dog while the helper and their dog are in the training space. When your dog can walk calmly into the room with the helper and their dog present, practice some simple exercises at a comfortable distance for your dog.

2. Have the helper enter quietly with their dog then move slowly to a location away from you and ask their dog to lie down. When you first see them coming into the room, toss some treats onto the floor so your dog is busy eating and not focused on the other dog. Stay at

the other end of the room, working on skill training with your dog. Keep him focussed on you, with his back toward the helper and their dog. Reinforce any non-reactive behavior.

MEASURING SUCCESS

Dogs learn by successful repetition. The criteria should gradually become more difficult but never so difficult that the dog fails to perform the desired behavior. Because the learning is gradual, it is easy to lose track of the success you've had along the way. To keep track, you should keep a measure of your success.

Measuring your success throughout the training process:

▶ Holds you accountable for really watching your dog and learning how to set up for success.

▶ Helps you learn what works and what doesn't.

▶ Helps you adjust and improve your training plan as you go.

Keeping a point system with a written log is the easiest and best way to measure success. Using a point system for success, you add points for success and subtract points for non-success. Failure is not an option.

Measures can be used to check whether your training is working as planned and adjust accordingly. For example:

If you are working on counter conditioning, your goal will be to keep the dog's arousal level below his threshold, to desensitize rather than sensitize his fear. Keeping your dog below threshold (so the dog doesn't react) is an art in and of itself. A simple point scoring system will help you "see" whether you are really creating a training/behavior modification program that is moving toward success. If the dog is more reactive over time you may be sensitizing him. If he is less reactive over time, you are sucessfully desensitizing him.

You'll have the best results if you keep a diary for a few months, to know whether you are gaining ground. By adding points for non-reactivity and subtracting points for over-arousal, you can objectively prove whether you are achieving correct behavior repetitions for your dog at a level where he can learn self-control.

The scoring system works as follows:

▶ Identify what you will use to measure a successful encounter. For example, if you are counter conditioning your dog against fearful reactivity toward other dogs, you might define success as your dog not losing impulse control or acting aggressively in any manner when another dog comes within his sight.

▶ Give yourself 20 points for each successful encounter. Deduct 2000 points if your dog loses control. Yes, this is a lot of points for not anticipating events in the environment and not watching your dog. But your goal is no over arousal and lots of positively reinforced moments of self-control. You can change how your dog feels, but it will cost you (and your dog) if you are inattentive or unprepared!

▶ Your goal is to accumulate 1000 points.

The point system will make you responsible for your dog's success. If you don't want to have to make up the 2000 points (100 successes!) then don't walk into a situation your dog might consider dangerous. Use distance to set your dog up for success.

This scoring system is a simple way to help you understand that single over-arousal events can set you back weeks or even months of training time. If you lost points, you moved too fast, were inattentive or did not carefully control the environment. Learn from what happened and go back to the level of difficulty where your dog was successful.

If going back to the last success isn't working, you need to backtrack until you find the threshold where your dog can handle the trigger stimulus. Changing an emotional association from fear to confidence takes time and repetition. When counter conditioning, remember the tortoise and the hare: fast progression leads to failure, slow progression leads to success. Settle into a plan that will take weeks, months or even a year or more of counter conditioning before your dog has enough good associations with the stimulus to change his reactions.

When climbing a mountain, you must wind your way up and down before reaching the top. Enjoy the journey and let your dog help you find the path. This is about companionship, not about finishing first. The point system will keep you on track.

SHY OR OVER-REACTIVE DOGS

Both shy dogs and aggressive dogs are over stimulated by certain events in their environment. We call them "reactive" dogs. The shy dog withdraws and avoids any action that might trigger scary things. While the growling or aggressive dog also thinks the stimulus is scary, he tries to solve the threat by making it go away.

> "A reactive dog is one who develops high anxiety when exposed to environmental or specific stimuli. This anxiety is displayed externally in a variety of ways. This is called the trigger or reactive response, and the behaviors that are witnessed (i.e. vocalization, lunging, lack of focus, shyness, spinning, panting, trembling, jumping up, snapping, biting, in-ability to eat and so many more) are symptoms of the dog's anxiety."

> *Jackie McGowan*

Technically these dogs are "over-reactive", since all dogs should react to stimulus. We strive to teach our dogs to react, but in a particular way. Preferably, this will be a way that (a) does not endanger the dog, people, or other dogs, and (b) results in a positive, not negative, experience.

Most over-reactive or aggressive behavior is based on fear or anxiety. Reactive dogs are difficult to live with, particularly those with aggressive behaviors. It may be only one situation, or many, that triggers a fear-aggression response. To modify the "reaction", you need to identify the trigger and change the dog's emotional reaction to that trigger.

Observation and analysis are critical for a successful behavior modification program. The program will reduce the stimulus to a level that elicits no response, allowing the dog to recondition his emotional reaction and learn more appropriate behaviors. These appropriate behaviors can be rewarded, therefore strengthened. The handler or owner will need to anticipate the situations, react appropriately, and guide the dog to the desired new behavior.

WHY DOGS BITE

Dogs are wonderful companions. They are loyal, friendly, affectionate and fun to be around. Why, then, are there so many dog bites in this country, with most of them inflicted on children?

Humans don't like to admit that, in addition to the fine qualities mentioned above, dogs are also aggressive, territorial animals with teeth, strong jaws and a hard-wired "bite or flight" instinct. In other words, a dog that bites a child who takes a toy from him is behaving normally. This is hard for people to accept, but it is necessary if we are to reduce the number of dog bites and the ensuing anti-dog legislation that is becoming more common every day.

In her book "The Culture Clash", Jean Donaldson says *"Dogs are unaware that they've been adopted into a culture where biting is considered a betrayal of trust and a capital offense"* (p. 58)

When a client calls saying *"My dog just bit me without warning!"*

I ask *"Have you ever scolded your dog for growling at you?"*

The answer is always *"Yes, of course I have."*

So what has the owner conditioned? Why did the dog bite?

Dogs don't consider biting a betrayal. It is just communication to them. How is a dog to understand that we can't accept biting of humans? We can't explain to a dog that biting a human may get him killed or cause him to lose his home.

Punishing a dog for biting or threatening to bite using the so-called "alpha" techniques, involving mild to moderate aggression toward the dog, can actually increase the likelihood that the dog will bite. Aggression tends to lead to aggression - not necessarily in direct return to the aggressor but potentially in a different direction and potentially at a different time.

Dogs can be reconditioned to accept what normally would not be accepted. For example, reconditioning using Exchange Games can cause a dog to think that having toys, contraband items, and even food taken from him is good - that it is likely to result in reinforcement, just like sitting for petting or lying down results in reinforcement.

PRACTICE PLACEMENT AND RESTRAINT

CLASSICAL CONDITIONING

Very often a dog reacts to unfamiliar or novel stimuli with unwanted behavior. Anticipation of this tendency and use of classical conditioning to change the dog's emotional reaction to unfamiliar stimuli can avert many issues in later life.

Many of us are unaware of the classical conditioning going on all around us. Whenever we wish to help someone have a pleasant experience, we pull out all the stops to "create" a pleasant atmosphere. Restaurants are aware of these powerful forces when they design a lovely ambiance, not just for eating, but for a "dining experience." Rather than using verbal cues to reach the dog's conscious mind, when we employ classical conditioning we use "pleasant, happy tones" and high-value luscious food treats to help create a positive emotional response.

Classical conditioning reaches parts of the brain that are lower, more primal, than conscious thought. A physiological response can occur without conscious thought. When we use classical conditioning to help a dog form a more pleasant mental association in the presence of other dogs or other people, we're thinking in Pavlovian terms. We use food (high-value powerful food treats) because eating makes a hungry dog feel good. That "feeling good" is a physiological response. (*See Conditioned Emotional Response page 24.*)

Classical conditioning can be used to counter condition something scary or aversive, such as fear of unfamiliar dogs or people, into something that evokes good emotions, such as an association with a favorite food treat.

The dog should be hungry before conditioning begins. For example, condition just before mealtime. Work at the dog's comfort distance from the scary thing (such as an unfamiliar dog or person). Set up the situation to operate well below the dog's threshold of fear or aggression. If the dog refuses food, he may be showing signs of distress. If the dog is showing raised hackles or other forms of anxiety, the scary thing is too close, or too loud, or moving too much. Reduce the stimulus, for example, by adding distance or making sure the scary thing is quiet and holds still.

Throughout the conditioning process, carefully observe the dog. Is he still feeling comfortable, while showing awareness of the strange dog or person at the distance? Is his demeanor happy and eager, and is he still readily accepting treats? If a dog appears uncomfortable or begins to alarm bark in fear of a person or dog, move away from the stimulus. Have ready high-value luscious food treats, such as tiny pieces of roast turkey or thinly sliced roast beef. Jean Donaldson's book "Dogs are from Neptune" suggests reserving special treats specifically for counter conditioning.

Watch the dog and begin feeding the dog at first sight of the stimulus, well before the dog begins to show signs of fear. Feed rapidly until the person or thing is out of sight, then stop the feeding. The message is "scary thing = yummy treats; no scary thing = no treats". The dog will begin to associate the sight of something that was once scary with great reward. Keep exposure to the scary thing brief. While the dog is still happy, turn and walk away with the dog, to a location where he no longer sees the scary thing.

Time these lessons for a period during the day when the dog is not experiencing other stresses. Otherwise, a series of high-powered distractions can mount up to create too much stress.

Counter conditioning aims to help the dog to relax in the presence of what he fears while those scary things are at a distance. Over time and with lots of practice the dog may be brought gradually closer to the scary thing. At that point, we are starting to reduce the distance. Attempting to rush in this progression may backfire. Carefully consider the individual dog's tolerance level for strange things or strange events and make sure the dog is truly conditioned to the current level before increasing the level (before moving closer, for example).

SELF-CONTROL SKILLS

An education in self control is one of the greatest gifts we can give our dogs, particularly over-reactive dogs. With self control, a dog can minimize his reactions to stressful situations and find inherent pleasure and reinforcement in his ability to control his reactions. When a dog discovers he has the power to turn bad situations to good situations by changing his response, he gains self-confidence. A confident dog is a happy and relaxed dog.

Dogs benefit from precise cues for appropriate behavior. If the dog can predict what behavior will lead to the reinforcement he wants, he is more likely to choose that behavior. Instead of allowing a situation to trigger an unwanted response, the dog finds opportunities for reward through self control behaviors for himself.

Self control does not come automatically. Particularly with over-reactive dogs, self control must be taught.

Be careful about getting caught in the old belief that all the dog needs is "more exercise." While exercise is great, it can also induce high levels of stress, leaving the dog in a semi-aroused state for hours, even days. Long sessions that leave the dog exhausted do not contribute to his ability to control his emotional state or to learn. They may further reinforce the "get revved and keep going till you fall over" pattern which can be difficult to break. Physical conditioning develops stamina. An out of control or over-reactive dog with stamina to spare can be difficult to train and live with. A more healthy balance is a short burst of activity interspersed with quiet times, which is what normal dogs do if given the opportunity. For example, activity for 5 to 10 minutes, then quiet for 20 to 30 minutes.

Far more important is teaching the dog how to deal with his emotional state when exciting things happen. Rather than a couple of intense exercise sessions that leave the dog physically exhausted, have many short sessions of controlled, directed interaction throughout the day. Games such as hide 'n' seek, scent work, recalls between two people who keep changing their position, short sessions of fetching combined with self-control behaviors such as sit or stay until released to fetch the article, are effective in burning the dog's mental and physical energy while teaching self control

Anticipate when the dog is about to feel energetic, and set a play session in motion before the dog begins to perform unwanted behaviors. Keep a diary for a few days to discover the rhythm of the day and know when best to engage the dog. Use a point system to help you gauge your success: 20 points for all successful encounters with no loss of impulse control, and a loss of 2000 points if your dog loses control. This way you will know where you stand. Your goal is to accumulate 1000 points. *(See Measuring Success page 83.)*

Dogs enjoy this type of relationship and training time, and are a real joy to train when they have not flipped into overload. Consistency and lots of practice give the best results.

Interrupting and re-directing inappropriate behavior early is a key component. While formal training is good, at the very foundation of this behavior is the issue of emotional self control. Focus on this issue, along with basic obedience, and you will have success. (*See* **SELF-CONTROL GAMES** *page* 180.)

CONFIDENCE

Many over-reactive dogs lack self confidence. They ride an emotional roller coaster between extremely high stress level peaks and subsequent exhaustion and depression. For these dogs the world can be a scary place. Sometimes these dogs show signs of stress that we misunderstand because we can't imagine why a particular situation could be frightening.

A dog will avoid any situation that frightens him. This is basic survival behavior. If he doesn't understand what is happening, then he won't feel safe. If he doesn't feel safe, his instincts tell him to get out or fight back.

Stress is increased when we force a dog to live in situations that are frightening to him. There are aspects of the human world we can't change. But we can build the dog's confidence to help him cope with scary things.

Through various self control and training exercises, including counter conditioning, we can begin to fill the dog's life with a range of strategies and learned behaviors that will reduce over reactivity. This will lead to a more confident dog, able to cope with new and previously scary situations, thus reducing the chemical soup of stress hormones floating around the dog's system.

Through these exercises, the dog will gain confidence and form a stronger relationship with his owner. The owner will become more confident in anticipating and managing situations and controlling the outcome of potentially alarming events. A strong human/dog relationship will develop which can be built into a life long friendship.

FAMILIARIZATION

Many dogs respond to different stimuli that have one thing in common: they are unfamiliar. Because their brains are still forming, young dogs are more easily able to assimilate new stimuli than older dogs. A lifetime of over reaction and stress can be avoided through familiarization and socialization. Positive introduction to a wide range of situations - various people, dogs and environments from an early age is critical for young dogs. Safe and positive exposure to novel stimuli is particularly important during the first 14 weeks of a puppy's life.
Appendix C contains a familiarization chart for use with puppies.

It is also during this period that puppies learn canine social skills. Puppies learn through play with siblings and socially adept (safe) adults. A puppy needs plenty of opportunity to develop his canine social skills so that later in life when he meets and greets other dogs he will know how to make friends and follow appropriate doggy protocol.

REWARD BASED LEARNING

Reward based learning is the pairing of reinforcement with specific behaviors as well as pairing of the reinforcement with the person who delivers it. A successful dog handler is 100% attentive to their dog when they are together, reinforcing good behavior and anticipating unwanted behavior at all times. The handler is always prepared to reinforce good choices that the dog makes regardless of whether it is part of the training plan.

For example: the dog is put into a relaxed down when the handler wishes to chat with someone. Even then one eye is always aware of opportunities to reinforce or supervise. If the handler cannot give the dog this level of attention, the dog should be placed in his crate or left at home.

Dogs learn what they practice. The successful dog handler sets his dog up for success. The successful handler never puts the dog in a position where he could possibly make a mistake. That way the dog never practices unwanted behavior.

For example: the dog is never free until he reliably comes when called. He never crosses roads until the handler releases him from a wait command. The dog is fenced or crated when unsupervised. The dog is not taken to a fireworks display until the handler is certain the dog has been desensitized to loud noises.

The successful dog handler is completely in control of the dog's reinforcements at all times. He knows what the dog wants to work for at any given time. He offers a wide, surprising and fun variety of reinforcements. There is a " no free lunch" policy. The dog only gets reinforcement for wanted behaviors.

The successful dog handler prevents his dog from discovering any reinforcements that come from a source other than the handler. No self-reinforcing behaviors are allowed to develop (crittering, chasing or playing with other dogs, sport barking, picking up sticks while hiking or searching, etc.) until the dog has strong foundation behaviors such as a solid recall and basic self control. Even then these reinforcements should be earned by the dog and presented by the handler. Behaviors that are hardwired or inherent to canine fixed action patterns - such as chasing critters - are highly reinforcing. These behaviors can become like drug addictions: they are intrinsically reinforcing and therefore extremely difficult to control. The dog that learns crittering is fun and is allowed to critter as and when he pleases will try to reinforce himself at every opportunity.

Management, the vigilance of the handler and the quality of reinforcement will determine the caliber of the human-dog relationship. If the dog believes the handler is the source of all good things then what the handler does or asks will be what matters to the dog. The development of a reinforcement history is a critical foundation in the human-dog relationship.

Behavior modification requires an understanding of the difference in training results between using reward (positive reinforcement) and punishment (negative reinforcement, positive punishment or negative punishment). Punishment stifles behavior, but also may lead to fallout such as fear and aggression. The human/dog relationship suffers.

Positive reinforcement builds confidence and strengthens relationships. The simple rule for positive reinforcement is: a behavior that is rewarded is more likely to occur again. By understanding the dog's currency (what the dog wants), developing a 'reward economy' and controlling reinforcement (both intrinsic and extrinsic), the handler can reward wanted behavior and not reward unwanted behavior. Dogs choose their behaviors. By making choices available that lead to positive outcomes, the handler ensures the dog will choose wanted behavior and the dog finds learning a pleasure.

Dogs live in the moment and make no attempt to hide what they are thinking and feeling. We just need to learn to observe, to better understand what they are feeling. (*See* **COUNTER CONDITIONING FEAR OR AGGRESSION** *page* 130, **COUNTERING LUNGING OR CHASING** *page* 133.)

CAUSES OF AGGRESSION

For behavior modification of aggression it is important to determine the triggers for the dog's emotional outburst. This will help determine the treatment protocol.

Aggression can be the result of one or more of the following:

CONFLICT-BASED - Aggression directed at owners or family members in response to perceived threats to status, control of resources, or social challenge. Fear and anxiety are major underlying components of the dog's behavior

FEAR-RELATED - Aggression in response to fear. Fearfully aggressive dogs tend to hold their weight toward the back, rather than the front, of their bodies when reacting aggressively. They appear conflicted; for example, moving forward while at the same time attempting to move backward, away from the object of their fear. Fear may be hereditary, the result of lack of exposure to new stimuli during the puppy socialization period (3 to 14 weeks of age), or learned from a previous painful, startling or unpleasant experience.

PREDATORY - Aggression when it involves all or part of the predatory sequence: freeze, stare, crouch, stalk, chase, bite, shake, dissect. Our society tends to accept what we feel is normal predatory behavior, such as stalking and chasing when it is directed toward squirrels, birds or mice. However, predatory aggression against larger animals or people is not considered acceptable. Potential victims that act as prey, such as children or animals that exhibit rapid or jerky movement or high-pitched squealing noises, may trigger predatory attack. For example, children running and screaming, small dogs running and high pitched barking, people jogging or riding bicycles, or limping elderly or disabled people may resemble prey in a dog's mind.

TERRITORIAL - Aggression directed at strangers approaching or entering the dog's territory. The dog may generalize the definition of home area to include areas beyond the owner's property. Guests invited onto your property, mail carriers, UPS or newspaper delivery folks, someone approaching your car or the car the dog is in may be viewed as intruders. The trail you are hiking, the yard you are in, the home you are visiting, the couch or bed the dog is lying on may become objects or spaces to guard. The breed should be considered in territorial or predatory aggression. A working, guarding or herding breed may simply be exhibiting behavior that it was selected for.

IDIOPATHIC - Aggression and its triggers cannot be predicted based on knowledge of canine behavior and body language; the episode tends to be explosive, severe, and out of context. You must rule out seizure disorders and medical issues first.

FEAR-RELATED AGGRESSION

In some cases, fear-related aggression is a learned response to a frightening or painful experience. The dog may associate a particular stimulus (location, noise, object or person) with the fearful experience and may have generalized the fear to other similar stimuli.

In other cases, no history of a painful or frightening experience exists. The aggressive behavior is consistently produced under the same set of circumstances and the dog's behavior and body language are indicative of fear. In these cases the type of aggressive reactive behavior can vary. For example, the dog may:

▶ Growl at the child who recently began walking or crawling.

▶ Back up, then snap at strangers when they try to pet him.

▶ Snap if cornered in a room when new people enter.

Punishment-elicited aggression is directed toward family or strangers who hit, kick or verbally assault the dog. The dog feels he needs to react by biting to protect himself.

Redirected aggression is directed toward family, strangers or animals who approach or touch the dog when he or she is aggressive in another context. For example, a dog is aggressing at another dog walking past his home, a child reaches out to touch the dog and the dog turns and bites the child. The dog is in an aroused state and redirects his aggressive response on the child.

MANAGEMENT

Identify the cause of the fear based on the behavioral history. Recommended management plans should include safety and avoiding fearful triggers so the dog does not continue to rehearse aggressive displays.

Use a muzzle, if deemed necessary, to prevent further injury. (*See* **CONDITIONING TO A HALTER OR MUZZLE** *page* 128.)

ENVIRONMENTAL MODIFICATION

If the reactive behavior is site specific, eliminate exposure to areas where it occurs. Use distance and good management to avoid aggressive displays.

AGGRESSION TOWARD OTHER DOGS IN THE HOUSEHOLD

Aggression within the household is disturbing to owners. Dog-to-dog aggression can occur between any combination of gender but is most common and can be very dangerous between females. When the aggression is between females, injuries tend to be more severe because neither dog backs down. (*See* **WALKING PAST OTHER DOGS** *page* 196, **COUNTERING LUNGING OR CHASING** *page* 133.)

TRIGGERS

Aggression can occur as a struggle for control of resources and social interactions. It is important to determine the triggers for the dog's display of aggression toward any other animals in the household. These are a few common triggers of aggression between dogs within the same household:

- ▶ At entry points and doorways.

- ▶ Over control of scarce resources.

- ▶ When a favorite person is present.

- ▶ When attention is given to one dog and not another.

▶ When new objects are found or explored.

▶ During greeting displays, particularly greetings with you.

▶ When excited. For example, at feeding time, when you return home, or during group play.

MANAGEMENT PLANS

Don't support incidents of dog-to-dog aggression. For example, don't allow one dog to act aggressively while taking a toy from another dog, thinking that the dogs will sort things out. Allowing the dogs to sort things out can lead to increasingly serious squabbles. Any new dog coming into the home should follow your rules, rather than making his own rules.

Teaching dogs to get along requires planning and management to address dog and handler safety by establishing clear rules. These rules should be enforced consistently. Modify the environment to avoid squabbles. For example:

▶ Use crates or baby gates to provide separate areas for dogs that tend to squabble when you are not at home.

▶ During feeding time, crate new dogs, or feed the dogs in stations while you supervise (don't allow them to move around until everyone is finished).

For further information on handling multiple dog households, read "*Feeling Outnumbered*" by Patricia McConnell and Karen London.

CREATING A SAFETY ZONE

Every dog, no matter how docile, needs an indoor spot that will allow him to relax undisturbed by children. When a dog is in his safety zone, children may not look at or interact with him. Using the safety zone correctly means greater safety for your child and his playmates, and more peace for everyone when it's time for a break.

Choose a place for the safety zone where your dog can still smell and hear household activities but be away from the thick of things. Provide fresh water, meals, edible toys and comfy bedding in the safety zone. The safety zone can be created with:

▶ A baby gate. This option allows you to confine your dog to a low-traffic room adjacent to family activity. Nowadays gates come in all heights and lengths.

▶ A crate. If your dog is already house-trained, consider using a larger crate for extra space and comfort.

▶An exercise pen ('x-pen' for short). It has panels so that you can fold it up to carry or store. If you're expecting a baby, start using the safety zone a few times daily no later than four weeks before the baby's arrival. If you already have kids, or if kids visit your home, introduce the safety zone right away. Despite what you may have heard, supervision does not prevent dog bites to children. You must be a "kid canine coach", which means you actively promote and reward good behavior by your child and your dog. Any time you cannot coach your dog and child through their interactions, use the safety zone. Examples:

--company comes over and things are a bit exciting--
--you are too busy or too tired to be an effective coach--
--your child's playmates are visiting--
--you have a babysitter or housekeeper over, or you're not home--
--front-door traffic might pose an opportunity for doggie escape--

As long as you continue to meet your dog's daily needs for aerobic exercise, affection, and training, there is no need to feel guilty about using the safety zone. It provides an important break for your dog.

HOW TO TEACH YOUR DOG TO LOVE THE SAFETY ZONE

1. Feed your dog all her meals in the safety zone using food-dispensing toys like a Kong (tm) or Busy Buddy (tm).

2. Between meals, when your dog is not watching, sprinkle a few outrageously good treats in the safety zone. Let her find the treats as a surprise in her own good time.

3. After a day or two of sprinkling surprise treats, introduce short periods with the baby gate or crate door closed using the following plan:

4. Offer your pooch her favorite edible toy in the safety zone. Then go take a shower, pay the bills, or check the mail. Start with five minute long activities, gradually increasing the time your dog is confined each time you practice. If your dog has been anxious about separation from you in the past, sit and read a magazine near the safety zone while she eats. At each of your dog's meals, position your chair another three inches further from the safety zone until you are out of sight while she eats.

SECRETS TO SUCCESSFUL SAFETY ZONE USE

How to prevent your dog from barking or whining while in the safety zone:

▶Provide your dog with plenty of aerobic exercise each day. A tired dog is generally a calmer dog.

▶Always provide safe, edible chew toys in the safety zone, such as stuffed Kongs.

▶Choose a spot for the safety zone near family activities and near your sleeping area at night. Dogs are social creatures and should not be isolated.

▶If you're using a crate, cover most of it with a light sheet or towel from the start (allow air flow).

▶Ignore whining or it will escalate. A much more effective strategy is to prevent it to begin with by following the above plan closely.

How to get your dog to go into the safety zone on your verbal cue:

1. Stand about two feet from the safety zone with your dog. Face the entrance together. Hold your dog by the collar.

2. Continue holding her by the collar and let her see you toss a tidbit into the safety zone. Pause so she strains forward a bit, thinking, "I really want to go in there!"

3. Release the collar and let her go. Just as she surges toward the safety zone, give a verbal cue like "nap time!" said just once.

4. She will hop into the safety zone and get the treat. Praise and encourage her to come back out to you.

5. Do this five to six times in quick succession.

6. Feed her meals like this for a couple of days, tossing in a handful of food at a time instead of a treat, and she'll soon have the idea.

7. Switch to first saying the verbal cue "nap time!" then releasing the collar and feeding the treats to your dog once she's moved into the safety zone. Now she's got the hang of going in on verbal cue.

8. Gradually increase your starting distance each time you cue "nap time," you won't need to stand near the safety zone to get your dog to go in on cue. This is very handy if you need to quickly get your dog out from underfoot or to move him away from your child.

Special thanks to Barbara Shumannfang, CPDT for generously allowing the use of her Safety Zone Handout. For easy-to-follow tips on how to be a kid canine coach see her book Happy Kids, Happy Dogs: Building a Friendship Right from the Start (Lulu, 2006).

INTRODUCING A NEW DOG INTO THE HOUSEHOLD

If you are adopting or adding a new dog to your home, it doesn't necessarily mean the dogs will end up playing together. Friendships and trust take time and understanding to build. The following suggestions are important to successfully introduce a new dog to your own dog.

CHOOSING THE NEW DOG

Younger dogs in the household are usually more open to new pups. An older dog may have some discomfort with the newly transplanted dog and disruption of routine. It's often best to introduce an opposite sexed dog into a home with an adult dog. Younger dogs are usually easier to introduce to the household than older dogs.

PREPARING THE RESIDENT DOG

Intact (unaltered) dogs tend to have a more difficult time than those who have been spayed or neutered before the new dog is introduced. It can take several weeks for hormonal surges to calm down after neutering, so the resident dog should be completely recovered before introducing a new dog, particularly since both neutering and introducing a new dog are so stressful.

PLANNING THE RESOURCES

Before you bring the new dog into your home you need to plan for the following: Toilet area, toys, treats, sleeping arrangements, feeding locations and daily exercise schedules. Have plenty of time to settle the new dog into your household. Take time off work to introduce a new dog to your dog and to his new home. This time will allow you to get to know the new dog and make the transition easier for all concerned. If you are unable to take time off work, at least plan for an entire weekend. If you have others living in your home, temporarily schedule overlapping days off. This way you will have two days to supervise the dogs, and then another family member can supervise the dogs for the next two days. Supervision, exercise, and hanging out together make fitting in go the most smoothly. Have realistic expectations and get help if you need it.

INTRODUCING THE DOGS

1. Introduce on neutral territory. Dogs naturally guard important resources such as their home, their car and their people. Meeting where they don't feel the need to guard anything will help them feel less anxious. Take your dog to a neutral place to meet the new dog. Have a helper so the dogs can be walked on leash separately. Avoid having anything nearby that the dogs might fight over such as toys, bones or food. When you start the process of introduction, walk parallel for a while so the dogs get accustomed to each other gradually. Keep them on a loose leash until they can ignore each other or are play bowing and want to interact, if both dogs look relaxed let them loose dragging their leashes. If all is going well, let them casually sniff each other. When they are comfortable (if you are in a safely enclosed area) let them off leash together. Once they have interacted well together, you can walk them home together (if possible) or meet in the front yard of the home.

2. Control and supervise. Supervise the new dog at all times until both dogs are calm with each other. This could be for a few minutes or for a few weeks. If the dogs are growling or avoiding each other, stay to watch them. If you haven't the time to supervise, crate one dog while the other is free and supervise the free dog. If the new dog hasn't learned house manners yet he can't be loose without supervision. Don't put your dogs in a position where they can make a mistake.

    Make sure all toys and food are up off the floor. If you are introducing a puppy and an older dog, hold the adult dog's leash and let the puppy drag his leash. How much freedom you give depends on how friendly the older dog is with the new puppy. Watch the dogs' communication signals as they interact. For information on dog communication signals, read Turid Rugaas' book "*Calming Signals*".

    A dog that is fearful or anti-social may take some special handling; he could bite if pressured too much by the other dog. If either dog is stiff or seems uncomfortable, defuse the situation by removing one dog from the area. Use a muzzle if you are worried If you use a muzzle, it should have been conditioned a long time before the new dog is brought home.

3. Remain calm. Dogs will sense your anxiety. Treat them all as if they are funny kids. If they are cranky or defensive or bossy, act as though they are funny. Don't act like there is something to worry about. Dogs can read us like a book. If we are worried they learn to be worried. Tell the dogs that they are silly, find them funny, and if things are going smoothly separate them before things begin to go badly. You can trigger aggression by tensing up or holding the leash too tight. Keep the leashes loose. If the dogs are tense, step away before the dogs are close enough to tangle. Don't walk straight toward another dog just circle closer from the side and then walk side by side. If you are calm and find the posturing amusing, the dogs will sense they don't have to worry either.

4. Gradually increase interactions. When you get your new dog home, don't just unclip the leash and let him loose. For a number of days, the new dog should only be out of his crate when on a leash or a drag line. If you don't have a crate, then keep the dogs in separate rooms until you are certain they are okay together. Gradually, as he begins to understand acceptable behavior, increase the length of time the new dog is loose. For the first month, the new dog should never be loose without supervision. This "easy does it" management is the best way to avoid a dog fight.

    Often, concerned owners will incorrectly interfere with dog interaction. Most of the time, it is better to ignore a situation and let the dogs work it out through posturing. It is okay to say something like "easy" or "be nice" in a calm voice. Do not rescue one of the dogs by picking him up or yelling at the unsociable dog. This will only make the situation worse. If you are constantly interfering, the natural dog social order between the dogs will never get established. Praise the dogs for tolerating each other. Praise what you like and ignore what you don't, unless one dog is being bullied or badgered too much. If so, put the aggressor in his crate for a timeout.

5. Provide each dog special time. Allow for special one-on-one time for each of your animals. Go outside and play with one dog while the other is in his crate, or inside with something good to chew on, such as a stuffed Kong or marrow bone. Be sure to pick up the bone or Kong before allowing the second dog to be loose.

6. Allow for settling in. Give yourself and the new dog time to learn how to live together. You should expect the "civilizing" process to take time. Be proud of yourself and your dog for every small improvement. They will add up and within months (not days) you will all be living happily together. Some animals adapt immediately while others take up to six months, so allow for ample adjustment time. Success depends on the new dog believing he or she can figure out what you want. That means lots of positive reinforcement for any good behavior and really good supervision so no fights occur.

7. Get help when you need it! Punishment will not teach your dog good behavior. Reinforcing good behavior and supervision (through crating and watchfulness) will change behavior. If you can't find a way to solve a problem, ask for help.

CHANGING PEOPLE CHANGING DOGS

RULES FOR PRACTICING EXERCISES

For safety, behavior consultants and handlers should adhere to the following rules throughout the training program:

▶ The behavior consultant should be well versed in all exercises recommended to clients.

▶ The handler must only handle his own dog, unless instructed otherwise.

▶ The handler must be proactive, not reactive.

▶ The handler must make sure the training area is safe to enter. For example, there should be no loose dogs or people exiting the area.

▶ If the handler has a reactive dog, he must have one-on-one training until the dog is no longer reactive upon getting out of the car or entering a training area.

▶ Before putting the handler in proximity to a stimulus or trigger that the dog is having difficulty with, the handler must have good leadership skills and a plan marking and reinforcing desired behavior.

▶ The dog must have good basic self control skills before introducing the trigger.

▶ Rehearse distractions so handlers can be successful on their own.

▶ The leash should be left on the dog until the behavior consultant feels 100% safe having the dog off lead.

▶ The behavior consultant should practice and fully understand all of the exercises before teaching the handler, so the behavior consultant is able to articulate exactly how the handler should work with the dog,

▶ Review EDITH. (*see Chapter 3.*)

▶ Safety for the handler and dog is always the first priority.

BASICS FOR THE HANDLER

When changing the dog's reactive emotional association to people, dogs or other scary things:

1. Work at a distance where the dog can exercise self control and focus on you when asked to do so.

2. Always go slowly, at the dogs pace.

3. As soon as the dog's body tells you that he is starting to respond emotionally, choose the best method to change his body and focus:

    a. Use food to bring the dog's eyes on you and change direction.

    b. If the dog is on a halter, gently slide your hand down the leash and up under the dog's muzzle, so you have control of his head. Pivot around the dog so that you are blocking the stranger dog (or other scary thing), then walk away. When the dog can focus on you, ask for a sit and treat. Turn around and start again. Stay further away from the scary thing so that the dog can remain relaxed.
    4. "No free lunch." The dog should comply with what you ask. No treat until you have his eye contact. Once you do have eye contact, pay the dog a CEO salary with bonuses. If you do, you will become more important than the scary thing.

5. Provide lots of exercise, particularly interactive play exercise.

Recognize that the dog and his environment may need to be managed his entire life. He may improve tremendously but he has practiced and learned the emotional stimulation of aggression. If you don't always insist on being the ONLY source of good stuff, he will look to other stimulation.

BASIC OUTLINE FOR CONSULTATIONS

The dog's behavior will be modified over the period of consultations. The handler must practice various exercises between consultations.

Have the handler fit the dog with the necessary equipment (leash, flat collar, harness, etc.) for loose leash walking skills and talk them through it. Most people allow the dogs to walk ahead of them. Convincing them that this is a big part of the problem can be a large part of the first consultation.

For dogs with little self control, use the Relaxed Down and Look Back exercises in Appendix A. These two skills can be taught to the handler during the first consultation. The Relaxed Down will teach the dog to lie quietly during the consultation. These two exercises can be the handler's first homework.

Practice the lured sit and down, eventually using these exercises together as "push ups".

For dogs that have spatial issues, perform the Head and Shoulder Desensitization exercise (*See page 155*)and work on leadership skills.

For dogs with fear or aggression when a person reaches for them, show the handler how to play the Gotcha Game (*See page 152*).

For dogs lacking in self-control, have the handler practice Wait at Doorways (*See page 193*).

Once the basic skills have been learned, work on duration of each skill in a relaxed environment, without stimulus or triggers. Once these exercises are perfected in a relaxed environment begin working on handling skills in and around the stimulus that is causing the dog difficulty. For example, introduce a dog who has good self control and can lie calmly while in the same room or introduce a person who can follow instructions well.

RECAP

ALL of these strategies require lots of positive reinforcement. Think of it like putting money in the bank! Success with dogs requires many "deposits" of positive reinforcements for calm and self controlled behavior before you start making any "withdrawls"!

"The single worst thing you can

do to an animal emotionally

is to make it feel afraid."

~Temple Grandin

Author of "Animals in Translation"

6   Specific Cases

The following real-life case studies provide examples of assessment, planning and analysis, and application of the techniques examined in this book. *All names have been changed in each of these case studies.*

CASE STUDY #1

Maggie's dog has bitten her husband several times and growls at her son when he walks past the dog's bed or crate. Maggie says the dog is wonderful, but wonders whether she should be concerned.

Household Members: Maggie, her husband and her teenage son.

Maggie's daughter and two young children sometimes visit.

Dog's Particulars: Charlie, a golden retriever, 10 months of age.

Medical History: Normal veterinary care, up-to-date on vaccinations.

Neutered at 6 months of age.

Nothing unusual in the dog's medical history.

BEHAVIORAL HISTORY:

Charlie is active and pushier than any other golden retriever the family has owned.

Maggie brought Charlie home when he was 12 weeks of age. Charlie's behavioral problems have been escalating over a period of several months.

Charlie growls at the family while he is eating. The breeder told Maggie to ignore Charlie's growling and feed him in his crate.

Charlie steals food off the counter and out of the trash. He growls at Maggie when she scolds him for taking things off the counter, but he has never snapped at her.

One evening, as the husband tried to climb into bed, Charlie growled at him. The husband laughed and climbed into bed. This type of behavior continued for several months.

A few months prior to the consultation, when Maggie's teenage son walked past, Charlie growled at him. The boy laughed and made fun of Charlie. Now whenever anyone tries to walk past his bed, Charlie growls.

The son recently tried to give the dog a kiss good night while the dog was asleep, and the dog snapped at his face. There was slight contact, with scrapes, but no punctures. The husband hit the dog and sent him to his crate.

ASSESSMENT

Learned aggression - Control conflict aggression - Possessive resource guarding

MANAGEMENT PLAN

I met with Maggie's family 4 times in 6 months. Each time, I taught the family a few more exercises. The family was advised to follow this management plan:

▶ Ensure that Charlie doesn't have the opportunity to rehearse the aggressive behavior .

▶ No more sleeping on humans' beds.

▶ Move the dog's crate to a quiet corner so people don't walk past it.

▶ Keep container of treats nearby so family members can toss treats to the dog while he is in his crate.

▶ Hand feed all meals.

▶ Condition the dog to a head halter or muzzle.

▶ Keep a leash on the dog at all times (*See* **Tag Line Use**, *page 45.*)

▶ Supervise heavily around children. If necessary, board the dog while the daughter visits with her kids.

FIRST CONSULTATION: RELATIONSHIP BUILDING

During our first consultation, we talked about behavior modification. I gave the family a manual of mine to read and to refresh their knowledge of the exercises I have asked them to do with Charlie.

Charlie doesn't seem very sociable to the husband or son so the following exercises were set up to improve the dog's relationship with everyone in the family:

▶ Follow the "No Free Lunch" (NFL) program for the next few months. *(See Strategies and Techniques, page 65.)*

▶ Practice and reward basic obedience exercises such as sit and down.

▶ Play the biscuit-toss game: Walk toward the dog while tossing biscuits.

▶ Have Maggie, her husband, and her son take turns hand feeding Charlie and playing the Food Bowl Game with him. *(See* **Food Bowl Game** *page 149.)*

▶ Play Attention Games. Voluntary Look Back. *(See Exercise page 191.)*

▶ Perform On-Off (Placement) exercises. *(See Exercise page 164.)*

▶ Play Gotcha games. (See *Exercise page 152.*)

▶ Lots of physical praise associated with food.

2ND CONSULTATION: YIELDING EXERCISES

▶ Perform "Wait at Doorways" and "Body Blocking". (*See Exercises pages 123 & 193.*)

▶ Teach Charlie to turn and sit, once on the other side of the doorway. (*See Exercise page 193.*)

▶ Practice "Leave It". (*See Exercise page 159.*)

▶ Begin Grooming and Veterinary Preparation exercises (in particular, have Maggie move her hands gently around Charlie's head and muzzle, to desensitise handling) he should be muzzled when starting to do the head and shoulder handling and gotcha games. (*See Exercises page 156 & 166*)

▶ Desensitise the dog to the eye contact of unfamiliar people through Attention Games. (*See Exercise page 121 & 165.*)

3RD CONSULTATION: INTERACTIVE PLAY

▶ Play Fetch Games, starting with the Two-Toy Game. (*See Exercise page 178.*)

▶ Practice puppy push-ups: Quick sits and downs.

▶ Practice stays and recalls.

OUTCOME

Today Charlie is 3 yrs of age. Resource guarding behavior is under control. He eats two meals a day in the kitchen, and anyone can walk past with no issues. He is not allowed on human beds unless invited. He is walked on a flat collar.

Charlie is social to all family members and guests. He is still supervised around children, although he seems to like them.

CASE STUDY #2

John's dog, Fred, has bitten his wife several times, each time more seriously.

Household Members:	John, male, mid-forties.
	Wife, married John 2 yrs ago.
	Three children: 6 months, 2 years and 8 years.
Dog's Particulars:	Fred, a Rottweiler, 5 years of age, intact male.
	John adopted Fred when he was an 8 week old puppy.
Medical History:	Not up-to-date on vaccinations.
	No known medical conditions.

BEHAVIORAL HISTORY

Fred has always been very dominant even at 12 weeks of age. John was single with a teenage daughter at the time Fred was adopted.

When Fred was a puppy, John took him back to the breeder because he was biting and drawing blood. The breeder held the puppy down for 20 minutes until he finally submitted. The breeder then showed the John how to do this and suggested he do it every day for at least the first year of the dog's life. John did as the breeder recommended, until Fred bit him when he was about 2 yrs of age.

Fred spends his days tied to his doghouse and is only brought inside when John is home in the evenings. Once in a while John's wife would feel sorry for Fred and bring him into the house, but then she couldn't take Fred back outside, because he would growl at her.

Fred growls at all the children. The 8 year old is afraid of him.

Fred sleeps next to John's side of the bed at night. Fred growls at John's wife when she walks past. Fred growled and bit John's wife when she tried to take away some food he had stolen. She needed 10 stitches but she was still willing to allow John to keep the dog.

John demonstrated that Fred is able to sit, stay and come (when not distracted). Fred is extremely food motivated.

Fred enjoys fetch. So, during the assessment I asked to see John play fetch with him. John's wife and 2 year old child came with us. When John threw the ball, Fred chased it but did not pick it up. Instead, he turned and came back, body slammed the child, and then jumped up at the wife's face. No contact was made with the wife and no growling occurred. But Fred was not playing; he was sending a message.

John admitted that he wasn't walking or giving Fred as much attention as often as he used to. He had been too busy.

I told John I felt, in this situation, that the dog's behavior could not be safely modified. I recommended euthanisia rather than rehoming. I felt (and still feel now) that the dog was /is potentially dangerous. However, I agreed to come up with a plan and work with them if they felt otherwise. John obviously had strong feelings for Fred, and chose to work to keep him and his wife agreed.

ASSESSMENT

Dominance aggression. Has little regard for humans. Extreme resource guarder.

MANAGEMENT PLAN

The family was advised to follow this management plan:

▶ Management 100% of the time.

▶ Have dog neutered ASAP.

▶ Keep shots up-to-date.

▶ Condition the dog to a basket muzzle.

▶ Install outside kennel with insulated dog house for Fred.

▶ Never allow dog loose in the house unless John is present and dog is muzzled.

▶ Wife has no responsibilities for dog.

FURTHER CONSULTATIONS

I talked to John about euthanasia again but he did not want to pursue that route at the time. John exercised Fred by playing fetch games. Fred enjoyed Two-Toy. (*See Exercise page 148.*) I worked with John on the dog's obedience skills over 4 consultations, in 30 minute training sessions. We used a different location each time. We worked on the following exercises:

▶ Relaxed Downs. (*See Exercise page 181.*)

▶ Eye contact and Attention Games, Look Back (*See Exercises page 121, 165 and 191.*)

▶ Recalls. (*See Exercise page 174.*)

▶ "Leave It" and the Food Bowl Game. (*See Exercise page 159 and 149.*)

▶ Gotcha exercises, modified to suit the dog. (*See Exercise page 152.*)

▶ Scent Games for exercise and structured supervised time outside with John, with no children running around. (*See Exercise page 179.*)

After 3 weeks, the client had desensitized the dog to the muzzle. During that time, if John went away he left Fred at a boarding kennel that specialized in Rottweilers. The kennel staff used food to move Fred from one place to another and had no issues with him.

OUTCOME

Today the dog is still living in an outdoor kennel, and comes into the house when John is home. He is still muzzled when in the home. The family has had two incidents with guests but Fred's muzzle was on so he did no damage. Fred has been good with all family members.

John asked if he could start taking the muzzle off in the home. I emphatically said NO!

CASE STUDY #3

Claire's dog, Buffy, bit a worker at her house. While Claire was holding Buffy, the man reached over to pet him. As the man removed his hand, Buffy bit him.

Household Members: Claire, single woman, mid-60's.

Dog's Particulars: "Buffy", poodle cross, 20 pounds, 2 years of age, neutered male

Medical History: Normal veterinary care, up-to-date on vaccinations.

No specific medical problems. In good physical condition.

Buffy is groomed several times a year, and groomer has no issues except that she muzzles Buffy to trim his nails. He is fine with grooming after nail trimming.

BEHAVIORAL HISTORY

Claire has owned Buffy since he was 8 weeks of age. She chose him because he was quiet and a bit reserved.

While outside he sometimes barks, but never charges after people.

In the past, Buffy has bitten Claire's friends. He tends to bite the ankles of Claire's guests when they stand up and move too fast or as they are leaving the house. On walks, if an unfamiliar person reaches out to pet Buffy, he often snaps at the person as they are removing their hand.

When Buffy snaps, Claire yells at him. If they are out, Claire walks away with him. If they are at home, she puts him away in a back room and he is quiet until let out of the room.

During the history taking process, it became clear that Buffy was uncomfortable with attention from unfamiliar people. The little dog had learned that, if he snapped at someone, they would leave him alone. Being put in a back room, or walked away worked for him, since he wanted to get away from the unwanted attention.

ASSESSMENT

Fear based aggression. Learned aggression. Territorial aggression.

MANAGEMENT PLAN

Claire was instructed to follow this management plan:

▶ Use an easy walk harness (such as the Sensation harness) or a head halter (such as the Gentle Leader) to teach Buffy to walk next to her.

▶ If Buffy becomes distracted by another dog or people while walking on lead, Claire should stop moving toward distraction, guide the dog's head around using food to lure him onto her other side so he isn't so close to the distraction and then walk in another direction if possible or to move out of the path of the oncoming stimulus.

▶ Manage guests. Guests should not enter the house until Buffy has been set up comfortably. Before guests arrive, Buffy should be put on lead or in the bedroom with a Kong. If Buffy is comfortable in a crate, that's another option, but he should never be put in a position where he's uncomfortable in the crate with guests around.

▶ Put the harness or halter and lead on Buffy before guests arrive. Being on lead will allow Claire to manage Buffy, keeping him a safe distance from the guests, so he does not practice unwanted behavior like snapping at people.

▶ If Buffy is on lead in the room with the guests, toss a handful of treats on the floor before the guests stand to leave, so Buffy is busy finding treats rather than getting nervous about the people moving around.

BEHAVIOR MODIFICATION

Claire was advised to perform the following exercises:

▶ No Free Lunch (NFL) program: All meals would be hand-fed, as reinforcement for wanted behaviors.

▶ Play Attention games, so she can use Attention by having him giving her eye contact when unfamiliar people approach. Voluntary Look Back (*See Exercise page 191.*)

▶ Desensitize to eye contact with unfamiliar people through Attention Games. (*See Exercises page 121 and 165*)

▶ Play the Gotcha Game and Grooming exercises. (*See Exercises page 152 and 156.*)

▶ Teach self control. (*See Exercises page 180.*)

▶ Teach Strolling on Lead. (*See Loose Leash Walking Exercise page 160.*)

▶ Practice the Body Block exercise, so the dog learns to move away from people if he is worried. (*See Exercise page 123.*)

▶ Pair treats with unfamiliar people who walk toward him, moving the dog out of reach of oncoming people. Don't pick the dog up, just let him walk along. Remind people not to touch or reach out to the dog.

▶ Teach Relaxed Down. (*See Exercises page 182.*) Down can be used as a timeout and to help regain control when dog becomes over stimulated.

▶ Put the dog on lead with the harness or halter before opening the door to guests. Have him sit and ask guests not to look at him. As he calms down the guests may toss a treat. Never let people bend over him.

▶ Keep the dog on a Tag Line in the house so if he starts to bark at something outside, you can pick up the lead and remove him from the area. Reinforce with food and praise when he has been quiet for 5 minutes.

▶ Desensitize the dog to the doorbell and knocking. Set this up with a helper so you can practice it many times over several months before trying it with real guests. Reinforce him with food or a toy for being quiet and calm when the doorbell rings. Do this repeatedly so the dog walks to the door and sits quietly instead of running around barking. Make it a game.

▶ Be prepared for visitors by having yummy treats near the front door. (See Case Study # 2.) Claire should give Buffy treats first, and the guests should ignore him. When Buffy becomes more relaxed around the guests, they may toss treats to him.

▶ If Buffy barks or growls at anyone, give him a timeout. (*See* **Think Positive**, Learning, chapter 2.)

FURTHER CONSULTATIONS

Claire had 5 consultations over the course of 4 months.

OUTCOME

Buffy consistently improved his behavior when guests came to visit. It was difficult to convince Claire to use the timeouts, but once she accepted them, they seemed to work.

Claire taught Buffy to move to a chair on the other side of her when guests walked toward them. She didn't allow anyone to try and pet him for a long time. Eventually he learned to approach Claire's close friends and sit in their laps, once they had been in the home for about 15 minutes. Claire is very happy with this progress.

Claire still calls Buffy to her when guests prepare to leave and scatters a few kibble on the floor for him to hunt. This keeps him busy as the guests leave.

Unfortunately, Claire failed to work on many of the exercises. Therefore, the result is primarily management (such as teaching him to move away when he wasn't feeling comfortable) rather than behavior al modification (teaching him not to fear guests).

CASE STUDY #4

Martha was knocked down the stairs when her dog, a German shepherd named "Sheba", jumped up on her.

Household Members: Martha and 3 children, ages 8, 10 and 12.

Dog's Particulars: "Sheba", 8 month old German shepherd, spayed female

Medical History: Normal veterinary care, up-to-date on vaccinations.

Spay occurred 2 months prior.

BEHAVIORAL HISTORY

Sheba jumps up and knocks the kids over. She also drags Martha downstairs, pursuing squirrels. The family walks Sheba around the neighbourhood for exercise, but she pulls on lead.

ASSESSMENT

Normal adolescent behavior

MANAGEMENT PLAN

Martha was instructed to follow this management plan:

▶ Find reinforcements Sheba will work for

▶ Use a halter (such as the Gentle Leader) or easy walk harness (such as the Sensation harness) whenever walking on 6 foot lead. (Not TO use a Retractable lead)

▶ If Sheba becomes distracted by another dog or people while walking on lead, Martha should stop moving toward distraction, guide the dog's head around using food, so he isn't facing distraction, to move her to her other side and walk in another direction if she can.

▶ If the halter is chosen, have the dog wear the halter or harness while supervised in the house or playing, allowing her to get completely comfortable with it before adding the lead.

▶ Put the dog on lead with the halter or harness before guests arrive, and use lead whenever guests are in the house. Being on lead will allow Martha to manage Sheba, keeping her a safe distance from the guests, so she does not practice unwanted behavior like jumping up on people.

▶ Keep the dog on a Tag Line in the house. This will allow Martha to get control of Sheba without having to grab at her.

BEHAVIOR MODIFICATION

Martha was advised to find reinforcements Sheba would work for, and perform the following exercises:

▶ Teach Loose Lead Walking. (*See Exercise page 160*)

▶ Attention, VoluntaryLook Back (*See Exercises pages 121, 165, 191*)

▶ Teach the dog not to jumping up: Have Sheba on lead with the halter before opening the door to guests. Move at least 10 feet from the door. Have Sheba sit or relaxed down at Martha's side. Ask guests not to acknowledge Sheba in any way. As the dog calms down, guest may give her a treat, or let her touch their hand and Martha rewards her. Only reward as long as the dog remains calm. A crate or tether can be used if Sheba can't maintain calm behavior .

▶ Teach Relaxed Down. (*See Exercise page 182*). Relaxed Down should be practiced every day, working up to a 10 minutes duration with the distraction of family members moving around the house, past the dog.

▶ Teach Wait Off Lead. (*See Exercise page 195*)

▶ Teach Wait at Doorways. (*See Exercise page 193*) Sheba should learn to wait until Martha has walked out the door and down the stairs, before being released.

▶ Teach Sheba how to greet friends. (*See Exercises page 186*)

FURTHER CONSULTATIONS

Claire had 2 additional consultations, during which Sheba practiced loose leash walking, self control games, scent games and the two-ball game. (*See Exercises pages 149, 181, 150.*) Games provide better exercise than walking Sheba around the neighbourhood.

OUTCOME

Once Sheba had learned a few self control skills, she and Martha joined obedience Foundation Skills class. Sheba learned how to search for each of the children and to use her nose to find toys they would hide around the home. The family adores Sheba, and she is turning into a wonderful companion with good self control skills.

CASE STUDY #5

While at the shelter, Bell showed lack of socialization and the beginnings of fear aggression toward a few of the staff members. We worked with her but she didn't seem to be improving with these particular people. Had the owner not shown up we probably would not have placed this dog.

Household Members: Mr. Smith 60 years old, his wife, 2 other dogs (both Labrador Retrievers).

Dog's Particulars: "Bell", a spayed Rottweiler shepherd cross.

Turned into the shelter as a stray, and then returned to the owner when she was approximately 1 year of age.

Medical History: Revaccinated due to unknown vaccination history.

BEHAVIORAL HISTORY

Mr. Smith said he hadn't noticed any aggression issues, but that Bell was a destructive chewer and out of control (he was unable to walk her on lead). Bell didn't see may people, just Mr. Smith and his wife. They have a lot of property, and go walking in their own woods.

ASSESSMENT

Lack of socialization, leading to fear aggression.

Note: Bell is what shelter staff refer to as a "thirdway" dog; a dog who has issues with self-control, lack of socialization and fear aggression that need addressing before adoption.

Bell needs a lot of exercise. She must be played with at least twice a day.

Bell has the potential to bite in response to fear, so should not be allowed to run free.

MANAGEMENT PLAN

Mr. Smith was instructed to follow this management plan:

▶ Use a halter (such as the Gentle Leader) or easy walk harness (such as the Sense-ation harness) whenever walking on lead.

▶ Have the dog wear the halter or harness while supervised in the house or playing, allowing her to get completely comfortable with it before adding the lead.

▶ Put the dog on lead with the halter or harness before guests arrive, and use lead whenever guests are in the house. Being on lead will allow Mr. Smith to manage Bell, keeping her a safe distance from the guests, so she does not practice unwanted behavior. If Bell is well behaved, Mr. Smith may drop the lead and allow Bell to be loose with the lead dragging.

▶ If Bell becomes distracted by another dog or people while walking on lead, Mr. Smith should stop moving toward distraction, guide the dog's head around using food, so he isn't facing distraction, and walk in another direction.

BEHAVIOR MODIFICATION

Mr. Smith was advised to perform the following exercises:

▶ Attention (for name recognition). Look Back (*See Exercises page 161, 191*)

▶ Strolling on Lead. (*See Exercise page 160*)

▶ Work on classically conditioning that new people are okay. Bell loves to play fetch so introducing fetch with new people would be a good way to help her.

▶ Relaxed Down. (*See Exercise page 182*). The down can be used as a timeout and to help regain control when dog becomes over stimulated.

▶ Use the long line when outside or walking in the woods. Step on it if the dog goes too far away or becomes distracted. When the dog turns to look back, reinforce with food and praise. Use a tag line in the house.

▶ Desensitize the doorbell and knocking. (*See Case Study #3*)

▶ Two-toy games and scent games. (*See Exercises page 148 & 179*)

OUTCOME

Mr. Smith had several additional consultations. He enjoyed working with Bell so much, he joined several training classes. Today, Bell is a sociable, non-destructive canine companion.

HAPPY ENDINGS

Follow up on the cases presented in this book as of October, 2007.

Example case number 1 from
Assessment Chapter 3

Black lab Female, 3 years of age.
Now 7 years old, she is now behind a permanent fence system and her owner has been
working hard to help her feel safe and that good
things happen when she sees other dogs walking down the street. There have been no incidents and she can now be walked on leash past
other dogs with out her getting upset and barking or lunging.

Example Case number 2 from
Assessment Chapter 3

Golden Retriever 18 months, Chance.
He is now almost 6 years of age and although his owners worked with him for a few months the
children were afraid of him. They asked if I would help find him a suitable home. I found a
retired couple with older grand children who only visit during the summer months. We worked
on creating a safe place for him. Today he is fine with their grandchildren and with the neighbor's children who visit occasionally. He loves to play fetch and swim so the children play with
him and he now feels very comfortable around children for short periods of time. His owners
carefully manage his environment to make sure no child gets into his space accidentally. There
have been no growling incidents or aggressive outbursts for almost 4 years

Case number 1 from
Specific Cases Chapter six

Charlie is now 7 years of age and is well adjusted and doing just fine. No incidents since the
behavior modification was started

Case Number 2 from
Specific Cases Chapter six

Fred the Rottweiler is now 9 years of age
His handler called me to say the Fred was doing great and that there had been no incidents for
the past 4 years. They still muzzle him at night time while he is sleeping in the bedroom. He is
still kenneled in an outside yard by himself during the day. When home he is allowed out with
family members to play fetch games and hide and seek games but when coming inside he is
muzzled.

Case Number 3 from
Specific Cases Chapter six

Buffy is now 6 years of age. When I last spoke to her owner, Buffy is still going to a chair when folks come to visit. Within a few minutes he will go say hello and get a tidbit and then go back to his chair and relax until the guests leave. He doesn't chase them out the door anymore.

Case Number 4 from
Specific Cases Chapter six

Sheba is almost 5 years of age and is social and polite. They all adore her. She keeps track of all the children and lies quietly while they have their friends over. Occasionally someone tosses a toy for her to go find. She is being the good sentry dog she was bred to be.

Case Number 5 from
Specific Cases Chapter six

Bell- Last I knew they were doing just fine but unfortunately I lost track of them and so have no follow up to report at this time.

7 The Journey

The Journey

When you bring a dog into your life, you begin a wonderful journey - a journey that will bring you more love and devotion than you have ever known, yet will also test your strength and courage.

If you allow it, the journey will teach you many things about life, about yourself and most of all, about relationships. You will come away changed forever, for one soul cannot touch another without leaving its mark.

Along the way, you will learn much about savouring life's simple pleasures - jumping in leaves, snoozing in the sun, the joys of puddles, drinking from a cool trailside stream and even the satisfaction of a good scratch behind the ears. There will be ups and downs along the way.

If you spend much time outside, you will be taught how to truly experience every element for no rock, leaf, log or hole in the ground will go unexamined. No rustling bush or falling leaf will be overlooked. Even the very air will be inhaled, pondered, and noted as being full of valuable information. Your pace may be slower - except when heading back home - but you will become a better naturalist, having been taught by an expert in the field for the dogs know the nose knows.

Too many times we hike on automatic pilot, our goal being to complete the trail rather than enjoy the journey. We miss the details - the colourful mushrooms on the rotting log, the honeycomb in the old maple snag, the hawk feather caught on a twig, the chip in the stone wall. When we walk as a dog does, we discover a whole new world. We stop, browse the landscape, kick over leaves, peek in tree holes, look up, down, all around. Ee learn what any dog knows: nature has created a marvellously complex world, full of surprises, and each cycle of the seasons brings ever changing wonders, each day an essence all its own.

Even indoors you will find yourself more attuned to the world around you. You and your dog will watch summer insects collecting on a screen or landing on the ceiling. (How bizarre they are! How many kinds there are!) Or note the flick and flash of fireflies through the dark. You will stop to observe the swirling dance of windblown leaves or sniff the air after rain. It does not matter that there is no objective in this; the point is in the doing, in not letting life's most important details slip by.

You will find yourself doing silly things that your petless friends might not understand. Like spending thirty minutes in the grocery aisle looking for the right dog food brand with the correct ingredients you must have, buying dog birthday treats or driving around the block an extra time because your pet is enjoying the ride. You will roll in the snow, wrestle with chewy toys, bounce little rubber balls until your eyes are crossed and point the laser along the floors and walls for a good game of chase. You'll even run around the house trailing your bathrobe tie, with a puppy in hot pursuit.

Your house will become muddier and hairier. You will wear less dark clothing and buy more lint rollers. You will find dog biscuits and kibble in your pocket after you have washed and dried your clothes. You'll feel the need to explain that the old plastic milk jug or cardboard box adorns your living room rug because your dog loves to play with it.

You will learn the true measure of love: the steadfast, undying kind that says "It doesn't matter where we are or what we do, or how life treats us, as long as we are together." Respect this always. It is the most precious gift any living soul can give another. You will not find it often among the human race.

And you will learn humility. The look in my dog's eyes often makes me feel ashamed. Such joy and love at my presence. Those eyes see not some flawed human who can be cross and stubborn, moody or rude, but only a wonderful companion. Or maybe they see those things but dismiss them as mere human foibles, not worth considering and so choose to love me anyway.

If you pay attention and learn well, when the journey is done you will be not just a better person, but the person your pet always knew you to be: The one they were proud to call beloved friend.

"He is your friend, your partner, your defender, your dog. You are his life, his love, his leader. He will be yours, faithful and true, to the last beat of his heart. You owe it to him to be worthy of such devotion"

~Unknown

Appendix A

Exercises

This section provides various step-by-step exercises for the handler and dog to practice.

Exercises can be chosen according to the dog's needs. Each step of each chosen exercise should be practiced to perfection before moving onto the subsequent step. Some exercises are prerequisites for others. Before beginning each exercise, be certain you have a thorough understanding of the exercise, its purpose and each of its steps.

These exercises have been listed in bold throughout this book.

ACTIVE ATTENTION

This exercise teaches the dog to respond to his name by giving you his attention.

BACKGROUND

All learning begins with attention. Paying attention to you is a learned skill and as such, attention requires repetition and reinforcement to be learned.

A dog responds with attention for two reasons: something good is going to happen or something bad is going to happen. Either way, that something is relevant to him. Friendship (respect, trust, and love) only result when the dog expects good from you.

Training for attention is the process of showing the dog that when you say his name something good is always going to happen. Luckily for us, dogs are eager for food, play and praise. By being prepared (having treats or a toy with us), we will always have something good to offer the dog when we call his name. Making yourself the most interesting thing in the dog's world will generate and maintain his attention.

PREPARATION

Have a pouch of yummy treats, and a hungry dog on leash.

Train in an area where there are no distractions, such as in a quiet house with no other people, dogs, cats, etc. around.

PROCESS

Step 1: Hold a morsel of tasty food in your fingers, just in front of dog's nose. Hold the food at the natural level of the dog's nose; not too high or he may learn to jump up to get it. When the dog focuses on the food in your hand, slowly walk backward a few steps, holding the food just in front of the dog's nose level. Sweetly speak the dog's name. If the dog follows you for a few steps, click (or say yes) and give him the morsel. Further reinforce the primary reward - the food, with verbal praise, pats and play.

If the dog gets distracted before taking a few steps, you probably moved the food away from his nose before he figured out what he smelled. Puppies cannot see well and haven't learned how to follow scent yet, so don't say anything, just start again. When you get his attention on the food, say his name, click and treat. Start pairing food and verbal praise by saying "goood" as the dog eats his food treat. Increase the value of the food reward with verbal praise, pats and play.

Spend some time reinforcing the dog's attention by drawing the treat feeding out. Break off little pieces while complimenting the dog in sentences such as "What a good dog you are. You're such a wonderful dog. You are so special." Mean what you say, since attention is about you both being together in the moment.

Move around to give the dog a minute to re-focus on his own business. Then start over again with the food morsel just in front of the dog's nose. This time, after the few steps, stand up straight and hold the food near your chest. Wait for eye contact. The instant you get eye contact, click and treat. Follow with praise, pats and play. Practice this throughout the day, for 2-3 repetitions at a time.

Step 2:   Continue the exercise in an area with no distractions, off leash. Begin to say the dog's name without putting the food right in front of his nose. Wait for the dog to look at you, back up a few steps, stop, wait for eye contact, then click and treat. When he looks at you, have the food up close to your face. Bend over for a puppy so he can see that the food is in front of your face and then stand upright and back up. Follow each click-and-treat with verbal praise, pats and play. If the dog doesn't give you attention when you call his name, don't go after him. Instead, run out of the room and hide. Don't call the dog. When he comes looking for you, click or say yes, treat and praise using physical contact.

DO NOT PURSUE YOUR DOG IF HE OR SHE IS NOT INTERESTED.

Instead, make yourself interesting by running and hiding, or by taking great interest in a toy. Talk to the toy, drop to the floor and pick it up quickly and enthusiastically play with it by yourself. The dog will come see what's happening. When he does, be ready to click and treat, and follow with praise and play. If something fun always happens when you call the dog's name, very soon he'll be sticking with you, waiting for you to give him your attention. Anytime he looks at you, reward his attention. Practice every opportunity you have.

Step 3:   Again, continue the exercise in an area with no distractions, off leash. If the dog gives you his attention every time you speak his name, begin to offer different fun responses to his attention. For example, every third call for attention, reward with an exceptionally fun toy and a physical play reward instead of a treat. Call the dog's name, and when the dog reaches you, throw the ball or use the tug toy as the reward. Vary rewards between food, play and praise.

Step 4:   When the dog is responding with attention 100% of the time indoors, you are ready to increase distraction by moving your training outside to a place of minor distractions, such as the backyard. Have the dog on a drag line, allowing the line to drag on the ground. You have increased the level of distraction, so you need to reduce the difficulty of the exercise. Return to the back-up-a-few-steps technique and click and treat when the dog is coming toward you. If he becomes distracted, step on the drag line to stop him from leaving the training session. Don't say anything. When he looks to you, click and treat, then praise and play for attention. If he gets distracted, turn and run, luring him with your unexpected change of direction. When he chases you, turn and run backward so you can make eye contact with him. Click and treat, and jackpot with fun physical play. Repeat 2-3 times. End on a really enthusiastic attention response.

If you cannot get the dog's attention outside, stop. Go back inside and continue attention training there until the dog has practiced the exercise enough to handle the distractions. Don't stay outside and teach the dog that he doesn't have to listen to you.

Every interaction is a teaching/learning opportunity. Every time you speak or interact with your dog you are training. Every time you use the dog's name and you do not positively reinforce his attention, you've taught him not to listen. If the dog is unable to offer attention because the distraction level is too difficult for him, you cannot reinforce attention, and you are teaching the dog not to listen. Positive reinforcement training depends on you setting the dog up for success. It takes more repetition and patience than punishment training but it is the only way to train a good friend.

Some dogs, regardless of how attentive they are indoors, find the lure of outdoors more reinforcing than you are. Some are extremely distracted by the smells, sights, and freedoms of the outdoors. Others are simply very independent. To keep highly distractible dogs safe outdoors, you may need to combine the cue "leave it" with use of the drag line and strong reinforcement for all levels of attention, no matter how small the criteria. Apply management skills and reinforcement skills to teach the dog how to behave outside.

PRACTICAL TIPS

Successful attention training means the dog knows his name is important. The dog's name is your key to his respect. To avoid teaching the dog that his name is irrelevant, don't use his name unless you want his attention. This may require tremendous self-control over your natural inclination to say his name frequently.

BODY BLOCK FOR CONTROL

The body block is a useful exercise to control the dog, without force if he becomes over stimulated. With the body block, you move into the space you don't want the dog to occupy or you move out of the space you want the dog to move into. This teaches the dog to move away or back off in response to your body cues. This is one of my favorite exercises to teach dogs that are rude.

PREREQUISITES

Before beginning this exercise, the dog should be comfortable with you standing in front of him, should be able to give you eye contact and should want to interact with you.

PREPARATION

Have a pouch of yummy treats, and a hungry dog on leash.

Teach the body block with a clicker or word marker at home.

PROCESS

Step 1: Find a wall that is clear and place a straight-back chair about 3 feet from the wall. Walk the dog through the channel between the wall and the chair. Repeat this until the dog is comfortable walking through the channel.

Step 2: Once the dog is comfortable with this exercise, move the chair closer to the wall, so it's just far enough from the wall to allow you to walk through. Walk through, encouraging the dog to walk behind you. Repeat this until the dog is comfortable with the exercise.

Step 3: Have the dog walk halfway through the channel, and turn directly in front of the dog so you are blocking his path. Step toward the dog and, as soon as he shifts his weight back, click. Do this several times until he is stepping back.

Step 4: Once the dog is responding consistently to your body cue, add the verbal cue "back".

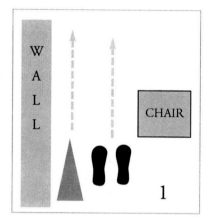
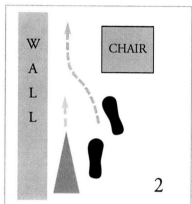
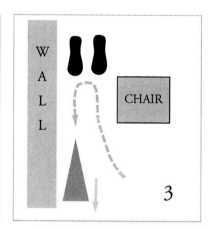

APPLYING BODY BLOCKING IN DIFFERENT SITUATIONS

If the dog is charging toward you to jump up in greeting, step forward toward him until he stops with all four feet on the ground. This effectively pushes his point of balance backward. Keep moving into him gently, not stepping on toes or using your knees, but moving steadily into his space until he backs up and pauses. Then you can ask for a sit. Always follow up good choices with reinforcement which, for this exercise, could be allowing the dog to pass through a door or get into the car.

In this case, you are stopping a planned move into your space. Don't wait for the dog to take your space. Show him that you will not allow him into your space except by permission. You are claiming the space and not letting the dog take it from you. You are requiring the dog to yield.

Use this for getting the dog to wait and back away from the open door. As he learns, just turning into him will be enough for him to back up.

CAVALETTI COURSE

When a dog is using the analytical part of his brain (the frontal cortex) the emotional part (the limbic system) becomes less active. This basic response can be used to help dogs, particularly over-reactive dogs, learn to cope with new stimuli.

One approach to this is navigation of an obstacle course where the dog must concentrate on where his next step will be and is reinforced for managing the course while ignoring any scary stimuli.

Dogs enjoy movement. In an obstacle course, the dog can be reinforced by movement as well as food treats.

This exercise desensitizes the dog to things that are scary for him. When "scary fake dog" is used, this exercise habituates the dog to the sight, sound, smell and movement of something similar to an unfamiliar dog while also allowing the handler to relax knowing there is no risk to another dog. This exercise teaches coping skills to the dog and the handler.

PREREQUISITES

Before beginning this exercise, teach the dog to walk on a loose leash.

PREPARATION

The room should be empty of other dogs and anything else the dog may be fearful of, such as unfamiliar people.

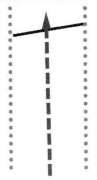

Have a helper, a pouch of yummy treats, and a hungry dog on leash.

Have cones and poles available for the cavaletti, or obstacle, course. (*See* **OBSTACLE COURSE EQUIPMENT**, *Chapter 4, page 55.*)

Set up two lines of cones to create a channel in preparation for holding the cavaletti.

Have available something slightly scary but completely controllable, such as "strange fake dog": A life sized stuffed dog, fitted with a jingling collar and ID tags on a lead so he can be slid slowly by as though he is a dog on a walk is helpful.

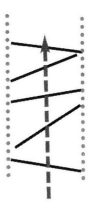

Lifelike
Stuffed Dog

PROCESS

The following steps can be followed over a series of separate training sessions. When beginning a new session, ease the dog into the exercise by running briefly through each of the previous steps.

Step 1: Have the helper drop treats with variable spacing in a line between the cones. Walk the dog at a casual pace in a straight line toward the channel and then through the channel allowing him to eat the treats as he walks. Click as he picks up each treat. Repeat several times.

Step 2: Have the helper add a couple of cavaletti poles, oddly spaced and at odd angles so the dog needs to think about where to put his feet to navigate the obstacle course. Have the helper drop treats with variable spacing in a line between the cones and through the poles. Walk the dog at a casual pace in a straight line toward the channel and then through the channel allowing him to eat the treats as he walks. Click as he picks up each treat. Repeat 5 or 6 times. Have the helper add one or two poles each time.

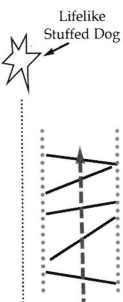

Step 3: Repeat Step 2, but have something very slightly scary (such as "strange fake dog" with the helper holding his lead) at the far end of the channel off to the side and as far away as necessary to avoid an adverse reaction from the dog. The helper should begin to raise the cavalettis keeping them at odd angles so the dog needs to think to navigate them. Keep the dog moving through the channel so he does not have time to think about the scary thing. He should be thinking about where to put his feet to navigate the poles, and be reinforced for every step or two as he picks up treats on the ground.

Step 4: Repeat Step 3, but have the helper jiggle the scary fake dog's leash so the tags on the collar jingle. The sound should be minimal enough that it does not elicit a reaction from the dog. Repeat, gradually increasing the amount of jiggling but only to the level the dog is able to cope with while still walking or trotting through the poles and picking up treats.

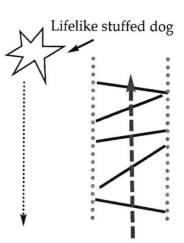

Lifelike stuffed dog

Step 5: Repeat Step 3, but have the helper very slowly slide scary fake dog alongside the channel. The movement should be minimal enough that it does not elicit a reaction from the dog. Repeat, gradually increasing the scary fake dog's speed and movement but only to the level the dog is able to cope with while still walking or trotting through the poles and picking up treats.

Step 6: Continue walking the dog through the poles, varying the layout of the poles so the dog always has to think about where he is stepping next. Continue to click or mark as the dog collects treats from the ground. Add variation to scary fake dog's movements (toward the dog, then alongside the dog) always maintaining a speed and distance that the dog can cope with and not react to.

PRACTICAL TIPS

▶ The handler should be relaxed and breathing normally to help the dog through the process. This exercise allows the handler to relax because the stuffed dog is completely controlled (unlike another dog) and cannot be hurt if the dog reacts.

▶ As the dog learns to work in the presence of minor scary stimulus, add other stimulus. For example: drape a dog blanket with the scent of another dog on it over the stuffed dog or lay the stuffed dog on his side.

▶ If the dog reacts to the stuffed dog by showing fearful body language, allow him to walk past and toss treats in front of him. Walking past is reinforcing because the tension is defused.

▶ If the dog reacts to the stuffed dog by charging him, let him sniff the stuffed animal until he disengages.

▶ Once the dog is comfortable with the stuffed dog, introduce a non-confrontational dog in the stuffed dog's place. Increase the distance, avoid dog-to-dog eye contact, and make sure the handler continues to breathe.

CHILL OUT GAME

This exercise teaches the dog controlled play with an on/off switch.

BACKGROUND

Easily aroused dogs are often the most fun to work with since they love to play and are easy to motivate with toys. These same dogs are frequently in the most need of impulse control.

Dogs that need to learn impulse control (self-control) are nearly always dogs that love to play hard. Play can be a high value reinforcer for these dogs. This exercise is designed to use play as a reward for self-control. This game will install an "on/off" switch by teaching the dog he can go from really high arousal to instant calm. This exercise will also give you the tools to calm the dog when any excitement occurs (such as response to a door bell ringing) and will help you teach the dog to substitute a calm behavior for agitated behavior.

Play exercise is great but even more important is teaching the dog how to deal with his emotional state when exciting things happen. Long play sessions that leave the dog exhausted do not contribute to his ability to control his emotional state. Generally, long hard play continues to reinforce the "get revved and keep going until you fall over" pattern of response. So, rather than a couple of intense exercise sessions that leave the dog physically exhausted but edgy, give the dog many short sessions of controlled play.

Interactive, controlled play with the dog has multiple benefits, including:

▶ Exercise for the dog.

▶ Play reinforcement relationship between dog and handler.

▶ A wonderful opportunity for you to develop and reinforce impulse control for the dog which will eventually transfer to all parts of the dog's life.

A dog that can be trusted to listen and respond calmly when aroused can go anywhere. Teaching impulse control will give the dog more freedom.

PREREQUISITES

Before beginning this exercise, teach the dog a reliable sit.

PREPARATION

Have a toy the dog really enjoys. Practice in an enclosed or fenced-off area until the dog has a solid recall.

PROCESS

Excite the dog by playing tug, chasing a toy, or play wrestling. In the middle of the game, stop all play, become still, and quietly ask for a sit. When the dog sits, immediately re-engage him in the game.

Repeat this exercise a few times. The dog will quickly learn that his sitting is what gets the game going again. Vary the requested behavior (sit, down, settle, or other behaviors the dog has on cue), the duration of that behavior, and the length of play.

CONDITIONING TO A HALTER OR MUZZLE

This exercise teaches the dog that having a halter on is rewarding. You can use a similar process to introduce the dog to a muzzle, allowing the dog to place his nose into the muzzle by himself until you can attach the neck strap. If a dog is gradually conditioned to accept a muzzle or halter, he will be able to move around the house wearing the muzzle or halter without attempting to get it off.

Safety Note: Some dogs can wiggle out of head halters. For safety, use a 'Snap Back' or 'Jerk-Ease' to connect the head halter to the dog's collar and connect the leash only to the head halter. Alternatively, clip the leash through the rings on both the halter and the collar.

PREPARATION

Have a really smelly and appealing food treat such as meat baby food in a jar. Preset the nosepiece of the halter to be very loose so it can be slipped over the dog's nose without unhooking the halter. Clip the lead to the dog's flat collar.

PROCESS

Step 1: Have the dog sitting in front of you and the open baby food jar behind your back. Present the jar and allow the dog to have a lick from the jar. Click for licking and remove the jar after only a brief lick. The dog will either light up because it LOVES this food or show moderate interest. If the dog has a less than enthusiastic response to the food, hold the jar under his nose until the smell encourages a lick. Let him have a few licks, saying "goood" softly while he learns that what you have tastes good. Now stand up and see if you can encourage an interest in another lick. Once he shows interest skip to Step 3. This may take a few days over many sessions, not a few minutes. Patience will pay off.

Step 2: Encourage the dog with an enticing voice "Did you like that? Do you want more? Wait for the dog to express interest and then deliver another click-and-lick to reinforce "engaging" with you. Repeat until you can turn and move and the dog will keep orienting to you, trying to pressure you to allow him a lick of the baby food. Begin to move around the room with the dog following. Deliver a click-and-lick each time the dog sits or stands in front of you. When the dog can move around and remain focused on getting access to the baby food, move to Step 3.

Step 3: Have the dog in front of you. Hold the halter in one hand behind your back, and the open jar in the other. Briefly show the halter to the dog, then present the jar and allow the dog a lick. Repeat, gradually working up to allowing the dog to sniff the halter. Once dog is comfortable with this step and thinks it's a game, repeat and begin to hold the halter as though you are going to place it around the dog's neck while allowing the dog a lick from the jar. Once the dog is comfortable with this step, repeat, but snap the collar together so the dog can hear the sound of the snap and see what you are doing. If the dog is noise sensitive, snap behind your back or far enough away from the dog so that he is comfortable and gradually move the snap closer to him. Repeat until the dog is comfortable with the snap near his head.

Step 4:   Put the collar part of the halter on (loosely on first) but leave the nosepiece hanging below the dog's neck. Present the jar and allow the dog a lick.

Step 5:   Once the dog has a strongly enthusiastic response to the food, slip the nosepiece over his nose. Deliver a click-and lick. Immediately slip the nosepiece off and step away, letting the dog pressure you for another lick. Repeat, gradually increasing the duration the nosepiece is on, making certain to maintain an enthusiastic response to the food.

Step 6:   Once the nosepiece has become part of getting a lick, leave it on after the lick as you move and let the dog follow and get another lick. If the nosepiece is so loose it slips off, make slipping it back on a way to earn a lick.

Step 7:   The dog should now be at a point where you can ask for some simple behaviors while the nosepiece is on his snout loosely to earn a click-and-lick.

Step 8:   When you are ready to attach the lead, attach to the dog's buckle collar too. This way the head halter will NOT close the dog's mouth and he will habituate to the halter much more easily and with less stress and resentment. Do this for at least the first two weeks or until he is completely comfortable with the halter.

PRACTICAL TIPS

▶ The baby food jar is a perfect treat delivery system. The opening doesn't allow for a lot of food to get licked out and the top can be easily screwed on and off.

▶ Meat baby food is generally very appealing but with a truly shutdown dog you may need to experiment. Try blending canned tuna with a little cottage cheese or meatballs. Find something that smells irresistible but is custard-like in texture and consistency so the dog can only get a bit of a taste when he licks it.

▶ The dog should only get a small lick for each click. Huge reinforcement value is added by tantalizing the dog; removing the jar after the dog has taken a quick taste. If the dog is shy, avoid frightening him in the beginning by gently delivering the food and letting him have a few good licks then gently easing the food away.

▶ Once the dog has become engaged with the food, deliver quickly and remove after just a brief chance to get a lick since removal makes access more important.

▶ Show the dog it's a wonderful game by making a fuss about delivering the food. Let the dog pressure you into getting the treat. You will only change the dog's feelings about the halter if you have a paycheck so powerful it overrides the dog's anxiety. So don't correct for pushiness.

▶ Only when the dog is really focused on getting the food should you move to slipping the nosepiece on.

▶ Don't jump to asking for other behaviors until the dog is so obsessed with the food that he ignores the nosepiece.

COUNTER CONDITION FEAR OR AGGRESSION

Teaching the dog skills to manage reactive behavior is one of the important ways we change how the dog feels about what he currently fears. This exercise uses classical conditioning to change the dog's emotional response from fear to anticipation of something nice, by pairing the hand-delivery of yummy treats with minor, then increasing, exposure to the scary thing. This is called counter conditioning, and is based on classical (or Pavlovian) conditioning. (*See "Learning", Chapter 2, "Counter Conditioning and Systematic Desensitization."*)

REAL LIFE EXAMPLE: DAZZLE AND SKATEBOARDS

Dazzle is an Australian shepherd puppy. Her owner is an experienced dog owner and trainer (me). I know all about the importance of socializing my pup to a variety of things in the early months of life. Early in life, Dazzle was introduced to all kinds of people, sights, sounds, animals, and so on. I thought I had done a pretty good job socializing Dazzle.

When Dazzle was seven months old, I took her with me on a trip to a large congested area in Massachusetts that she was unaccustomed to. During this trip, we encountered a lot of new people and stimuli, one of which Dazzle took a strong dislike to. I was chatting with my husband and not really paying attention to her, when all of a sudden she was barking and growling. What was this all about?

As I watched Dazzle, looking for clues, I realized she had tucked her tail between her legs, folded her ears straight back, raised her hackles, and was barking and growling as she was "escaping" to a safe distance. I then looked around and realized she was barking and growling at the boys riding skateboards along a wooden walkway, which made a really weird loud sound. Aha! This was something Dazzle had never seen or heard before. Imagine what it must have sounded and looked like from a puppy's perspective! I tried to convince Dazzle that it was safe to approach, but she would have none of it. So my homework was to get her accustomed to the sight and sound of a skateboard on different surfaces.

I turned and went another way, distracting her by tossing treats in front of her and asking her to target my hand, but she kept looking back because the noise was quite loud.

We spent training sessions at our local skateboard park, giving her treats and playing games. I would avert my eyes from the kids so they would not stop to talk while I was with her. Over time, a combination of systematic desensitization and counter conditioning reduced her reactivity when in the presence of kids riding bicycles or skateboards. The exercises changed her emotional response to strange noises and people moving on skateboards or bicycles. To this day, when she sees kids on skateboards, she looks to me for that extra special treat.

PREREQUISITES

This exercise assumes the handler or trainer assisting the handler, has expertise in observation and timing. Expertise in observation means the handler watches, identifies, and responds appropriately to the slightest tension in the dog's body (facial muscles, such as the eye ridges and ears, tail carriage, body muscle, etc.). This is required to ensure the dog never experiences a stress response during counter conditioning sessions and therefore never has the opportunity to practice the unwanted behavior.

Before beginning this exercise, the dog should have solid foundation skills, such as attention and sit and have a strong positive relationship with the handler.

Teach the dog to look at you in response to his name, to come toward you in response to a recall cue, to relax on cue and to walk on a loose lead. Reward each of these behaviors step by step, building them incrementally. Teach all of these foundation skills in a calm, non-demanding environment so the dog can succeed. Over time, gradually begin to move the dog out of the house (an environment with minimal distractions) and into the yard or street (environments with more distraction). Work with the dog patiently so he is able to respond to the same cues while moving into an increasingly distracting environment.

PREPARATION

Counter conditioning should be set up such that the dog cannot possibly fail. That takes planning. Practice around the scary thing (other dogs, people, or whatever), but be sure to have adequate distance between the dog and what the dog fears at all times. Adequate distance means the dog is happy and relaxed, showing absolutely no signs of stress. If you see physical signs of stress, stress hormones are being produced. If the dog shows even subtle signs of stress, you are sensitizing, rather than desensitizing the dog.

The goal in counter conditioning is to avoid stress chemicals and elicit only "happy" or calm chemistry. Work with the dog at his or her comfort level while other dogs or people are way off in the distance. If that means the fearful dog can only work happily with you and ignore the scary things that are 200 feet away at a park, then that's where you will start.

You'll experience success if you plan each exposure to the scary thing as a controlled session, rather than just a "let life happen" with an attempt to recover from unpleasant episodes. Every time the dog rehearses undesirable behavior, you lose precious points gained when the dog rehearsed desirable behavior.

While counter conditioning, use a head halter or no-pull front ring harness to safely manage the dog. Teach foundation behaviors, such as sit, down, leave it and watch me so that you have alternative behaviors you can cue when needed. Combining sits and downs as though the dog is doing doggie push ups is a good exercise to practice and rehearse.

Have a pouch of yummy treats, and a hungry dog on lead.

PROCESS

Step 1:   Have the dog,on leash, an adequate distance from the scary thing. This might be 30 feet or 200 ft. Use as much distance as needed so that the dog is non-reactive. As long as you work with adequate distance, you will have stimulus control: if you ask for a behavior and the dog can give it to you, you will know that he is still thinking rather than reacting. He is using the analytical part of his brain (the cerebral cortex) rather than his emotional (limbic) system. We call this working sub-threshold.

Wait one second, give a yummy treat and then turn around and walk away. You are aiming for the dog to stay focused on you while giving a casual glance to the scary thing. Repeat several times for up to 10 minutes then allow the dog to rest. Practice many times each day for 5 to 10 minutes each session. Training sessions should end with a good play session within a safe area, particularly if the dog has experienced any stress. Play sessions help the dog learn that dealing with potentially stressful and challenging situations can be fun. For example, scent games are a great way to relieve stress and they are fun for both handler and dog. Dogs love to hunt!

Step 2:   Begin to increase the duration of the exposure from one second to several seconds. Be aware of just how long or short the time is while increasing duration. For example: start by exposing the dog to the scary thing for only 3 seconds then turn the dog around and walk away.

Step 3:   Once the dog is working well with increased duration begin to reduce the distance from the scary thing very gradually over many training sessions. Classical conditioning is powerful, but it takes repetition over time to change an emotional response from fear to the expectation of something nice. Moving too quickly will reverse the conditioning. If you spend a year counter conditioning the dog, consider it a year well spent. When you decrease the distance, go back to the 1 second duration.

Step 4:   Dogs that are fearful of other dogs may benefit from meeting one dog at a time using appropriate distances over several months. Begin with low-level distractions such as letting the dog see a strange dog in the distance when another person is around without attracting the dog's attention.

Step 5:   **Once classical conditioning begins to change how the dog feels about the scary thing, you can begin clicking for behavioral change. If the dog is upset, I do not recommend clicking.** During successful counter conditioning of a fearful dog, the dog begins to look for the response that earned the reward. For example, if the dog consistently gets a reward for looking at the scary thing, the dog will begin to look at the scary thing to earn the reward. This is called operant conditioning: the dog is operating on his environment. Operant conditioning is a powerful tool because it teaches the dog that he has some control of his environment.

The operant behavior of "looking at the scary thing, then looking back at you" is the behavior that you are substituting for the fear behaviors. Instead of barking or growling, the dog turns away from the scary thing to make eye contact with you. When this begins to occur, it is time to start marking the behavior with the clicker (or "yes"). Ask the dog for a few sits and downs.

Look for calm, happy, thoughtful body language as the behavior that will earn the click. This is a new and valuable response to what used to be a fearful reaction. We want the dog to understand that this new behavior is being rewarded. The click means a treat is coming, which brings the dog's focus to you rather than to the scary thing.

ADDITIONAL EXERCISES

Practice entering a new or potentially arousing area using food and movement as a distraction so that the dog does not focus on the scary things around him. Before entering the area, toss wonderfully tasty treats onto the floor and click-and-treat along this path. You are Hansel and Gretel-ling your way through the new scary area dropping yummy treats instead of breadcrumbs. Make sure the dog sees the treats you have tossed onto the floor. Don't allow the dog time to think about the scary things around him; he should be concentrating on the food and the movement. If possible, enter backward so the dog is following you and can see your face.

If the dog is scared of other dogs, arrange some "dates" with dog-owning friends, particularly friends with non-reactive dogs and go for parallel walks (walk at the same time but at a distance from each other). Parallel walks should start at a distance of 20 feet or more, depending on the dog's needs. Make sure you know where the other dog is going to be walking before you set out. (*See* **SIDE-BY-SIDE WALKING**, page 184.)

PRACTICAL TIPS

When counter conditioning a reactive dog, don't fade out the food until the dog is completely conditioned and has a positive emotional response to the scary thing at any distance and in any environment. Once the dog is offering alternate behaviors in the presence of the scary thing, you can start weaning the dog off the food rewards.

Of course, life does happen. Occasionally when we're walking with our dog on a loose lead, a scary thing (person or stray dog, for example) will come up too close and personal. If this happens use the situation as a learning opportunity. Say, in a happy voice (I sometimes wish I had taken acting lessons) "*Oh look, it is Fido!*" and start rapidly feeding the dog little pieces of yummy food treats while the scary thing is nearby. Do this every time as a response to whatever the dog fears. Gradually, after some practice, when the dog first notices distractions at some distance he will begin to look at you offering eye contact and waiting for those special treats. In other words, the dog has learned that the sight of the scary thing predicts that good things are going to happen. Once this begins to occur, you have classically conditioned a change in how the dog feels about scary stimulus. This success itself is a great reinforcement for your efforts!

I've seen counter conditioning help various dogs overcome their fears or hypersensitivities. For instance, some dogs are extraordinarily reactive when around young children who make jerky motions or who shout and run. Others fear men, women in funny hats or people in big bulky jackets. Some dogs cannot tolerate motorcycles. Others hate the sound of lawnmowers. We can help them improve, step-by-step, using this simple process.

The counter conditioning process is very rewarding, but it must be done slowly, step-by-step, without missing any steps or moving on to the next step too soon. The dog will tell you when he is ready to move forward. Listen to the dog!

COUNTERING LUNGING OR CHASING

Dogs that lunge at or chase moving objects, such as traffic or people riding bicycles are in danger of hurting themselves or others.

Lunging can be a fear response or a natural response to movement particularly in herding breeds. If the response is due to fear, it can be counter conditioned so that the dog begins to learn that traffic means something good is coming. If the response is due to prey drive or herding instinct, an alternative behavior can be conditioned.

The following step-by-step process shows how lunging due to aggression or fear can be counter conditioned. The subsequent real life example illustrates teaching an alternate behavior for a prey-drive chase response.

PREREQUISITES

This exercise assumes the handler or the trainer assisting the handler has expertise in observation and timing. Expertise in observation means the person watches, identifies, and responds appropriately to the slightest tension in the dog's body (facial muscles, such as the eye ridges and ears, tail carriage, body muscle, etc.). This is required to ensure the dog never experiences a stress response during counter conditioning sessions and therefore never has the opportunity to practice the unwanted behavior of lunging.

PREPARATION

When counter conditioning lunging, use a Gentle Leader or Sensation harness to safely manage the dog. Teach foundation behaviors such as sit, down, leave it and Active Attention, so that you have alternative behaviors you can cue when needed.

Have a pouch of yummy treats, and a hungry dog on leash.

PROCESS

This process shows how lunging due to aggression or fear can be counter conditioned.

Choose one or more of the following exercises, depending on the needs of the dog:

▶ Park the car across the bottom of a driveway or in a parking lot and sit in the back with the dog with the car doors and tailgate closed, watching the traffic. The dog may feel safe in the car and thus be less reactive. Reinforce good behavior. If the dog shows reactive behavior, you are too close to the traffic, so park further away.

▶ If the dog reacts toward moving people or bicycles, ask as many pedestrians and (stationary) bicyclists as possible to feed the dog. The dog will begin to associate people and bicyclists with something good, so they will no longer be scary.

▶ Dogs are usually better if the moving object is coming up behind them rather than toward them, so walk on the side of the road in the same direction as the traffic (if there is a safe pedestrian pavement/sidewalk area) with yourself between the dog and the traffic.

▶ If the dog is less reactive when you aren't close to him, walk with him securely on a long line. Occasionally let him get ahead of you toward the road (but only if he is not practicing reactive behavior).

PRACTICAL TIPS

▶ During the counter conditioning process, continuously pop treats into the dog's mouth, using both hands (one hand, then the other) in rapid-fire fashion. This will distract the dog from the traffic. If the dog is more interested in toys than treats, play games such as tug.

▶ Keep session short: Many short repetitions support strong learning.

▶ Watch for the dog's particular body language that precedes a lunge, such as alert ears, intense stare or lowering of the head. If you see the dog about to lunge, hold the leash right underneath the dog's chin and turn the dog around and away from the moving object, saying "Too Bad". You can follow this with a cue to lie down and a cue to "Leave It" until the moving object has gone past. When the dog is walking properly beside you again praise and treat.

▶ While counter conditioniong, keep the dog as far from the traffic as needed to avoid reaction. If the dog is practicing lunging, or is highly aroused by the situation at any time, he is too close to the traffic or there is too much traffic. Reduce the stimulus by moving farther away or by selecting a quieter place for this stage of his training. For example, train in parking lots where traffic moves slowly, or sit on a bench in the park at a distance the dog is comfortable with.

▶ Look for every opportunity to reinforce the dog for NOT lunging, spinning or aggressing toward cars or other moving objects.

▶ A dog that practices lunging learns to lunge. Manage the dog's environment so he does not have the opportunity to practice lunging. For example, house him where he cannot see moving objects pass. Manage your training sessions so he is distracted by other reinforcement (food treats, tug games, etc.) so he has no time to think about lunging.

REAL LIFE EXAMPLE OF TEACHING AN ALTERNATIVE BEHAVIOR

My Australian Shepherd, Tucker, wanted to chase the horseback riders that trot by our house. Chasing horses is a high-excitement behavior and is inherently reinforcing for a herding dog. I needed to create a new behavior that would eventually become more rewarding than chasing the horseback riders, so I conditioned playing ball-fetch until these became wonderfully rewarding for Tucker. During this time, I managed Tucker caerfully so that he was never allowed the opportunity to chase passing horseback riders and practice and be reinforced for that unwanted and dangerous behavior.

Once I had Tucker hooked on ball-fetch, I called my neighbor who owned a horse and asked him to please let me know when he would be riding down my way. He appreciated my concern and willingness to train my dog. Before he arrived, I placed several tennis balls in the house in plain sight.

When I heard my neighbor approaching on horseback, I asked Tucker to find the ball. Tucker hesitated for a moment, so I ran to a tennis ball and picked it up quickly before he could get it. Then I ran around the house playing with it myself. Once I had his full attention, I began playing fetch games in the house. I repeated this exercise each time my neighbor trotted by that day.

Once Tucker was ignoring the sound of horses trotting by and playing ball with his full attention indoors, I moved my training outside. I placed Tucker on a drag line and had some yummy treats (just in case) and several balls within sight. When I could hear the faint drumming of horse hooves, I asked Tucker to get his ball. By the second horse, he was running to where we left the ball. He had it! He understood the game. The sound of horse hooves now meant it's time to play ball. I rewarded him with a big jackpot of playing fetch.

For the next few days, I repeated the exercise outdoors. Eventually, I was able to shorten and then remove the drag line. For the next month, whenever a horse trotted past, Tucker would immediately begin searching for his ball and we would play fetch until the horse was gone.

Today, Tucker will still find his ball when a horse passes, but I no longer play fetch with him every time. He is happy just carrying the ball in his mouth and I verbally reinforce him for finding his ball.

CRATE CONDITIONING

Providing a dog with a crate as his safe haven is a great kindness. The crate will be familiar so he will feel comfortable in it practically anywhere. If you need to travel, the dog will feel safe and at ease with friends, in a motel, or at a quality kennel. The dog's crate should be his safe zone where children are not allowed to bother him.

A crate allows the handler to restrict the dog's freedom for safety and control without punishment. Crate training is the best solution for management to ensure a dog or puppy does not rehearse unwanted behavior. A dog or puppy can be confined to his crate when not supervised, preventing mistakes such as elimination inside the house or chewing household items.

This exercise teaches the dog that his crate is a safe, comfortable and rewarding place to be.

PREPARATION

Crate training is best done after the dog has been exercised, so he is relaxed and prepared for a rest. Have comfortable bedding inside the crate, preferably bedding familiar to the dog.

Have a hungry dog and some yummy treats.

PROCESS

Step 1:   Tie the crate door open and toss treats inside the crate allowing the dog go in to get the treats and come out as he pleases.

Step 2:   Once the dog is comfortable going into the crate, untie the crate door and begin to move it slightly as the dog goes in to get the treat. Gradually increase the amount of door movement.

Step 3:   Eventually (over several training sessions) the dog should become comfortable with you closing and immediately re-opening the door. At this point, gradually increase the amount of time the door is closed. Continue to toss treats inside the crate while the door is closed, or put a stuffed Kong inside the crate to occupy the dog so he's barely aware the door has been closed.

Step 4:   When he is comfortable with a closed crate door, begin to step away (one step, let him out, repeat with two steps, etc.). Vary the number of steps so he cannot be certain when the crate door will open. Continue to toss treats inside the crate, or provide a chew.

Step 5:   Eventually, the dog will feel comfortable enough for brief stays in the crate. Keep a chair by the crate and drop treats in the crate while you read or watch television. Let the dog out after a few minutes and have a game of fetch or tug. Repeat this several times so that the dog learns going into his crate is rewarded and that he will be able to come out again shortly. Gradually (and separately) increase distance and duration until the dog has a strong positive association with his crate.

▶ Never force a dog into a crate. Use positive reinforcement training to teach the dog that his crate is a good place to be.

▶ Each dog has a different level of sensitivity, so adjust the training to the particular dog. For example, if the dog is worried about the sound of the door hinges, desensitize or counter condition the dog to the sound of the door hinges while he is outside the crate. Oil the hinges to change the sound.

▶ Be patient, not rushed, to allow the dog to learn a positive association with the crate.

COUNTER CONDITIONING RESOURCE GUARDING (DOG TO DOG)

Resource guarding is natural dog behavior. Most people with multiple dog households have witnessed posturing and threatening around food, toys, bones and coveted people. The human, as the leader in a group of dogs, should manage the dogs to avoid conflict caused by resource guarding and should intervene (safely) to stop any fights that occur.

Counter conditioning can be used to reduce resource guarding between dogs. A dog with resource guarding issues can be classically conditioned to enjoy having other dogs around him in situations that were previously tense. The objective of counter conditioning resource guarding is to teach the resource guarding dog that the presence and proximity of other dogs is an indicator of good things. *(See "Learning", Chapter 2,* **COUNTER CONDITIONING AND SYSTEMATIC DESENSITIZATION***, page 22.)*
Once the dog is feeling relaxed he can be taught appropriate alternative behaviors to guarding that will allow him to retain possession of what he wants without fighting. Examples of good alternative behaviors are moving away from other dogs or waiting for permission to take the resource.

A dog without resource guarding issues, but who is guarded against by a resource guarding housemate dog, can be taught to respond to subtle guarding cues by moving out of the guarding dog's area.

MANAGEMENT

A management plan is vital for avoiding resource guarding conflict and to keep the dogs safe and avoid rehearsal of resource guarding behavior. To create a management plan:

1. Notice when resource guarding occurs. Some triggers for resource guarding fights are:

   ▶ Excitement when the handler returns home.

   ▶ Excitement when the handler prepares to take the dogs out.

   ▶ Multiple dogs entering and exiting doorways.

   ▶ Areas where food is prepared or provided to the dogs.

▶ Presence of resources such as toys, toy boxes, crates, beds and attention-giving people.

2. Set up the daily routine to avoid resource guarding triggers and manage the dogs' access to each other when resource guarding triggers are present. Use baby gates, X-pens or crates to separate dogs at times of high excitement or resource availability.

For Example:

▶If resource guarding involves high-value items such as marrow bones, pig ears or meaty bones, dogs should be gated away from each other or crated before providing these items and all traces (including tiny scraps) of these items should be picked up before the dogs are allowed to mix.

▶If mealtimes are tense, feed the dogs at a comfortable distance from each other. Have each dog down-stay. Release each dog to his food bowl individually and stand by and supervise while the dogs eat. When each dog is finished, have him lie down until all the dogs are finished eating. Pick up the food bowls as soon as the dogs are finished, and ask each dog to leave the room one at a time. If necessary, feed the dogs in different rooms or crates or at different times.

▶If the dogs squabble over toys, only allow access to toys when the dogs are separated, or when you are available to supervise play. When playing with multiple dogs, provide a toy for each. Make all experiences around the coveted items enjoyable for each dog. Avoiding practice of posturing or guarding behavior by distracting each dog and reinforcing appropriate social behavior.

PREPARATION

Have a bowl of yummy treats and two dogs, the resource guarder and the non-guarder.

For safety, tether the guarder. If necessary for added safety, tether the non-guarder also. (When the dogs are more advanced, the tethers can be removed.)

Clear the room of any unnecessary resources (toys, bones, etc.).

If the handler is the resource, provide whatever distance necessary between the dogs to avoid tension. If needed, put a visual barrier between the dogs.

PROCESS

STEP 1: CLASSICAL CONDITIONING

(using Counter Conditioning Techniques)

Sit both dogs a few feet away from each other. Say the non-guarder's name and give him a treat. Immediately say the guarder's name and give him a treat and lavish praise. Pause for several seconds. Repeat 10 times, always giving a treat to the non-guarder first. It is vital to keep the guarder well under threshold to achieve a positive CER (Conditioned Emotional Response) to the other dog's presence. If at any point the guarder presents any sign of guarding toward the other dog, even warning signals as subtle as tongue flicks, hard glances, or lowered head, move the dogs a few feet further apart. In the beginning, it is likely the dogs will be so far apart that the handler will need to walk from one dog to the other to deliver treats.

Variable reinforcement is the most effective means of achieving strong and reliable behavior. Vary the amount of time between treats and avoid falling into a predictable rythym.

Gradually decrease the distance between the dogs, maintaining calm and relaxed body signals from the guarder.

Repeat this step over many sessions until you see a clear calm response from the guarder as soon as you feed the other dog. Dogs can learn when one dog gets something that they are next. It will take multiple sessions, but have patience.

STEP 2: MORE CLASSICAL CONDITIONING

Wait to attempt this step until it is clear that the guarder presents a positive emotional response to the presence of the non-guarder as a result of many repetitions of Step 1.

Sit in a closed room with the guarder and a supply of yummy treats with no other dogs or resources in the room. Sit for about 20 minutes, quietly reading or watching a television program. Then get up and open the door to allow the non-guarding dog into the room. Have both dogs sit, reinforce with a treat, and then lavishly praise and quietly jackpot the guarder. Stretch the jackpot out for 20 or 30 seconds. Take the non-guarder out of the room. Repeat the exercise several times, varying the amount of time between putting the non-guarder out and letting him back in.

Perform this exercise until you see a clear happy response from the guarder when the non-guarder appears. This may take anywhere from a few trials to a few sessions.

Repeat the exercise but provide the guarder access to a previously guarded resource such as a bone, toy, empty food dish or coveted sleeping location. If there are clear gradations in the guarder's hierarchy of resources, use the lowest value resource to begin with.

The resource may gain value when the other dog enters the room, especially if the other dog demonstrates any interest in it. To reduce the likelihood of a guarding occurrence, place the resource away from the door and remain alert to the guarder's body signals throughout the exercise.

Tether the guarder to ensure he won't be able to move to a location more likely to evoke guarding when the other dog is allowed into the room. Introduce the other dog on leash to maintain distance. Keep the other (non-guarding) dog's attention on you to avoid tension in the guarder due to eye contact with him or his prize. The resource should be within the guarder's proximity, whether he engages with it or not. Repeat the exercise until the guarder has a clear happy and eager response to the entrance of the non-guarder.

Proximity and orientation are variables that are independent and so they warrant counter conditioning separately. Repeat Step 3, without tethering the guarder but while retaining the leash on the non-guarder to prevent any proximity to the guarder and his prize. When the guarder is relaxed and demonstrates a happy response to the other dog's approach, increase proximity to a couple of feet away, increase distance and allow the non-guarder to orient toward the guarder.

STEP 3: GENERALIZE THE BEHAVIOR

Repeat Step 2, but generalize to other areas by moving to another room, the backyard, etc. over many sessions. Each time you move to a different area, repeat from the beginning of the sequence, over many training sessions.

STEP 4: INCREASE THE VALUE

Repeat Step 2, but gradually increase the value of the guarded resource, starting from the beginning and proceeding through the sequence over many sessions each time a higher value resource is introduced.

STEP 5: OPERANT CONDITIONING

A dog with resource guarding issues can be taught an alternative response, such as moving away from other dogs rather than threatening or fighting in order to retain possession of a resource. The resource guarder can be taught that this type of behavior prevents having the guarded item removed permanently.

Classical conditioning is always taking place even while training through operant conditioning. Therefore, a well-executed operant technique achieves a collateral conditioned emotional response (CER). With operant conditioning, the guarder offers a response and feels happy and relaxed, rather than just feeling happy and relaxed (as with classical conditioning alone).

Dogs trained to sit, down, do tricks or other behaviors, develop CER's to salient aspects of the training stimulus package. For example, when the trainer reaches a hand into the treat pouch, a dog trained through positive reinforcement experiences a "yippee" feeling. In the case of counter conditioning of resource guarding, the presence of another dog becomes the contingent cue to be reinforced for performing a specific behavior, so the CER will likely become strongly attached to the other dog. The net result is not only a behavior that is mutually exclusive to guarding (such as sitting and giving the handler attention) but a warm fuzzy feeling about other dogs around coveted resources.

Before beginning operant conditioning, have a nicely polished behavior that is incompatible with guarding, such as sit, attention, or stepping away from other dogs. Repeat Step 1 but cue, mark and reinforce the resource guarding dog for performing the chosen behavior. Repeat several times each day for 5 or 10 minutes each session over a period of weeks or months (depending on the dog).

PRACTICAL TIPS

▶ Be aware of the proximity of the other dog to the guarder. At no point should the guarder feel the need to guard. If the dog feels the need to guard, the dog will associate other dogs with tension, arousal and guarding, rather than with relaxation and good things.

▶ Between counter conditioning sessions, manage vigilantly. Every time guarding is practiced, it reverses hours of counter conditioning. It is vital that the guarder is not triggered in day-to-day life. This may mean removing all resources or even separating the dogs from one another other whenever resources are present.

► Introduce cold trials that simulate random, planned "management lapses" in day to day life.

► Practice cold trials once per day (more often if guarding is creeping back) to maintain the conditioning.

For more information on resource guarding, read *"Mine"* by Jean Donaldson.

COUNTER CONDITIONING AND PREVENTING TERRITORIAL AGGRESSION

Protective, or territorial aggression, may be exhibited toward people or other animals that approach the dog's property or human family members. Generally people and other animals that are unfamiliar to the dog or unlike the members of the dog's household are the most likely "targets" of territorial aggression. While most forms of territorial aggression are likely to occur on the dog's home property, some dogs may protect family members regardless of the location. Territorial aggression can be prevented or minimized with early socialization and good impulse control skill training.

MANAGEMENT

To reduce potential fear and anxiety toward visitors, young dogs should be taught to sit and receive a reward when meeting new people. You should also ensure that a wide variety of visitors come over to visit the puppy, while the puppy is young and sociable. (*See* **PUPPY SOCIALIZATION CHART,** Appendix C.)

PREPARATION

Most dogs will be happy to alert the family by barking when strangers come around. The dog that has been well socialized and has self-control skills can be taught to quickly settle down and relax. Teaching to the dog to "Go to place" ensures that the dog is never right at the door. (*See* **DOWN ON MAT** - Placement, *page* 146)

PROCESS

For dogs exhibiting territorial aggression, you will need to train enough impulse control to be able to have the dog sit, stay and when calm, take a reward at the front door. Generally a leash and head collar will give the fastest and most effective management until you have taught the dog to go to its place. Using a desensitization and counter conditioning program as with dog to dog resource guarding, you can begin retraining with low levels of stimuli. Examples of low-level stimuli could be you knocking at the door yourself, people arriving in a car and walking past the front of the house, or perhaps even a family member knocking on the door or ringing the bell. (*See* **GREETING AT THE DOOR** *page* 153.) Each time someone arrives at the house or rings the bell, the dog will come to expect a favored reward (toy, cheese, hot dog slice or play session) as soon as he stops barking. Once the dog can be controlled and receives rewards in this environment, gradually more intense stimuli can be used.

DESENSITIZING SEPARATION ANXIETY

Dogs are great companions because they become so attached to their people. But that attachment can sometime backfire in the form of separation anxiety. Separation anxiety is a dog's negative response to being left alone and can vary from mild distress to full-blown panic.

Most dogs just curl up for a nap and await your return. However, some dogs do exhibit panic-like behaviors that may include excessive barking, household destruction and inappropriate elimination. These dogs are not acting out of spite or anger. They are unable to manage separation from their social group.

This program of exercises can be used to desensitize a dog against separation anxiety by changing the dog's response to your getting-ready-to-leave cues.

PREPARATION

Start your desensitization program on a weekend so you have at least one to two days to begin the process of reconditioning the dog.

Do not leave the dog alone until he has shown obvious improvement. The dog must not be left alone during this desensitizing process which may take a month or more depending on the dog.

Prepare to change your getting-ready-to-leave cues as follows:

▶ Write down exactly what you do when you get ready to leave the house.

▶ Observe the dog carefully to identify the point in your getting-ready-to-leave sequence at which he begins to show anxiety.

PROCESS

Desensitization training can be used to recondition separation anxiety using the following steps:

Step 1:   Begin your getting-ready-to-leave sequence. At the point where your actions begin to cause the dog to have an anxiety response such as panting, pacing or whining, break away from your getting-ready-to-leave sequence and do something completely out of the ordinary. For example, start to clean the room, fold some clothes, or sit down and read a book. By breaking the sequence, you change the association the dog has with the getting-ready-to-leave cues.

Step 2:   When the dog is calm (this could take 5 to 10 minutes), repeat using a different type of activity to break the sequence. For example: play a good game of fetch or tug with the dog. He'll be really surprised.

Step 3:   Repeat until you can get through the entire sequence and right to the door without the dog experiencing an anxiety response.

Step 4:   Repeat, finishing by putting your hand on the doorknob (but don't open the door). Let go of the doorknob, turn around and go sit down or do some other task, until the dog is calm. When you turn around, be calm and aloof. Don't give any effusive greetings or make a fuss. Just go about some type of normal household activity.

Step 5:   Repeat, adding opening and closing of the door without leaving. Continue to allow the dog to rest until he is relaxed in between steps.

Step 6:   Gradually progress to walking out the door, closing it behind you and immediately walking back in. When you can go out and return quickly with no adverse behavior from the dog, lengthen the amount of time you stay outside. Start with seconds, then work up to minutes. Make sure the number of minutes is variable (1 minute, then 3 minutes, then 2 minutes, then 4 minutes, then 1 minute, gradually increasing the minutes at a variable rate) so the dog cannot guess how long you will be gone.

Step 7:   When the dog is not reacting to you leaving for a few minutes, repeat the sequence but add getting into the car, driving out of the driveway and returning immediately. When you come back inside, don't acknowledge the dog until you have performed a small chore and the dog is calm and quiet. Speak to him quietly but don't make a fuss. Be calm and aloof.

Step 8:   Repeat the entire getting-ready-to-leave sequence, but take the dog with you when you leave. Take him to work, to a friend's house, or on an errand.

Step 9:   Each morning repeat the getting-ready-to-leave sequence until the dog isn't stressed by any of the getting-ready-to-leave cues. Lengthen the amount of time you are gone from the house. First 2 minutes, then 5 minutes, then 1 minute, then 10 minutes. Vary the times you are gone from shorter to longer to shorter again, gradually increasing the overall time. Soon you will be able to leave for longer and longer periods.

ADDITIONAL EXERCISES

Practice sit-stay or down-stay exercises using positive reinforcement. Gradually increase the distance you move away from the dog until you are briefly out of the dog's sight while he remains in the "sit" or "down" position. The dog will learn that he can remain calmly and happily in one place while you go to another. Practice this during the course of your normal daily activities. For example, if you're watching television with the dog by your side and you get up for a snack, cue him to stay and leave the room. When you come back, give him a treat or quietly praise him.

When the dog is up to a 10-minute stay with you in the same room, leave him in another room (but within sight of you) while you sit down and read a book. When you add distance, decrease duration to help the dog succeed. Begin with 1 or 2 minute stays, gradually increasing the amount of time to 10 minutes. Reward the dog for being away from you and not following you around. If he stays lying down while you are someplace else, toss him a treat. Do not call him to you; reward him in position so he associates being away from you as something safe and rewarding.

PRACTICAL TIPS

▶   Avoid getting into patterns that the dog can read. Play ball or go for walks at different times and in different sequences. If you see anxiety developing in the dog, defuse it by changing the behavior pattern you are in. Avoid patterns in your actions and activities that may feed or reinforce the dog's anxiety.

▶   Don't expect too much too fast from the dog. Separation anxiety is based in emotions such as fear. Changing fearful emotions takes time and patience. You may need to take a few days leave from your job to work on this but the results will be worth the effort, since it will reduce the stress and improve quality of life for both of you.

▶ Give the dog plenty of exercise, particularly just before you plan to leave him home alone. This will help burn off excess energy and set him up for a nap while you are out.

▶ Give the dog a special, long lasting treat whenever you leave to distract him from your absence. A Kong or marrowbone filled with peanut butter or yogurt will keep him busy for hours. Give him the long lasting treat daily, even if you're not leaving the house, so it does not become a cue for you leaving. When you give him his long lasting treat, place him in a room by himself with the door closed or a baby gate across the doorway or close him in his crate. This way he will learn that it is okay not to be with you all the time.

INTERIM SOLUTIONS

Desensitizing a dog to separation anxiety can take time. In the meantime, an anxious or distressed dog can do serious damage to himself or to your home. The following suggestions may be helpful in dealing with the immediate problem while allowing you to leave the home for work or errands:

▶ Have a trusted friend, family member or neighbor dog-sit.

▶ Take the dog to a dog daycare facility or a high quality boarding kennel that provides environmental enrichment through games, toys and play.

▶ Take the dog to work with you, even for half a day, if allowed.

▶ Consult your veterinarian about the possibility of drug therapy. A good anti-anxiety drug should not sedate the dog, just reduce his anxiety while you're gone. Such medication is a temporary measure and should be used in conjunction with a behavior modification program.

WHAT NOT TO DO

▶ Don't use punishment. Separation anxiety is based in fear and insecurity. Punishment works by causing fear and it is not an effective way to treat separation anxiety. If you punish the dog when you return home, it may increase his distress.

▶ Don't get another pet. This usually doesn't help an anxious dog as his anxiety is the result of his separation from you, his person, and not merely the result of being alone.

▶ Don't crate the dog. The dog will engage in anxiety responses in the crate. He may urinate, defecate, howl or even injure himself in an attempt to escape from the crate.

▶ Don't leave the radio or television on unless you normally have a TV or radio on when you are at home. If you typically don't have TV or radio on it can become a cue for the dog.

▶ Don't enroll in obedience school. While obedience training is always a good idea, it won't directly help a separation anxiety problem. Separation anxiety is not the result of disobedience or lack of training, it's a panic response.

DOWN AND DOWN/STAY

This exercise teaches the dog to lie down and stay until released.

PREREQUISITES

Teach Attention and Sit before beginning this exercise.

PREPARATION

Have a hungry dog and some yummy treats.

PROCESS

Step 1:   Teach the Down: Have a handful of treats and have the dog sitting in front of you. Hold a treat between your thumb and the middle of your forefinger in such a way that the dog cannot take it from you, up to the dog's nose. Move your hand from the dog's nose to under his chin, and then down his chest, stopping with your food hand between the dog's front legs. As the dog backs down to the floor to get the food, slide your food hand forward slightly on the floor towards the dog's toes. Click and treat any movement to drop the body toward the floor. Toss the food treat so the dog moves and start again when he comes back to you. Repeat, gradually increasing the criteria until the dog eventually lies all the way down. Fade the lure as early in the process as possible, by luring without a treat in your hand and gradually reducing the lure. Allow the dog a moment to think what behavior earned the reward and he'll soon figure out that the down is what you want. Jackpot the big steps toward the goal. Repeat, working as soon as possible to have the dog offer the behavior without being lured into position. Once the dog offers the behavior 100% of the time without being lured, add the "down" cue. Increase duration by gradually and variably lengthening the time between the down and the click. Proof the down by varying the location and beginning to add distractions during separate training sessions.

Step 2:   Teach Down-Stay with Self-Control: (*Note: The clicker is not used for this part of the exercise*). Once the down is on cue, ask the dog to "down", kneel next to him, give him the "stay" cue and place 3-5 food treats on the floor in front of the dog within your arm's reach. Be prepared to pick the food up if he moves. If he gets up, simply start over, keeping the duration short enough to allow him to be successful. When he has held the down-stay position for a few seconds, pick up the treats and give them to him. Don't release him. Say "goood, stay" as you feed him the treats one at a time. Repeat several times, then release him and give him lots of praise and have a game of tug or ball fetch, or something he really enjoys. Once the dog is consistently waiting in the down-stay, begin to place the food further away. Always take the food back to the dog. Add the cue "stay" but begin without food on the floor. Once he is consistently responding to the cue by staying in place, begin to move around while he stays, starting with one step, then gradually and variably adding more movement. Practice in different locations with no distractions, and then gradually add the distractions.

PRACTICAL TIPS

If the dog is not easily lured into the down position:

♦   Work on a carpeted surface or put a mat or towel on the floor. Dogs with sensitive skin may not like to lie down on a cold or hard surface.

♦   Train new behaviors in an environment where the dog feels safe. A dog that is worried about other people or dogs around him may not feel comfortable lying down.

♦   Use food to lure the dog under an obstacle that causes the dog to lower his back and bend or crawl into the beginning of the down. For example, sit or squat on the floor and stretch out your leg for the dog to lie under, or use a low table or chair. Keep making the bridge the dog has to duck under ever lower until he begins to understand what earned the click.

♦   Shape the down by clicking any movement that isn't standing up straight, such as bent front elbows.

♦   Jackpot the down when it happens.

DOWN ON MAT

This exercise teaches the dog that lying down on his mat out of the way is rewarding.

PREREQUISITES

Teach the dog "down" (lie down) before beginning this exercise.

PREPARATION

Have a chair, a rug or mat, a pouch of yummy treats, and a hungry dog.

PROCESS

Step 1:   Place a treat on the mat. Allow the dog to go to the mat to get the treat. Repeat this a few times. This will build the dog's interest in the mat.

Step 2:   Reward (mark and treat) for any contact with the mat. When the dog figures out that every time he goes to his mat he gets a cookie, he will offer it willingly and often.

Step 3:   When the dog is standing on the mat, ask for the down (alternatively, the down can be shaped on the mat). When he lies down, mark the behavior and toss a treat a couple of feet away from the mat, so he has to leave the mat to get it. This sets him up to repeat the behavior of going to the mat and lying down. Repeat.

Step 4:   Once the dog automatically goes to the mat and lies down every time he finishes the tossed treat, gradually add distance (place yourself farther from the mat). Separately, add duration (wait a moment before clicking and tossing the treat). Then add minor distractions.

Step 5:   When the down-on-mat behavior is strong, add the cue "go lie down".

PRACTICAL TIPS

If you are unable to get the dog to lie down on the mat, lure him into a down position by holding the treat in your hand on the mat and waiting a few seconds. When he lies down, open your hand so he can get the treat.

EXCHANGE GAMES

These exercises teach the dog to accept and enjoy giving up valued objects such as food, bones and toys to you.

BACKGROUND

Resource guarding is natural behavior. As carnivores, dogs defend their "kill", whether it's a caribou carcass or a tennis ball from others.

Reconditioning training is never a chance to prove who the boss is. If you turn it into a power play, you may get bitten. You aren't exerting your "control" over the dog in any way, but rather making your presence around the dog's possessions a sign that even better treats are coming.

Sharing is a learned behavior. You can teach the dog that if he shares he will get what he wants. Through exchange games, you can condition the dog to feel relaxed instead of worried or aggressive about giving up a toy. This is accomplished by teaching the dog that giving up something of value means exchanging it for something better.

There are three situations where resource guarding is likely to occur:

1. Eating meals, bones or rawhides. This problem is an easy fix and very manageable: Place dogs in different rooms or in their crates if necessary until you have the time to work on this.

2. Playing with highly treasured toys or what the dog perceives as his (which can include your underwear, socks, table napkins or tissues from the trash). Always exchange for a higher valued item that YOU have.

3. Dogs who guard space are of greater concern. (*See* ON-OFF EXERCISE, *page* 164.)

REAL LIFE EXAMPLE: TUCKER AND THE VALUED ITEM

My Australian Shepherd, Tucker, is an extremely confident, pushy representative of a confident and pushy breed. I adopted him from Aussie Rescue when he was 13 months old and was told he had resource guarding issues. The first time I tried to put him in a crate, he growled and snapped at me. I used positive reinforcement training to recondition Tucker and it paid off. While crated at an agility show, Tucker, managed to pull a zip-lock bag containing my daughter's make-up (which we had foolishly left within reach) into his crate. Tucker was happily chewing the make-up and was about to start on the blush and metal barrettes (yes, Aussies will eat anything!) when two strangers noticed what was happening. They opened his crate and removed the contraband from his mouth. Tucker's response was to wag his tail at them, willingly give up the stuff, and smile happily, as if to say, "Hi there - so whatcha got?" The people were amazed. Their admiration of Tucker's good manners was great positive reinforcement for me. Here Tucker was, on his own turf, approached by total strangers. Why did he just let them take what he was so obviously enjoying? Because from the time he came to live with me, I have worked with him regularly on two exercises which are the object exchange and food bowl games.

Tucker had been reinforced so many times for exchanging things with us that he never even thought twice about allowing someone else to open his crate and reach into his mouth. Many other dogs would have bitten or at least growled - normal dog behavior. Tucker's reconditioning enabled him to accept what does not come naturally to dogs. By reconditioning his natural possessiveness, he now really believes that giving up an object means getting something better.

PREPARATION

Have some toys, a pouch of yummy treats, and a hungry dog on leash.

PROCESS

GAME 1 - TOY EXCHANGE

Start with a toy the dog feels lukewarm about. Show him a treat and when he drops the toy, mark and treat while taking the toy. Then give the toy back to him. This will teach him that he not only gets something of higher value than he gave up, he also gets back what he gave up.

Once he's dropping the toy consistently, add the cue "give." Then try the exchange with a slightly more valuable toy. Once this is going well, begin to touch the toy with your hand and say "give," reinforcing heavily with food. Over time, increase the criteria by using more valuable toys, then bones, then food. The food or object you give in exchange should always be of higher value to the dog than the one he gives up.

GAME 2 - TWO TOY

Have two toys (squeaky toys, hoses, Frisbees, or other toys) ready. Toss one of the toys a short distance, only a few feet away, to where the dog can see it. With a puppy you may need to start with just a short roll of the toy in front of his nose.

If the dog doesn't react by chasing the toy, chase the toy yourself to pique the dog's interest. Increase the distance gradually.

Once the dog gets the idea of chasing and picking up the object, back up with the second toy calling his name, teasing with the toy so he runs toward you to get it. Call "come" as you run backward, teasing the dog with the second toy. Don't throw the second toy until the dog drops the first one.

Toss the toy in the air and catch it yourself or slap it on the floor to make it seem more attractive than the one the dog has in his mouth. When he drops the first toy, throw the second toy, pick up the first and repeat the exercise. He'll quickly figure out that dropping the toy makes you play, while keeping it makes you quit.

Once the dog is fanatical about the retrieve, begin to use the cue "give" when showing the second toy. As the dog learns to love the game, add, "sit" to the game before you throw the toy. Ask the dog to "down" when he brings the toy to you. Mix it up, don't ask the dog for all these skills in any single throw. Make them a fun part of the game.

GAME 3 - FOOD BOWL

The food bowl game is a self-control exercise that is easy to teach because the dog is so motivated to get what is in his food bowl. With the food bowl game, you can teach a dog that hands near bowls are harbingers of good things.

The food bowl game is best played with puppies under 5 months of age. If you are starting with an older puppy or adult dog that is an avid resource guarder, you may be taking risks with this exercise and should obtain the assistance of a professional dog behavior counselor or trainer who uses positive reinforcement methods.

Have the dog's food bowl with at least 10 pieces of some really good and smelly treats for the dog. The goal is for the dog to stay sitting while you lower his dish onto the floor and then wait until you release him to eat.

1. Start standing up, facing the dog, with his food bowl in one hand. Cover the top of the bowl with your other hand so he cannot get food from the bowl until you offer it. No free treats!

2. Ask the dog to sit. Begin to lower his food bowl. If he stands up or moves toward the bowl, lift it up so he cannot get it. Have him sit again. If he sits, give a treat from the bowl so he knows he can earn a reward for sitting.

3. Start to lower the bowl again. Stop and give a treat just before the dog moves. If you watch the dog closely you will learn the signals he gives before breaking a sit. You want him to succeed. If he gets up again just stand up straight and say "too bad". Ask the dog to sit. Don't give him another reward (you don't want him to think that is part is the game). Once again, begin to lower the dish. Before he breaks his sit, mark his good behavior and reinforce from the dish (take a piece from the dish with your free hand and feed it to him).

4. By the sixth or seventh time the dog should be waiting while you lower the food dish, rather than diving for it. This exercise is a wonderful way to link good manners with something the dog really wants without any scolding, pushing, pulling or correcting. The dog is learning that he can get what he wants by exercising self-control.

    Once the dog will stay sitting while you take your hand away from the dish on the floor, you can then pick the bowl up and place right in front of the dog saying "ok" the dish is now his. Gradually stretch the time the dog will wait, until you are able to walk around the room before returning the bowl to the dog so he can eat the rest of the food.

    If the dog has ever growled at you while he is eating, follow the above sequence. Be sure when you get to the point where you can put his dish on the floor only a few pieces of food are in the bowl. When he has eaten the few pieces reach for his dish and add a few more pieces. As you reach to add food to his bowl the dog should back up to let you put the food in. If he dives for the bowl remove your hand and put no pieces in the dish. Each time you move your hand to drop in food, pull it back immediately if the dog moves forward before you release the dog to eat. The dog will learn he doesn't get more food until he is polite and waits for you to release him.

With this exercise, the dog should begin to look happy and expectant when you approach his bowl. If he appears nervous, return to the first step.

If the dog is responding well to the food bowl game, you can begin to work on more advanced exercises. Do NOT perform this next step if the dog is in any way nervous or aggressive (tense, growling, or otherwise) during the food bowl exercise. Play the food bowl game, but keep your hand in the bowl for a few seconds while the dog eats a few bits. Occasionally pick up the food bowl, add some treats and immediately put the bowl back down, releasing the dog to eat.

If the dog is happy with you adding treats to his bowl, you can begin to have other adult family members and friends the dog knows and likes play the game. Have each new person start with the first step and work through the exercise over time.

An extension to the food bowl exercise is to have the dog sit-stay, letting him see you with his bowl of food. Take his bowl to another room and hide it. Return to the dog and release him to go find his bowl to eat. The "hide the food bowl" game becomes two training exercises in one session; it teaches self-control and it also becomes a scent game.

Play the food bowl games regularly for about a year and then occasionally throughout the dog's life to keep his response to you approaching his bowl one of anticipation of good things to come.

PRACTICAL TIPS

Children should be closely supervised around dogs, regardless of the dog's training or reconditioning. Given the range of behaviors both kids and dogs exhibit, it is not possible to make a dog completely "kid proof". By reducing the dog's motivation to guard objects, you are increasing the chances that if something happens beyond your control, he'll have a relaxed response rather than an aggressive one. And that could save his life.

For more information on resource guarding behaviors, read "*Mine*" by Jean Donaldson.

GAME 4 - SIT/STAY FOOD TREAT GAME

How wonderful to have our dog believe that calmly "staying in position" is how to make us give him what he wants (food, toy, play, or just going out the door)! In other words, our job as owners and trainers is to teach our dogs that holding position - not moving - is the key to get the gumball to drop into their paw.

1. Ask the dog to sit, and then hold a treat about 2 feet away from him. Stand sideways with one shoulder toward your dog.

2. If your left shoulder is closest to the dog hold the treat in your right hand (the hand furthest from your dog). Begin to lower the treat straight down to the floor. As you are lowering the treat, if the dog moves or gets up, you should say very matter-of-factly "TOO BAD" or "OOPS" (your No Reward Marker) AND at the same time move the treat away and out of his reach. Ask the dog to sit again (you may need to step out of position so you can face your dog and body block him back into position if he has scooted forward).

3. If the dog maintains position, give the dog the treat while he is in position.

4. You are bending down with the treat and pulling back with the treat until you can place the treat on the ground about 2 feet from the dog and the dog HOLDS POSITION.

5. You want the dog to hold position AND make eye contact with you before you lift the treat and move toward your dog to give it to him. Remember, we want the dog to realize that to get us to give them the treat they must:

> a. Hold position, and
>
> b. Look at us (not the food or toy).

6. When you have progressed so that you can put the treat on the ground, you should start moving away from the dog while the treat is on the ground. Of course, you have to be ready to pick it up if the dog moves. You are now developing duration of the holding position behavior. You can try this with a ball or toy too.

Keep it fun, laugh when your dog hopes to fool you and tries to cheat, reinforce for trying.

FINDING THE HEEL POSITION

The leash is not a tool for controlling the dog. It is your public relations tool. It is a training aid. It is a safety net.

PREPARATION

Have a pouch of yummy treats, and a hungry dog on lead.

PROCESS

Step 1: Stand by Me: With loose leash, click and treat the dog three times for standing by you (no eye contact needed).

Step 2: Look at Me: Click and treat three times for looking at you while on a loose leash.

Step 3: Come by Me: Toss a treat past the dog's nose so it lands about 3 feet away. When the dog looks back at you, click and treat from your pocket or treat pouch. Take a step or two to the side and repeat process.

Step 4: Follow Me: Wait to see if the dog stays with you or tries to go for the tossed treat. If he stays with you, back up a few steps. If the dog turns to follow you, click and treat.

Step 5: Head in Heel Position: The dog is in front of you. Give the dog about 3 feet of slack in the leash. Have the remainder of the leash secured around your waist. Do not call the dog's name, just begin walking backward. If the dog turns and walks toward you, lure his nose to your left side using a treat (he will be facing you but his nose is at your left pant seam). Click and treat. Repeat several times.

Step 6: Find Heel: Once the dog is responding consistently, you are ready to add forward movement. Walk backward until the dog's nose is by your left pant seam, then immediately move forward. The dog will need to turn his body to follow you. Click and treat as he begins to turn. Once he is in place, with his nose lined up at your left pant seam, click and treat again. (This time he will be facing the same direction as you.) Repeat several times, making sure you reinforce the dog while he is in position.

Step 7:   Maintain Heel: Once the dog is moving fluently into the heel position, you are ready to add a pivot. Count out 6 treats and hold them in your hand. Walk backward and as soon as the dog's nose is at your left side, pivot right and begin clicking and treating. Continue clicking and treating as long as the dog is in heel position, until all 6 treats are gone. Release before failure. Repeat several times.

Step 8:   Add the Cue: When you can walk 10 steps forward after moving backward and pivoting, add the cue of "let's go" before you back up and pivot. Repeat several times.

Step 9:   Proof the Heel: Once the dog is able to get into heel position (as in step 6) on cue, and walk 30 steps without forging, cue "heel" and begin walking without first setting up the dog in heel position. If the dog drops into heel position, reward and praise. Repeat several times. If the dog forges, stop moving forward, follow step 6, and begin walking forward again.

GOTCHA GAME

Positive reinforcement training using the clicker is very hands off. You'll be learning how to make the dog operant - meaning how to get the dog to do a desired behavior without using your hands or the lead. This training method is all about getting the dog to freely choose a behavior on his own because the dog believes that trying or offering behavior will earn him a reward. This makes for smart, happy, and eager dogs. It is a really fun, humane way to train.

Using a clicker is so effective, that we don't really need to reach and hold our dogs by the collar very much. But we've discovered that this really humane, effective, training method sometimes creates dogs that back away when we do reach for the collar because we haven't desensitized them to collar handling. Unfortunately there may be times, particularly in emergencies when grabbing the dog's collar will save his life. If the dog is not used to having you grab his collar, and something is happening that has him aroused, then it's possible you'll get bitten, or the dog will dodge away fearfully out of your reach.

So as we train with our clickers, we need to be sure we don't neglect touch as reinforcement. By training the "Gotcha" game, the dog will enjoy being grabbed because being grabbed is rewarded.

PREPARATION

Have a pouch of yummy treats, and a hungry dog.

Train in an area where there are no distractions, such as in a quiet house with no other people, dogs, cats, etc. around.

PROCESS

Start by reaching out calmly for the dog's collar with one hand. Just as you take hold of the collar, click and treat. Hold the collar while you feed and praise. Repeat this daily (you can incorporate Gotcha in with other training exercises).

As the dog gets comfortable with you holding his collar say "Gotcha" before you reach. Click as you get hold of the collar, treat and continue to hold onto the collar as you praise and scratch his neck or behind his ears. In the dog's mind, you have now made touching his collar something positive, instead of something negative.

Once the dog knows what the word "Gotcha" means, come up behind the dog and put your arms around his belly from above, saying "Gotcha". Treat and then play.

Once the dog enjoys being grabbed around the belly, begin lifting him up and holding him. Rough-house a little, grabbing his collar while giving him a treat. Then let him go and run away from him, rewarding him with a chase game (have a tug handy, if he enjoys tug). Continue to make "Gotcha" a fun game. If you ever need to grab him, you can say "Gotcha" and he'll come toward you rather than back away.

PRACTICAL TIPS

When you start this training sequence, move slowly and calmly as you reach to take hold of the collar. If you progress carefully, you will be able to grab the dog by the collar or around the belly and he won't pull away, panic or bite in response.

Always use the cue word of "Gotcha", so the dog knows this is a game that will be rewarded. Your goal is to have a dog that thinks being grabbed is fun.

GREETING VISITORS AT THE DOOR

This exercise teaches the dog the correct behavior for greeting guests at the door.

BACKGROUND

The most common complaint I receive from clients is that they cannot teach the dog how to greet people at the door. When the dog gets excited, he is not being disobedient. He reacts the way he does because he has not been taught how to behave with visitors.

Most of the situations I see are families who have chosen a dog to protect them from intruders. They may have chosen a dog bred for his protective qualities, such as a full or mixed-breed Doberman, German Shepherd or Rottweiler. As the puppy grows up, his natural guarding instincts begin to show. The dog may begin to bark at people who come to the door. This is what the family wanted, but now the family members are afraid the dog is going to bite their friends and begin to react to the dog's guarding behavior by yelling at or manhandling the dog. Their reaction gives the dog more reason to feel threatened and worried about strangers. This cycle continues until the some dogs become dangerously reactive in response to visitors at the door. No amount of reassurance will calm the dog. He is doing what he has been bred and taught to do.

Another common scenario is the opposite problem: A happy and over-stimulated dog. This is the happy-go-lucky type of dog who is overly sociable with everyone he meets. As the doorbell rings, he runs exuberantly to the door to greet his new friend and hopeful playmate. As he does this, the owner holds him back, grabbing onto his collar while letting the visitor enter. The guest then makes a fuss over the dog, touching him and giving him attention while telling the owner "Oh, he is fine. See? He likes me!" All the while, the dog is leaping around and out of control. No amount of yelling, scolding or shoving will deter the dog from rushing excitedly to the door each time the bell rings. He is a fun loving dog who gets so excited he will sometimes even urinate all over the guests' feet.

In both of these situations, the dog is being reinforced for undesired behavior. In the first scenario the dog will never understand that he is the cause of the stress and tension. Each time a family member shows anxiety or fear when someone comes to the door, the guarding dog thinks the guest is something to be concerned about. The over-excited happy dog has his excitement enhanced by the restraint and by the attention from the visitor. In both cases, the dogs interpret the owner's reassurance as praise for their behavior. Both of these dogs are being inadvertantly rewarded for inappropriate behavior with guests.

Their owners certainly didn't plan on this happening, nor do they even understand what they were doing. They inadvertently taught their dog improper greeting behavior.

The dog's brain has two separate systems, the limbic system (the emotional system, or "Lizard Brain") and the cerebral cortex (the analytical system). When one works, the other is inhibited. When a dog is in a highly emotional state (excitement, anxiety, fear or stress) the analytical portion of his brain is compromised. He is less able to think and learn. This is something that the dog cannot control; it is a biological response. The dog is not being bad. He is just unable to express self-control or impulse control.

The dog cannot learn better greeting behavior when the occasional visitor comes to your door. The dog's level of stress will be too high and his brain will not take in what you are trying to teach. You must set up situations to rehearse the behaviors you want. It is not a case of being bad, stubborn or spiteful, but a genuine inability to learn when in an emotional state of mind. Help the dog into a place where he can think about what he needs to do instead of mindlessly reacting to the situation.

Correcting the dog physically will further convince the dog he cannot feel safe around guests. Instead, find out what the dog really likes and use classical conditioning to change his emotional reaction to guests.

PREREQUISITES

If the dog is fearful of people, he should first be counter conditioned. See Counter Conditioning Fear or Aggression exercise. This is no small issue and can take quite a while to accomplish. Good management of the situation, including being proactive so the dog doesn't have to react, is vital for success.

PREPARATION

The dog should be on a buckle collar and leash for this exercise.

Place a non-skid rug about 6 feet from the door. This will be the dog's 'spot'. Even if you have carpet near the door, you need to make it easy for the dog to identify where he needs to be.

Place a big bag of very special treats (chopped no bigger than 1/4 inch square) outside the door, and another just inside the door. These should be treats that the dog will drool over, such as liver, roast beef, cheese, or chicken. Experiment to see what the dog will do anything for.

PROCESS

Step 1:   Have an adult that the dog knows well and likes, such as a spouse or partner, come to the door. Do what you always do when you let guests enter your house, except stand back where the rug has been placed. As the guest enters with a treat in hand, stand calmly and hold the dog at a distance from the guest so he cannot jump up. Wait until the dog settles down and sits on the rug. Then have a guest move forward one step at a time until he can give the dog a treat (the dog must remain in a sit position). Tell the dog that he is good and escort your guest into the room together.

Step 2:   If the dog responded well to step 1, plan to have the dog meet neighbors or close friends whom you see regularly and who the dog knows and likes outside. If the dog enjoys fetch, have the guests toss the ball for him to fetch. Or go for a short walk and have the guests give the dog a few treats along the way. If the dog is responding well, go into the house together with the guests. Some dogs may never be trustworthy. So don't jeopardize your friends until you are certain the dog is ready for this step.

Step 3:   If the dog responded well to step 2, invite these same guests to a "training party". Make sure they completely understand what you want them to do: Enter the house when you say to "come in" and bring a tasty treat with them from the bag outside the door.

Have your first guest come to the door. Follow the process in step 2. Repeat this process with the next guest. When each guest has been through the process, wait about 10 minutes and start the process over. The dog should encounter people coming through the door a total of 40 times in this training session. So, if you have four people, they will cycle through the door ten times. If the dog is responding well by the 4th time through this cycle, your guests may now pet the dog under the chin giving the dog a treat at the same time. By the 10th time, the dog should be sitting quietly to be touched under his chin. Note: If the dog is shy or fearful, then no petting allowed.

As you rehearse this exercise, it will become boring and predictable. That is just what we are looking for! The dog will calm down about halfway through the session and learning will start to take place. Initially the dog may not understand what you want. A second "training party" a week or so later will continue to help the dog become familiar with the process when guests come to the door. Invite guests whom the dog doesn't know very well, and repeat this step all over again the following weekend!

HEAD AND SHOULDER DESENSITIZATION

This exercise associates touching with praise and yummy treats teaching the dog not to feel threatened when people touch or restrain him.

PREREQUISITES

Teach "Gotcha Game" before beginning this exercise.

PREPARATION

For dogs with restraint issues it is important that all meals come from the handler. All things good must come from people. No free feeding (leaving food down for the dog to access freely).

Have a hungry dog and some yummy treats.

PROCESS

Start with touches by a very familiar person; the person that the dog feels the most comfortable with. For the first two weeks, hand feed treats to the dog while moving your hand about 8 inches above his head and back. Feed treats at a high rate so that he receives a treat within a second or two of finishing the previous treat. Gradually move your hand closer but watch to be sure he is still comfortable. If he is uncomfortable at any time, increase the distance between your hand and his body. Sessions should be short; end each session before he becomes stressed or tired. When your hand is near his head, neck or shoulders, the bar is open (lots of treats, delivered one at a time). When your hand is not near, the bar is closed (no treats). Eventually, you should be able to run your hand down his neck so you are touching his side, shoulders and sides of his head (work on one side at a time).

Call the dog to you and repeat the routine many times throughout the day. This is how you will feed the dog his meals.

PRACTICAL TIPS

The Gotcha game can be taught alongside this exercise, in separate training sessions.

Teaching the dog to target body parts, such as his nose, to your hand or another object is also complimentary to this exercise. (*See* NOSE-TARGET, *page* 163). Use the same process as for the nose, but shape targeting with shoulders, hips, chest, neck, etc.
(*See Kay Laurence's book "Clicker Dances with Dogs" for more information on teaching targeting of various body parts.*)

For additional information about desensitizing the dog to touch, see "*Mine*" by Jean Donaldson or "*Aggression in Dogs*" by Brenda Aloff. Both books are listed in References section of this book.

GROOMING

This exercise teaches the dog to tolerate, or even enjoy, grooming.

PREPARATION

Do all your grooming in the same area. Have all the tools you need ready and within easy to reach before you get the dog.

GROOMING TOOLS:

► Brush (slicker, pin or bristle brush).

► Comb if needed (mat splitter if longer coat).

► Rake for undercoat.

► Nail clippers, file and quick stop for nail bleeding.

► Eye wipes, ear wipes (baby wipes with no alcohol).

► Q-tips.

► Baby oil or ear oil.

► Damp towel.

PROCESS

Don't call the dog to you. Go find him, put him on leash and bring him to the grooming area. Give him a treat for coming with you.

Start by inspecting his entire body, from nose to tail, with your hands. The more you do this, the better you will learn what the dog looks and feels like so you can detect any swelling, lumps, scabs, ticks or fleas. Look in his ears and check his nails. Give him a treat.

Brush or comb out areas that need it. Always start in the same place and work around his entire body. Give him a treat.

Check his ears for wax and dirt. Use baby wipes wrapped around your index finger to swab out dirt. Be gentle; only work as far into the ear as you can with the baby wipe wrapped over your index finger. Use a Q-tip with a little baby oil on it to clean out the folds you cannot reach with the baby wipe. Don't go in too far, and be sure the cotton tip doesn't stay in the ear. Give him a treat.

Hold up his lips and check for tartar on his teeth. Look at his gums and the general condition of his teeth. If his teeth are dirty, gums inflamed or he has bad breath, talk with your vet. A change of diet, harder food to chew and brushing or scaling his teeth can help. If he is eating the right food, has good mouth care and does not have other medical issues, a dog should always have clean breath.

Have your vet or groomer show you how to clip nails safely, so you don't cut into the quick. Buy good clippers and use them weekly so you can easily keep the dog's toenails the right length. Clip the nails on one paw at a time. Be sure to clip the dew claws if present (some dogs have none, and others have them only on the front paws). Check the dog's foot pads for cuts or abrasions.

End your session by misting the dog with mixture of 1 part Keri bath oil to 20 parts water and wiping the mist off with a towel. This will remove any dander on the coat from brushing.

▶ Groom small dogs on a table to save your back. Put a rug or skid mat on the tabletop so the dog has traction.

▶ During hot weather, keep a quart of water with lemon slices in the fridge to daub on any red or itchy areas. Lemon changes the pH of the skin surface and isn't sticky. Trim the hair around any hot spots to allow air circulation so they will heal quickly.

▶ Give the dog a vegetable treat each day. Raw vegetables (such as carrots or broccoli stems) help clean the dog's teeth, are low in calories and are high in fiber. Note: Some fruits and vegetables, such as grapes, raisins and onions, are toxic to dogs so should not be fed.

▶ If the dog has wrinkly skin, look in the folds. Check that they are clean and wipe with lemon water if any skin problems appear. Wipe dry with a towel.

Make this grooming time special. Use it as an opportunity to bond with your dog. Give treats throughout the grooming session and have a jackpot treat (such as a ball fetch or tug game) for the dog when grooming is finished.

LEAVING THE HOUSE

This exercise teaches the dog not to charge out when the door is opened. This exercise is particularly useful in a multiple dog household.

PREPARATION
Have a handful of yummy biscuits, kibble, and hungry dogs.

PROCESS

Go outside, without the dogs and hide a few biscuits. Allow the dogs out, one at a time by name, and help them find a hidden biscuit. Use the cue "find the biscuit". If the wrong dog attempts to get out, body block him and ask for a sit. Then invite and allow the chosen dog out. This will teach the dogs their names, along with self-control.

When each dog understands the game, let them out together and cue "find the biscuit". Once the dogs learn the game, they will focus on finding the hidden treat when they leave the house, rather than charging around mindlessly looking for things to chase. As an alternative, show the dogs a handful of dry kibble. Have them wait at the door while you toss the handful of kibble outside in front of them. Allow them out one at a time. While the dogs are hunting for the biscuits, recall them one at a time. Reinforce successful recalls with treats and release each dog to continue his biscuit hunt.

To teach the dogs to come back after finding the treats, touch the dog you are going to call, say his name and run backwards. When he reaches you, give him a treat. Eventually, you'll be able to call each dog back to you even though he is focused on finding a treat.

Note: For those with single dogs, just toss a handful of treats or kibble outside the door to slow them down, or let them out and then ask for a sit and toss.

LEAVE IT

This exercise teaches the dog self-control.

PREPARATION

Have two treats for this exercise, one that has high value and one that has lower value.

PROCESS

Step 1:   Hold the high value (smelly and delicious) treat in your left hand. Hold the less valuable treat in your right hand. Hold both hands behind your back. Offer your right hand (with the lower value treat) to the dog, keeping the treat inside your fist so the dog cannot get it. Let the dog nibble on your fist as he tries to get the treat. The instant the dog stops trying to get the food, say "leave it" and bring your left hand from behind your back with the smelly treat visible in the opened palm of your hand. Give this treat to the dog while saying "take it".

Step 2:   Repeat step 1 until the dog actively ignores the right hand, waiting for the left hand to appear with the high value treat.

Step 3:   Switch which hand holds the good treat and repeat steps 1 and 2, using the opposite hands.

Step 4:   Put the more valuable treat in your pocket and hold a less valuable treat in one of your hands. Repeat steps 1 and 2, but bring the valuable treat out of your pocket. Practice this exercise a couple of times a day, until the dog consistently responds to the "leave it" cue.

Step 5:   Put two or three plates of yummy food on the floor (you don't need much food on each plate). Separate the plates by at least 10'. Walk the dog on lead toward one plate; stop short of the plate and say, "leave it". Don't let dog get the food. Calmly hold the lead and wait. Don't say anything; just wait. When the dog glances away from the food, click and treat.

Step 6:   Continue to next plate and repeat. Gradually increase the criteria, reinforcing the dog for glancing away from the bowl, then reinforcing glancing at you, then reinforcing looking at you with his full attention. Repeat each level of criteria until the dog is fluent at that level. When the dog consistently looks at the food, then looks back to you for reinforcement, add the cue "leave it".

Step 7:   Practice this exercise at least 20 times over a period of weeks. When you can walk up to a plate and the dog looks at you rather than the plate of food, jackpot him and have a game of fetch or tug. Be sure to pick up the plate of food so you don't inadvertently allow the dog access to them.

Step 8:   Once you have taught the "leave it" cue indoors, you are ready to generalize it to any object of the dog's attention. Take the dog outdoors, on lead. Wait until he begins sniffing, trying to greet other dogs or people, wandering off, or not giving eye contact when you use his name. Step on the drag line and say "leave it". The moment the dog changes the distracted behavior and looks at you, click and treat. Then play, making yourself so fabulous that the dog will learn "leave it" means it is very worthwhile for him to stop what he's doing and see what you have.

Step 9:   Have a helper run by your house while you are carefully holding the dog on leash. Be ready for the dog to respond when he sees the runner. Say "leave it" calmly as soon as the dog makes any muscle movement to lunge or bark. When the dog looks at you, click and treat. Repeat this distraction, changing your position in relation to the runner as many times as it takes for the dog to ignore the distraction and look immediately at you.

Step 10: Practice in locations with distractions, such as a park. If the dog can't look at you, the level of distraction is too high. Move farther away from the distractions, until the dog can ignore them and look at you.

"Leave it" is a primary management skill. Reward it throughout the dog's life.

LOOSE LEASH WALKING

This exercise teaches the dog to walk on a loose lead, and builds the dog's self-control.

BACKGROUND

By letting the dog lead you toward his own interests, you successfully train him to pull. Every time you let a dog pull, he learns that pulling is how he gets to go his own way, to sniff what he wants, with you in tow. The dog may feel he should be on alert, since you have put him in a decision-making position. As a result, he may feel he needs to protect you and the space around you.

The solution to this is to stop reinforcing pulling and begin reinforcing walking without tension on the lead. From now on, the positive reinforcer is continuing to move forward, and the negative is NOT getting to move forward.

Change your view of taking a walk. The walk is yours. It is the dog's privilege, not his right, to accompany you on this patrol.

Rules for the dog when strolling on lead will be:

▶   If you stay by my side and keep the lead slack, we move forward.

▶   If you move ahead and pull, we stop.

For chronic pullers who go to the end of the lead and then pull and ignore you:

▶   When the dog leads and tension is on the lead, STOP MOVING.

▶   When the dog looks back, gently guide him back to the "acceptable side" using the shortest route.

PREPARATION

Use a flat buckle collar. For well trained pullers, use the Sensation Harness™ or Easy Walk™. If you really need extra help, use a head halter. (*See Training Resources and Equipment Chapter 4.*) The lead should be at least 6' long, made of flat cloth or nylon webbing or leather and comfortable for you to hold. Have some yummy treats and a hungry dog.

PROCESS

It is easier for a dog to learn where he is supposed to be when strolling on lead if you consistently choose one side for walking during this teaching period. Inconsistency encourages dithering in front of you, and in front of you is your space.

If you prefer having the dog on your left, slip the loop handle of the lead over your right wrist and grip the lead firmly in your palm where it joins the loop. Use your left hand as a light guide supporting the lead so you don't trip over it. If you prefer having the dog on your right, use the opposite hands.

Start walking. Walk as though you own the world. Lead the parade, head up, shoulders back. Say ABSOLUTELY NOTHING. The dog will need to look at you for information instead of just listen.

Whenever the dog moves ahead or pulls, stop. Guide him back to the acceptable position. Stand still and count to ten. If he stays with you and is calm, begin your walk again. By continuing the stroll when he is by your side you reward a loose lead position.

If you stop and the dog ignores you, jiggle the lead. Don't tug, just jiggle. By jiggling, you are making yourself a nuisance; nagging without words. When the dog turns to notice you, take a step backward and guide him to your side.

If the dog needs incentive to stay at your side, place a treat on the ground next to your foot when you stop. If the dog makes eye contact while in position by your side, give him a treat.

If you are consistent, you will build a strong foundation for loose leash walking.

This method of teaching the dog to walk on a loose lead without pulling is from "Walk With Me" by British trainer Kay Laurence, available in booklet form from www.learningaboutdogs.com

---

NAME RECOGNITION

Successful name recognition training means the dog knows when his name is spoken, something really important to him will always happen. This exercise teaches the dog an eager, happy and willing response with eye contact and his full physical and mental attention when you say his name.

PREREQUISITES

Teach association of the clicker and food before beginning this exercise.

PREPARATION

Have a hungry dog and some yummy treats.

PROCESS

Step 1: Start by saying the dog's name when he is looking at you and clicking and treating. Repeat a few times. Next, toss a treat on the ground. When the dog finishes eating, say his name. As he turns his head toward you, click. Wait until he comes to you for the treat. When he's eaten the treat, toss another treat in a different direction and repeat many times, over many training sessions. Gradually increase difficulty by turning sideways and stepping away from him a little. This will encourage faster movement toward you.

Step 2: Before you add distractions, he should have a head-snap-toward-you response to his name. Once he does, begin saying his name when he is mildly distracted. Be prepared for him not to respond quickly. Be sure he has on a leash or drag line. Give him a bit of time to hear you because of the distraction. If he doesn't respond and begins to move away from you, step on the lead, but don't say his name again. Wait until he turns to look, then click and treat. If he doesn't turn his head and look, the distractions are too difficult and/or the treats are not high enough value (or he's not hungry). Train when he is hungry, with higher value (and varied) treats, in a less distracting environment. Gradually raise the distraction level so that you can work on helping the dog believe that even if there are chipmunks shouting rude things at him, when you say his name you are always worth listening to. Your reinforcers have to be wonderful to be more interesting than the kitty, bicycle or smart-mouthed chipmunk.

Be sure the dog is not being rewarded until he gets to you. If you are using a toy reward, wait until he is moving toward you and toss the toy behind you, which will help improve the speed he uses to return to you. The instant he turns to see what's happened, turn and move away holding onto the leash or long line. The minute he follows, click, and make a big fuss with lots of praise and treats.

PRACTICAL TIPS

Training for name recognition is the process of vigorously reinforcing the dog's attention to his name.

▶ Always reinforce the dog's head-turn response when you say his name.

▶ Don't use the dog's name unless you are prepared to reinforce.

▶ Don't use the dog's name if the distractions are more interesting than your reinforcers.

▶ Be prepared to insist on a response. The dog should wear a drag line outdoors or a tag line indoors until he has consistent name recognition behavior.

▶ If you goofed and said his name without being ready to reinforce, make an exciting game of running to get a cookie to reward his name recognition.

▶ Don't use the dog's name unless you are going to make it worth his while. Don't cry wolf! Don't waste the dog's name.

NOSE-TARGET

Target training teaches the dog to touch his nose, paw, or other body part to a specific object or person.

PREPARATION

Have a pouch of yummy treats, and a hungry dog.

PROCESS

Step 1: Squeeze a smelly food treat into the space at the base of the second and third fingers. The scent of the treat will encourage the dog to sniff in the direction of your hand. Standing sideways with the target hand nearest the dog, wait for the dog to turn his nose toward the hand. Follow success with a click or "Yes" and allow the dog to take the treat. Repeat this step 10-15 times.

Step 2: Begin again, but without the food reward in your hand. When the dog sniffs or touches your hand with his nose, click and treat from the other (non-target) hand. If the dog is confidently stretching out to touch the hand, move the hand a little so his nose has to follow it before the click and treat. Repeat 10 - 15 times. Vary the position of the hand in relation to the dog and gradually increase the distance (move 3 steps, 5 steps, moving through doorways etc.). At each stage, reinforce 10 - 15 times to build the dog's confidence and understanding. The goal is to create a nose-touch to the hand that is a confident, strong push.

Step 3: Transfer the target to an object, such as a chair. Rub the treat on the surface of the chair and lead the dog's nose to chair with the target hand (scented with treat). Click when the dog's nose is near, or touches, the chair. When the dog gets the idea of touching the new object with his nose, begin sending him to the chair from an increasing distance. When the dog is hooked on touching his nose to the target, add the verbal cue "touch".

Step 4: When the dog is confident about the targeting concept and targets on cue, you can teach the dog to nose-target a "new" (unfamiliar) person. This is a good exercise for shy dogs. The new person should be relaxed, hold their shoulders and head sideways to the dog, and avoid making direct eye contact. The new person should sit in a chair with their hand down by one side, palm facing outward. The yummy treat should be squeezed between two fingers, but easy for the dog to lick out. At this stage, don't click when the dog takes the treat from the new person. Both the handler and the new person should be calm, quiet and still, letting the dog make his own approach. Gently replace the treat each time, until the dog has taken a treat from the new person 10 times. Then let the dog rest.

Step 5: When the dog is confident taking the treat from the new person's palm, you can move to the next stage. The new person has no treat in the hand. The handler stands still calmly talking to the new person. When the dog touches the new person's empty palm, the handler immediately clicks and treats. As soon as the dog finishes his treat, the handler gives the verbal cue "touch". If the dog goes to the stranger's palm, the handler clicks, and a big jackpot is well deserved. Build on targeting stranger's hands with very gradual changes in posture, location, gender, etc. Targeting a hand makes contacting strangers a comfortable behavior and provides the handler with a positive way to reward social interaction. The dog learns to make the contact themselves as opposed to being forced to stand still and tolerate contact. This can make all the difference when building confidence and social skills in a shy dog.

Step 6:   Take your targeting outside to generalize the skill. Start somewhere safe and familiar and gradually move to less familiar places. Stage the exercises by having friends walk up quietly and ask the dog to target the friend's hand. When first training in a new environment, you may need to go back to the first step for a while until the dog can perform the behavior reliably. Fearful or shy dogs have a much harder time becoming operant, so never be afraid to back up to an easier step. New environments can be scary for shy dogs, so developing a reward for nose-targeting a hand gives you a way to move the dog around the environment while encouraging the dog to feel safe and reinforced. With shy or over-reactive dogs patience is key. Don't expect too much too soon.

For more information of targeting techniques see Clicker Trainers Series: Foundation and Novice (Kay Laurence).

ON-OFF (PLACEMENT)

Some dogs have issues moving off the bed or other furniture. When you approach and ask him to get off the couch, he may snap or growl at you. This can be a learned behavior. Perhaps moving off furniture has, in the past, led to consequences not beneficial to him. With some dogs, it can be due to resource guarding issues such as guarding of his body or personal space which may have roots in fear or insecurity.

This exercise teaches the dog that moving from one place to another, such as from the couch to the floor, is rewarding and fun.

BACKGROUND

One of the least understood causes of problems with dogs is defensive behavior. This problem is both genetic and caused by how the dog has been handled in the past. Defensive behavior is about survival. It is the fight-or-flight survival response triggered when a dog is thrown into a panic state by fear, pain, or both. Different dogs have different defensive tendencies ranging from not very defensive to quite highly defensive.

People can inadvertently increase a dog's defensive tendencies, often in dramatically damaging ways.

Punishing defensive behavior can begin a vicious cycle leading to increased aggression. This on-off exercise can be used to prevent or to rehabilitate undesirable defensive behavior, such as snapping when asked to move off the bed by building a desired response, or moving off the furniture when asked (and being rewarded for doing so).

PREPARATION

Have a pouch of yummy treats, a comfortable piece of furniture (chair or bed) and a hungry dog on a tag line (about 3 feet or 1m in length).

Step 1: Invite the dog to get on the furniture using an upward motion of your hand as a cue. You may need to lure him up with a treat at first. Give him a treat when he jumps up on the furniture. Then ask him to get off, motion of your hand away from the furniture as though tossing a treat on the floor. If he does not get off within two or three seconds, toss a treat on the floor a few feet away from the furniture. If he still doesn't move, pick up the end of the tag line (don't reach for the collar) and turn your back to him. Gently put a bit of pressure on the tag line. As he steps forward, praise and give a treat. Use lots of verbal praise. Repeat this process, 10 or 20 times per session. Remember to stop before the dog becomes tired or bored with the game. Eventually, as the dog learns that he gets a treat for getting off, and then is allowed and invited to get back on the furniture, you will no longer need to prompt the dog with the tag line.

Step 2: Practice every day for 10 days.

Step 3: Once the dog is responding to your motioning hand by getting on and off the furniture, add a verbal cue for each, such as "on" and "off". You have now patterned new behaviors for getting on and off the furniture on cue.

Step 4: Practice weekly or so for the remainder of the dog's life, to keep the behavior strong.

PASSIVE ATTENTION

This exercise teaches the dog to give you attention even when you are not giving him any attention. This means that you can be talking to a friend, taking a walk, or watching TV, and the dog will be aware of you and waiting for you to give him a cue or a click and reward for attention.

The passive attention game allows you to give the dog a cue at any time and rewards the dog for his ability to respond quickly.

PREPARATION

Have a pouch of yummy treats and a hungry dog on leash.

Train in an area where there are no distractions, such as in a quiet house with no other people, dogs, cats, etc. around.

PROCESS

While talking to another person, use your peripheral vision to see if the dog is watching you. Click and reward the dog for watching you.

When you look away from the dog, have a friend click the dog when he is watching you. After your friend clicks, you treat the dog. It is important when you play passive attention games that all reinforcement comes from you.

PREPARING FOR VET VISIT

A visit to the veterinarian's office or dog grooming parlor can be stressful for many dogs. This list of exercises is intended to start you thinking about all of the weird stressful things that can happen on a trip to the vet or groomer and help you condition the dog to accept a veterinary examination or grooming visit with minimal stress.

GETTING THE DOG READY TO BECOME THE BEST PATIENT THE VET HAS EVER SEEN.

PREREQUISITES

If the dog has handling issues, perfect the Grooming Exercises, The Gotcha Game and Head and Shoulder Desensitization exercises before attempting this exercise. *(See pages 156, 152 & 155)*

PROCESS

Practice the following "events" as often as possible. The dog should always be relaxed and comfortable during these exercises since the intent is to teach the dog it is pleasant to be handled. Repeat the various exercises, increasing duration or difficulty when the dog is ready. Practice all of these exercises in various locations; the more locations, the better. Continuously reinforce each exercise with food treats, praise, massage, petting or play.

THE SIT, STAY, ROLL-OVER EVENT:

1. Have the dog stand with one hand on his head or neck, and the other hand gently resting under his abdomen.

2. Teach the dog to sit on cue.

3. Teach the dog to lift one paw (shake) on cue.

4. Have the dog lay on each side with legs away from you and your hands holding both lower legs gently (typical restraint for most lameness exams).

5. Teach the dog to tolerate you giving him a bear hug around the neck. This is a typical restraint position.

6. Teach the dog to lie on his back (for a belly rub).

7. If possible, gradually and with someone else's help, teach the dog to lie on his back with front and back legs extended. Then teach him to lie on his side with front and back legs extended. These are X-ray positions.

THE PEOPLE DESENSITIZATION RELAY EVENT:

1. Have another family member whom the dog trusts and has no issues with approach in positions 1 and 2 above.

2. Have the approaching person wear a long jacket, white if possible.

3. Have above person wear a rope or ideally a stethoscope around the neck (cheap imitations come in dress up kits for kids or ask your vet).

4. Teach the dog to allow another person to hold their paw (great for catheters or drawing blood samples). Start by having the person wipe the dog's feet with a towel one at a time while you feed the dog yummy treats.

5. Have the dog lie on each side with his legs away from you and your hands holding both lower legs, gently. When the dog is comfortable with this position have someone else look between his toes and gently manipulate his legs.

6. Teach the dog (using lots of yummy treats) to enjoy someone else holding him around the neck in a bear hug. This can upset some dogs enough to bite so go very slowly and only do this if you are comfortable that it won't push the dog beyond his bite threshold.

7. Teach the dog to walk politely on a leash away from you led by someone else (this is particularly important if you own a 100+ pound dog!).

THE TOUCH MY DOG EVENT:

1. Teach the dog to tolerate you handling his paws. Wipe them off with a towel.

2. Get the dog accustomed to his ears being handled and his mouth being opened.

3. Look at the dog's eyes and shine a penlight in them.

4. Teach the dog to sit with you holding him around his muzzle and gently lifting his head to expose his neck. Then have a helper gently press on the dog's neck. Have the helper pour a tiny amount of alcohol on the dog's neck. (This simulates jugular blood samples.) Then swap positions with your helper.

THE NEW PLACE GENERALIZATION MARATHON:

1. Teach the dog to stand and stay on a table (you may want to do this on a special mat, and take that mat to the vets or groomers with you).

2. Repeat the stand stay and various other behaviors on the table.

3. Repeat the stand stay and various other behaviors on a park bench outside. Remember lots of yummy treats!

4. Repeat the stand stay and various other behaviors at a friend's house (with their permission of course!). IF the dog has never met them, don't ask them to approach and touch him at this time, but do have them give some yummy treats or better yet, ask them to play with a toy with the dog - outside of course.

5. Go on short car rides. Treat extensively during trip and when you arrive. If the dog tends to get carsick, try treating for car trips to the end of the driveway (very short!) or go to the closest park and play.

6. Drive to the vet's when they are closed or slow (always ask the veterinarian's office permission first, so they can recommend slow times). Play with or practice obedience in the grass outside, the parking lot or in the waiting room.

7. Teach the dog that crates are safe, comfortable places at the vet's and elsewhere. Crate

trained dogs fare better if they require a stay in a crate at the vet's.

8.   Teach the dog it is fun to be crated in strange places with you and various other people coming and going and delivering treats (simulates hospitalization or being kenneled).

WEIRD AND SCARY EQUIPMENT EVENT:

1.   Help the dog tolerate or even enjoy nail trimming by teaching him that clippers are a source of treats. Leave them in plain view while he is eating his own food or place them in the dog's own toy basket.

2.   Teach the dog that muzzles are fun. Many dogs will growl or snap when hurt, and must be muzzled for human safety. (*See* Conditioning to a Halter or Muzzle *page* 128.) Veterinarians can't risk bites to you, them, or their staff and even nice dogs will bite if they hurt enough. Making the muzzle a fun thing ahead of time and knowing how to put one on will ensure safety and reduce the dog's stress.

3.   Teach the dog to enjoy being brushed. Make it fun and rewarding for the dog . Make it a daily or at least a weekly event. Remember not to call the dog to you for grooming. Go to him, put the leash on and lavishly reward him as you take him to the grooming area.

4.   Desensitize the dog to a stethoscope (toy stethoscopes work fine). Use it first, then have others use it. The dog should face forward and stand calmly. If the dog pants, gently close his mouth.

5.   Teach the dog to enjoy baths. The vet may find it necessary to give the dog therapeutic baths.

THE GOLD MEDAL FINALISTS EVENT:

1.   Teach the dog to allow you to brush his teeth.

2.   If you have a breed with a tendency toward ear problems, clean the ears starting at a young age with a mild ear cleaner (ask your vet for recommendations). Repeat every week or two.

3.   Teach the dog to enjoy other people getting him out of and putting him into a crate. Crate transfering is a possible time when dogs might bite - especially a nervous dog. Be careful and go slowly.

4.   Teach the dog to tolerate his temperature being taken.

PRACTICAL TIPS

This is not a complete list and is not broken into all the mini steps needed to desensitize the dog. For those dogs with handling and restraint issues, you must go slowly and pair lots of treats, toys and games the dog enjoys with any of these exercises.

These steps will, however, dramatically increase the odds of the dog having a more pleasant trip to the vet's or groomer's facility.

Most training involves breaking behaviors into the tiniest bits and teaching them step by step but few people take the extra time to teach the unusual behaviors needed for when the pet is sick and needs to be handled by medical staff.

Ask your vet or groomer about their policies involving giving treats during exams, after exams, and during various procedures. Do not get upset if the dog fusses or if the vet thinks it is better to have a qualified technician handling the dog. Many owners and veterinary staff members get bitten due to improper or inadequate restraint. Those staff members need their fingers to be able to do surgery, put in catheters, and otherwise take care of your pet.

A visit to an emergency clinic means your dog will see a new set of people. This may mean that a dog that is good at his regular veterinarians will be upset and stressed at the emergency clinic.

Always have the dog on a lead or in a crate when you take him to the vet. Dogs left to wander the waiting room can escape and get hit by a car, get into a fight with another dog, or cause stress to a cat quietly minding his own business.

QUIET AT THE DOOR

The ring of the doorbell can send many a dog into a frenzy of jumping, barking and general misbehavior. Desensitization can be used to change the dog's response to the doorbell.

These two exercises teach the dog an appropriate response to the doorbell. The first exercise teaches the dog not to respond to the doorbell. The second exercise teaches the dog to respond to the doorbell by sitting quietly.

PREREQUISITES

Before beginning Exercise 1, the dog should be taught to lie down on a mat on verbal or hand-signal cue.

Before beginning Exercise 2, the dog must be conditioned to a head halter and should be taught to respond to light pressure forward and up on the head halter by sitting. Use a food lure to teach the sit.

PREPARATION

Have a hungry dog, a helper and yummy treats. For Exercise 1, have a mat for the dog to lie on. For Exercise 2, have the dog on a halter (such as a Gentle Leader) and a 4-foot lead.

PROCESS

EXERCISE 1: DESENSITIZATION AND COUNTER CONDITIONING

Step 1:   Choose a door inside the house to begin with. Have your helper stand beside the closed door and knock on it. As the dog runs toward the door barking, toss treats one at a time on the floor in front of the dog. Toss the treats regardless of what the dog is doing until he stops barking. Repeat until the dog no longer barks when you knock but instead comes running to find the treats.

Step 2:   Have your helper go to the other side of the same door and knock. Immediately open the door and toss food in front of the dog. Repeat until the dog no longer barks when you knock and open the door, but instead comes running to find the treats. This may take several training sessions.

Step 3:   Repeat Step 2, but begin to toss the treats toward the mat, set a few feet away from the door, gradually shaping the dog to go to his mat. Once the dog aims for the mat when you knock on the door, ask the dog to lie down on his mat, then toss more treats (one at a time) to the dog so he can get them while remaining in a down position on his mat.

Step 4:   Repeat Step 1, but use the outer door most often used by guests. Start by having your helper knock, as in Step 1. Once the dog no longer responds by barking, repeat the same exercise using the doorbell (a different sound, which may trigger barking again). Repeat until the dog no longer barks when you ring the doorbell. Then repeat Step 2 and Step 3 in sequence, from the outer door using the doorbell. Jackpot particularly good behavior.

Step 5:   Have a helper ring the doorbell while you sit in a chair and read or watch TV. Ignore the doorbell (don't get up). When the dog takes a breath (so is quiet for an instant) begin to toss treats on the floor one at a time. Repeat this sequence, gradually shaping the dog to go to his mat (by luring him with tossed treats) and then lying down on his mat as in Step 3.

Step 6:   Repeat Step 5, but have the helper enter and toss treats on the floor one at a time, rewarding tiny gaps in barking. Repeat this sequence until the helper can enter and the dog moves to the his mat waiting for the helper to toss treats to him on the mat.

Step 7:   In real life the person at the door may require your attention before you can treat the dog, so begin to build the dog's self-control by building in delayed delivery of the treat. Start by waiting a few seconds before treating. Then bounce back and forth between a short time interval and a longer one, gradually increasing in variable amounts (1 second, then 3 seconds, then 2 seconds, then 4 seconds, then 3 seconds, etc.) until you can achieve 5 minutes. This will take multiple training sessions.

EXERCISE 2: SIT RESPONSE

Have the dog on lead, about 4 feet from the door. Have the helper ring the doorbell (or knock on the door). Slide one hand down the lead to take hold of the halter just under the chin and pull up and forward to get the dog to sit. The dog should remain sitting as you open the door. If the dog tries to jump up, pull up and forward a bit until the dog sits again. Have the helper give the dog a treat while the dog is sitting.

Repeat this process numerous times per session. This exercise will help the dog learn to sit and wait quietly for a treat when he hears somebody at the door. Gradually, as the dog learns to sit when someone knocks or the doorbell rings in anticipation of a treat, reduce the pressure on the halter.

PRACTICAL TIPS

If you have more than one dog, put the dogs not practicing the exercise someplace where they cannot be heard by the dog practicing the exercise. Each dog should be worked alone until that dog is reliable. Then work them together, adding one reliable dog at a time. When working them together at first, alternate one on-lead dog and one dog loose. Have the loose dog on a tag line, so you can help him if needed.

If the barking gets worse before it gets better, don't be concerned. This is a normal part of how dogs learn. Eventually, the doorbell (or knock on the door) will become a cue for the dog to go and sit quietly on his mat waiting for a treat.

Some dogs find barking inherently rewarding. If the dog continues to bark after 6 or 7 trials of tossing food, add distance (take the dog to a place further from the doorbell sound, such as the back room or yard) and gradually decrease the distance or reduce the noise level (buffer the doorbell noise) and gradually increase the noise.

To change any really ingrained or self-rewarding behavior requires LOTS of repetitions in a controlled environment. Be sure the dog has relearned how to be calm and quiet when the doorbell rings before testing his new behavior on real guests. Little steps and lots of repetitions are keys to success.

REFRESHER ATTENTION GAMES FOR A WEEK

This week full of attention exercises is to fast-track the dog toward a deeper relationship and understanding of eye contact. It is especially helpful for dogs that easily lose focus on you in a training class or forget you exist when you go to the dog park. Building a solid foundation of attention for a few minutes each day for a week will greatly improve the dog's ability to focus on you and respond to cues in a distracting situation.

These exercises can also be used to desensitize a dog to eye contact, first by very trusted and familiar people, then (once the dog feels secure) by less familiar people.

Never allow an unfamiliar person to stare at the dog. (*See Communication, Chapter 2.*)

With a sensitive or fearful dog, eye contact by unfamiliar people should be fleeting and side-facing rather than a front-facing direct stare.

Set up the environment for safety (dog on leash with head halter, helper at a safe distance, etc.). For sensitive or fearful dog, always watch the dog's body posture and remove pressure to relax the dog before he reacts.

PREPARATION

Have a pouch of yummy treats, and a hungry dog.

Train in an area where there are no distractions such as in a quiet house with no other people, dogs, cats, etc. around.

PROCESS

DAY ONE

Watch the dog's eyes. Whenever the dog looks at you, mark the behavior and give the dog a treat. Don't do anything special to get the dog's attention, just wait for it and capture it. Repeat this exercise throughout the day.

In addition to rewarding the dog's attention, begin rewarding eye contact. Mark and treat every time the dog looks at you as many times as you possibly can in one minute. Repeat this a few times. My personal best was 60 times in 60 seconds. Have someone time you and count!

With a few treats in your hand, hold your arm out to one side, hand closed. Don't say anything to get the dog's attention, just wait patiently while the dog stares at the treats to try to "will" them out of your hand. The moment the dog moves his eyes off of your hand and glances at your face, click and treat.

By the end of this day, you should have marked and rewarded the dog for looking at you one hundred times or more.

DAY TWO

If you can predict that the dog will look at you, say the dog's name first. When he looks at you, mark and treat. If you guessed wrong, and the dog didn't look at you after you've said his name, you've set yourself back a tiny step. Do not assume that the dog understands the relatively sophisticated concept of an individual's name. You will be teaching the dog that hearing his name is an opportunity to get a reward if he chooses the right action - looking at you.

If he didn't look at you, immediately go back to rewarding him for looking at you for as many times as you can in a minute. Now you will probably be better at predicting when the next eye contact will come.

Continue to notice anytime the dog looks at you during the day. Mark and reward each time.

Try to have 100 successful repetitions of dog's name, the dog looking at you, and mark and treat.

DAY THREE

Take the dog to a place that is interesting and potentially distracting, such as a friend's home, public park or post office. Move away from the interesting activities. Go far enough away so the dog is able to work with you. As far as a block away may be the right distance for the dog.

Wait for the dog to look at you. When he does, mark and treat, then celebrate. Is he still looking at you? Mark and treat again. Do your one-minute round of rewarding eye contact. If you can predict when the dog will look at you, use the dog's name before he looks. Reinforce all attention and eye contact.

By waiting until the dog looks at you rather than trying to get the dog's attention, you teach the dog to **choose** to give his attention. We also call this the Look Back. Patience will pay off because you will have a partner who checks in with you on his own. *(See* **VOLUNTARY LOOK BACK** *page* 191.)

For safety and control of the dog's training environment, the dog should be on a drag line. But your goal is to get the dog to look at you even when there is no drag line so don't use the drag line to get his attention. It's there for safety not for getting the dog's attention. The cue to look at you should be his name and not a tug on his collar. If you have a hard time handling a drag line, clicker and treats, drop the drag line on the ground and stand on it.

Throughout the day, mark and reward each time the dog looks back at you.

Add a good game of fetch after the training session.

DAY FOUR

Return to the place of distractions to the distance where you were previously successful. Practice one minute of rewarding attention. If you are able to reward as many times in one minute as you could at home, move a few feet closer to the interesting activities. If not, then stay at this place or move a bit further away. Practice another minute of reward. If all is going as planned and you are able to predict that the dog will look at you, say his name just before he looks.

Studies show that dogs need to hear a cue paired with a rewarded action 30 to 50 times before they make a strong association between the cue and the action that earned the reward. Every time you say the dog's name and he responds by looking at you you are successfully conditioning the dog's attention response to his name. Every time you say the dog's name and he doesn't look at you, you're conditioning the dog to ignore (not respond to) his name.

If another dog or other distraction comes too close for the dog to ignore, either wait until it's passed and the dog turns his attention back to you or move a few feet away. Move away by moving backward so that your dog ends up facing you.

In addition to these exercises, mark and reward the dog for looking at you at anytime during the day. Verbally reinforce with a happy voice and smile.

Note: Don't ever use someone else calling the dog's name as a distraction during any training!

DAY FIVE

Return to the place of distractions. Warm the dog into the exercise by rewarding attention at a distance from the distractions. Then move gradually to the closest distance where you were last successful, stopping occasionally and working him as you go. Practice a one-minute round of rewarding the Look Back while continuing to move closer to distractions. Add the dog's name if and when you can predict him looking back at you. Move calmly away if the distractions become overwhelming.

Continue to mark and reward the dog for looking at you at anytime during the day and add a good game of fetch after the training sessions.

DAY SIX

Repeat the exercises from Day Five.

Move a little closer, allowing the dog to notice the activities then immediately call his name and move backward excitedly. As soon as he turns toward you, click and treat. Reward him several more times for looking at you.

Repeat this as many times as you can in five minutes.

DAY SEVEN

Repeat the exercises from Day Six, gradually moving closer to the distractions.

You have now spent a few minutes each day building up a history of rewarding the dog for looking at you even around some attractive distractions. If you've managed to mark and reward the dog's attention over 100 times each day you should be nearing 1000 successes already! This is the foundation for strong attention. You may need to continue this training and refresh it by occasionally rewarding attention especially in highly distracting situations throughout the dog's life.

Remember a good game of fetch after the training sessions helps the bonding process!

RECALL GAMES

If you train the recall as a game, and if you make it the best game the dog ever plays, "come" will always signal the best in your relationship with your dog.

A reliable recall means "come as fast as you can to me, no matter where you are and what you are doing". These exercises teach the dog a reliable recall.

PROCESS

There are hundreds of variations to teach recalls. Here are a few that I use:

GAME 1: REWARD THE RECALL

Anytime the dog is actually doing the recall behavior on his own (running at top speed toward you) call out the cue word "come". Do not call "come" when the dog is standing there just about to come; ONLY CALL WHEN THE DOG IS ACTUALLY ENGAGED IN THE ACT OF RUNNING TO YOU. When the dog gets to you, click and treat and have a really good round of play so the dog remembers how wonderful it was to come to you.

GAME 2: THE BACK AND FORTH RECALL GAME

Have two people (later three or more can play) sit facing each other on the floor with the dog in the middle. Each person should click and treat every time the dog comes running toward them. Once the dog catches onto the game each person can begin to say the cue word "come" when the dog is running toward them. Don't use "come" to get the dog's attention. If you need to get the dog's attention, use his name. Raise the criteria by having the people stand rather than sit, then add more people and gradually make the circle bigger. Raise your criteria again by having the people call the dog one at a time and only reinforce (click and treat) when the dog moves toward them after being called.

GAME 3: THE OPPOSITION REFLEX

Before starting this exercise, the dog must understand that the cue "come" means running fast toward you. Have someone hold the dog (preferably by crouching behind the dog and wrapping their arms around his chest) so the dog is facing you. Tease the dog with food or a toy, rousing the dog's interest in you. Turn and run about 20 feet away. Look back over your shoulder and call "come". Use a really positive, strong, excited call. The dog should be released just after the cue is called. As the dog moves toward you, move away to help entice him to come faster. Reinforce verbally and give a jackpot reward (of praise, play and/or food) when the dog arrives. Use all your reward tools to keep the dog focused on you for 15 to 30 seconds. Repeat this sequence once or twice more.

PRACTICAL TIPS

▶ Do not test your recall until you have practiced many repetitions. Be sure you practice the opposition reflex recall in distracting situations before using the cue without the agitation of being held and lured.

▶ Never use the recall cue in situations the dog may find aversive. For example, crating, clipping nails or grooming. If you need to get the dog to do these things attract him to you and spend 5 minutes playing. When finished playing, ask him to sit or down. Clip on a leash where you were playing and then proceed with what you need to do (crate, groom, etc.). This way the dog is rewarded for coming to you and won't connect coming with something aversive.

RECALL FROM DISTRACTIONS

This exercise builds a bombproof recall for those times when the dog is moving away from you and there are distractions present. The objective is to train the dog to run away from you at top speed and then to turn on a dime and run toward you when you give the recall cue.

PREREQUISITES

Before beginning this exercise, teach the dog to enjoy retrieving a ball or other toy.

PREPARATION

Have a helper, a pouch of yummy treats, a ball or toy and a hungry dog. For this exercise, a ball is used as the example for this exercise, but another toy can be substituted.

Set up the training situation so you have complete control over distractions.

PROCESS

Have a helper stand 30 or 40 feet away. Aim the ball to land near the helper. The instant the ball leaves your hand, call out "<dog's name> come!". If the dog turns toward you, click and back up several steps as quickly as possible creating even more distance between you and the ball. If the dog follows you instead of chasing the ball, when he reaches you feed him generously for a full 60 seconds. Talk to him while you feed, praising "*Oh what a good dog. I'm so glad you stayed with me!*" and so on. If you have a second ball, toss it once you have done the 60 second praise party with food.

If the dog ignores the recall cue and continues toward the thrown object, the helper picks up the ball and ignores the dog. When the dog eventually gives up trying to get the ball and returns to you, praise him lavishly but don't feed. Once the dog begins to respond to recall off of the thrown ball, begin mixing in occasional tosses where you throw the ball but don't call him off of it and allow him to fetch and retrieve. This way the dog will retain his enthusiasm for retrieving.

When you can successfully alternate trials of fetch and recall (come back to me rather than fetch) you can increase the difficulty of the recall by increasing the distance or pausing a few seconds between throwing the ball and calling the dog (letting the dog get closer to the ball before being called off). If he fails to respond to the recall cue, have your helper pick up the ball as usual so that the dog is never rewarded for ignoring the recall cue.

Gradually shape this recall behavior so you can call the dog even when he's so close to the ball he can almost grab it.

Practical Tips

▶ If your aim is poor, use an object that doesn't roll such as a squeaky toy or Frisbee.

▶ If the dog isn't toy motivated, throw a chunk of food that will show up against the ground, such as a piece of bagel, tortellini or cheese.

▶ In the early stages of training, click at the very the moment the dog turns away from the ball (or toy or food). Don't wait until the dog returns all the way to you.

▶ Once the dog is fluent at switching directions in the middle of a predatory-type chase, set up the situation so the object of distraction is more like real life. For example, have your helper ride a bike if the dog is a bike-chaser or have a dog friendly dog (or a very brave cat) with the helper.

▶ Teaching the dog not to chase moving objects such as critters, cars, bikes or joggers, is best handled first as a management issue. Management means "don't put the dog in a position where he can make a mistake". Chasing is naturally reinforcing for many dogs, which makes it hard for us to offer a better reinforcement. Therefore, chasing moving objects (other than you, when recalled) is a behavior best not learned and best not practiced. Do not set the dog up to fail, and don't allow him to rehearse the problem behavior. Do not let the dog off lead if you don't have control of the distractions. Use a drag line until the dog is desensitized to distractions and knows that listening to you means a great reinforcement.

RECALL USING PREMACK

This exercise is for dogs that love to chase things, such as critters and who can't hear you call when they get into "chase mode". This exercise is not for dogs that aggressively chase or charge at people. This exercise teaches the dog to come to you in order to be released to run or play. (*See page 20 for more about the Premack Principle*)

PREREQUISITES

Before beginning this exercise, teach the dog attention.

PREPARATION

Have a pouch of yummy treats, and a hungry dog on a drag line. Note: A harness is safer than a collar for this exercise, in case you accidentally stop the dog suddenly when using the drag line.

PROCESS

Step 1:   Allow the dog to run free, with the drag line dragging on the ground. When the dog is no further than 10 feet (3m) away, ask for the recall. If the dog responds successfully, praise and release him (this is his reward). If the dog does not stop, use the drag line to slow him down, then stop him. Don't stop the dog suddenly; this is a positive training exercise, so punishment should be avoided. The call must be timed at least 6 feet (2m) before the end of the line to avoid the risk of the dog hitting the end. You can tie a small knot that you can feel before this point so you know when the end of the line is coming close.

Step 2:   Increase the recall distance. Continue until the dog can be in full pursuit, yet be called off and come back to you.

Step 3:   Once the dog is fluent with the recall, add another off-lead dog as a distraction. Because you have increased the distraction level, reduce the recall distance. Gradually increase the recall distance as the dog progresses.

Step 4:   Continue this training until the dog flies toward you on the recall even when other dogs are going in the other direction.

Step 5:   Once the dog has a solid recall, even with distractions, gradually reduce the length of the drag line, repeating these steps. Shorten it by 2-4 foot intervals before removing it altogether.

With repetition, the dog will come to believe that to be able to run into the woods, she will need to return to YOU first. It will take a lot of practice to achieve this new behavior, so be patient and encouraging. Repeat this exercise throughout the dog's active life.

RETRIEVE GAMES

This exercise teaches the dog to go out, pick up an article that you've thrown, and bring it back to you.

PREPARATION

Have a pouch of yummy treats, and a hungry dog on leash. You can teach retrieve games while you relax or even while you watch TV.

PROCESS

Offer the dog a toy. As he mouths or sniffs it, say "fetch". Reward him with praise or a treat. When he consistently touches the toy with his nose or snout on the " fetch" cue, offer it with the cue but don't reward him. He will expect a reward, so when you give the cue again (straight away) he will be a bit keener; he will probably knock the toy with his nose or even take hold of it with his mouth. This is the behavior that earns the reward.

Only increase the criteria when you have 100% response to the current behavior. By very slowly raising the criteria in this way, the dog will go from sniffing to nosing to taking hold of the toy in his mouth.

Once the dog is taking the toy in his mouth, drop the toy and give the cue "fetch". If the dog does not pick up the toy, return to the previous level (holding the toy and letting the dog take it in his mouth). If the dog picks up the toy, praise and reward with play or a treat. You can then begin to drop the toy slightly further away, backing up as you call the dog, to encourage him to bring it back to you. Reward the dog for bringing it to you, even a few steps. Give plenty of praise and fuss once you have the toy so it's clear the praise is for fetching the toy back to you, not just for picking it up.

There are toys on the market with Velcro pouches to hold treats and handles for this type of game.

SCENT GAMES

Dogs naturally enjoy scenting. This exercise teaches the dog to use his nose to find things such as toys, food, and people.

PREPARATION

Have a toy, pouch of yummy treats, and a hungry dog.

Practice in an enclosed or fenced-off area until the dog has a solid recall.

PROCESS

GAME 1: TRACK IT

Have the dog out of the way (in a down-stay, a crate, or a fenced-off area) while you lay a "track". The track will consist of tiny food treats laid out in a line and spaced about 3 inches apart. Escort the dog to the start of the track. Use a cue, such as "track it", and show each morsel to the dog.

As he catches on to the game, make the morsel track longer and the spacing further apart.

As extra incentive place the dog's favorite toy at the end of the track. When he picks up the toy, praise and run backward using his name and the word "bring". This will develop attention and retrieve.

Have food or a second toy in your pocket and exchange this for the toy in the dog's mouth, using the word "give".

GAME 2: SEARCH AND RESCUE

Have a helper restrain the dog by kneeling on the ground and holding their arms around the dog. Tease the dog by showing him a toy in your hand, moving the toy around and tossing it in the air a couple of times. Then run straight away from the dog 50 feet or so. Drop flat to the ground and lie still.

The helper should continue to restrain the dog while you run away, encouraging the dog the watch you and using a cue such as "watch".

Once you have dropped to the ground and are laying still, the helper releases the dog saying "Find". When the dog gets to you, play with him with the toy. Repeat several times, then swap places with the helper (the helper runs away while you hold the dog).

GAME 3: FIND IT

This is a really wonderful teaching game. It will help you develop a dog with self-control and rock solid stays. You can use food or toys, whichever is high value to the dog.

Have someone hold the dog's leash. Secure the leash to a solid object (such as a tie-down) or ask the dog to sit-stay. Show the dog that you have an item he wants. Place the item on the ground in front of the dog far enough away from him so he will have to move to get it. Walk back to the dog and take control of the leash.

When the dog stops pulling to get the desired item, say "find it" and let go of the leash. When the dog gets the item, say "yes" and offer praise and play.

Bring the dog back to the spot where he is required to wait and start again. This time, place the item a little further away. Gradually increasing the distance will build the dog's sit-stay as well as building the game from a visual search into a scent-driven search.

As training progresses and the dog begins to enjoy the exercise, begin to ask the dog for a more solid stay. Don't let the dog get the item if he breaks from the stay. Ask him to sit and wait a moment before allowing him to get the item.

PRACTICAL TIPS

Raise criteria slowly. Don't make the scent games too hard too soon. If the dog can't find the item, help him by getting your body near the hidden object. Letting the dog successfully problem-solve will build his confidence. Confusion and failure will reduce his confidence, so let the dog win the game!

SELF-CONTROL WITH DISTRACTIONS

Self-control cannot be imposed on any animal. It develops when the individual sees the positive benefit coming to them by waiting rather than acting on impulse.

Practicing with distractions of increasing appeal will teach the dog self-control. He will begin to understand that when he shows self-control, he is much more likely to get what he wants.

This exercise teaches the dog to stroll alongside you even when surrounded by distractions.

PREPARATION

Have a handful of yummy treats, a hungry dog and an enclosed backyard or fenced area. Practice only with distractions that the dog can tolerate.

PROCESS

Step 1: Place something the dog wants on the ground about 20 feet away from you. It should be something he really wants, such as his ball or favorite toy, food dish with something yummy in it, or another dog in a fenced in area. Start walking toward the distraction. If the dog pulls on the leash, back up and guide him to your side. Walk in another direction if needed but don't continue to walk toward the distraction while the dog is pulling on the leash. The dog is allowed to be a foot or so ahead of you but the leash should be slack.

Step 2: Click and treat the dog for all good behavior as you begin to practice with distractions. If the dog hasn't learned that self-control works, show him that the effort to ignore the distraction will be noticed and rewarded. Each time you practice, the dog should improve. If not, the distraction level is too difficult. Add distance or choose something slightly less distracting to help the dog succeed.

Step 3:   Once the dog can walk by the distraction without pulling, the best reward is to allow the dog to have what he wanted when he expressed self-control. Have the dog sit a few feet away, waiting a moment. Then give him the toy and play for a while, or let him eat the food, or allow him to play with his doggie friend. These are the ultimate jackpots! They teach the dog that self-control leads to what he wants.

SETTLE: RELAXED DOWN ON LEASH

GOAL

The dog can maintain a quiet relaxed down position next to you while you sit, stand, work or talk with others. The relaxed position has the dog lying over on one hip, not in a crouched down, and with no tension on the leash. The dog will learn that she can relax and be attentive without needing to interact.

Note: Because we are looking for a calm, off duty-but watchful behavior, instead of marking the right position with your clicker, you will quietly say "good" and then, as you see the duration lengthen give the food to the dog while they are in position. This is the beginning of more self-control taking shape.

For several days before you start this exercise, be sure you have been using a good food treat to lure the dog into the Relaxed Down position. As you lure with food you might also need to place two fingers in the dog's collar, putting slight pressure downward.

PURPOSE

We are looking for a dog to yield to the pressure on the back of his neck, so that if the dog ever gets stuck by its collar, he will stop struggling and just lie down quietly. I have had two dogs over the years become stuck by their collars and fortunately they knew this exercise and did not panic, but waited patiently for me to help them.

This also teaches huge self-control on the dog's part in all situations.

1.   Clip the leash to the dog's buckle collar and place your foot on the leash shortening the length of the leash so that the dog only has a few feet to move around. You may sit in a chair if you can still maintain pressure on the leash with your foot. You are limiting the dog's movement and options so that lying down will be the most logical position. Place a mat on the floor for the dog to help him think about lying down.

Think of this as a puzzle to solve. If no distractions are around, you may give the dog a bit more length of leash and quietly wait for the dog to become bored and think about lying down and settling. BE PATIENT. Give the dog as much time as he/she may need to figure out how to be comfortable. If you are in too distracting an environment, ask someone to set something up to block out the stimulus or move to a new location. You are not forcing the dog down. This should not be stressful.

You are setting up a situation that the dog will solve by lying down. Do not give the dog any cues. Be very calm & relaxed. The moment the dog lies down and relaxes his muscles say "yes" and treat and step off the leash.

PROBLEM SOLVING

If the dog is sitting or standing but won't lie down even after waiting 4-5 minutes, take a treat and lure him to the ground. As soon as the dog goes down, say "yes" and treat. As you give the dog the treat, make sure you look at his position. If he is lying so he looks as t hough he is ready to spring back up, then you need to take the treat close to one elbow and slowly move it back towards the dogs belly staying very close to the body and ground. If the dog stands up, you have gone too fast, so try again. You want to reinforce the dog when he is lying flipped over on to one hip. This is the relaxed position we are looking for.

2. When you have done step #1 enough times so that the dog immediately lies down when you begin to place your foot on the leash you are ready to lengthen the time the dog stays down. Now wait for 5 seconds after the dog is down before the "yes" and treat. Remember that the dog can get up after the "yes". Each time you will add just a few more seconds to the time the dog remains down before the "yes" and treat. Make sure you vary the times from shorter to a longer time. (Don't always increase the time frame or the dog will quit.) You are working up to 10-15 minutes or until the dog goes to sleep.

3. When the dog is able to lay quietly next to you with no pressure on leash, begin to ask the dog to "relax" as you are putting your foot on the leash. Use the dog's name first to get his attention and when you have eye contact, step on the leash and say, "relax". "Yes" and treat when he is down and settled quietly.

4. Now get the dog's attention by saying his name, say "relax" smile, maintain eye contact and give the dog a few seconds to process the request. If he doesn't go down, simply put your foot on the leash and "yes" and treat when he is down, calm and settled. Don't say "relax" again. It's the dog's job to listen. "Yes" and treat. From now on, each time you want the relaxed down, say the "relax" cue and wait briefly to see if he acts before putting your foot on the leash. Now wait for a few seconds, taking your foot OFF the leash and then say "Yes" and treat for staying down, relaxed and calm. Start working on the 4 D's (*see Learning, chapter 2).* Do not lose your patience. If you remain matter of fact, you will see the moment the dog thinks, "Oh, I know how to do this". Whenever the dog avoids responding to a distraction during the relaxed down, say "yes" and treat. Let the dog know that you will reward good choices. Be alert for those times when the dog is relaxing quietly, looking around, being quietly watchful - reach down quietly and give a treat - this is exactly what you want him doing!

SHAPED RELAXED DOWN

The relaxed down teaches self-control. The dog learns that he can quietly, calmly be with you. He can watch and wait. He doesn't always have to act. It teaches the dog that he can comfortably and safely wait next to you while exciting things go on around him. A self-controlled, calm watchfulness allows the dog to learn and exercise judgment.

This exercise teaches the dog a quiet, "relaxed" long down position, with no tension on leash, while you relax or chat with others. The dog can relax and be watchful of everything going on around him, without needing to interact.

PREREQUISITES

Before beginning this exercise, teach the dog the "down" cue.

PREPARATION

Have a chair, a rug or mat, a pouch of yummy treats, and a hungry dog on a long leash.

PROCESS

Step 1:   Sit in a chair with the rug or mat on the floor next to you. Click and treat any interaction the dog has with the rug (one paw, pushing with nose, standing on it, etc.). Only click these behaviors 2 or 3 times before the dog has to offer you something that gets him more onto the rug. You are working toward a sit or down on the mat. Once the dog lays down on the mat, jackpot and end the session.

Step 2:   At the next training session, put the rug on the floor and wait. When he lies down, click and treat. If the dog doesn't remember the down on the rug, click and treat the best the dog will offer, and work toward the down.

Step 3:   Once the dog is giving you the down on the rug, begin to wait for 5-10 seconds before click and treat.

Step 4:   Once you are certain the dog will lie down on the rug as soon as he sees it, put the behavior on the verbal cue "relax". Say "relax" and wait for the behavior. Click and treat.

Step 5:   Once the behavior is on verbal cue, begin to fade the click and treat. Use your voice praise to continually reinforce the dog's quiet watchfulness. Work toward longer periods of relaxing on the mat while watching TV or eating.

Step 6:   Work "relax" in many locations and then begin to ask for it without the rug.

Step 7:   Once the dog can be quiet and watchful without any pressure on the leash, begin to practice "relax" in increasingly distracting situations. Go into town and do a "Relax" on leash outside a store. Until the dog can stay in the "relax" position, no one should be patting or talking to the dog. Ask people to ignore the dog but to talk with you.

Step 8:   Let family, friends and strangers pat the dog briefly while in the "relax". Re-cue the position if the dog moves or gets up. Don't let anyone, particularly children, distract the dog from the quiet, calm watchfulness of "relax". Avoid allowing the dog to play (with children, etc.) while in the "relax" position, since you are teaching the dog to relax.

PRACTICAL TIPS

If the dog is sitting or standing but won't lie down, even after waiting 2-3 minutes, lure him to the ground using a treat. As soon as the dog goes down, say "yes" and treat. As you give the dog the treat make sure you look at his position. If he is lying so he looks as though he is ready to leap up, take the treat close to one elbow and slowly move it back towards the dog's belly, staying very close to the body. If the dog stands up, you have gone too fast. Reinforce the dog when he is lying on his side. This is the relaxed position we are looking for.

SIDE BY SIDE WALKING

Face to face meetings with other dogs are difficult for dogs and are especially difficult for insecure dogs. Instead of meeting face to face, join other dog handlers and walk together side by side. Side by side walking allows the dogs to give each other as much or as little attention as they are comfortable with.

This exercise teaches the dog the skill of walking calmly alongside another dog on leash.

PREREQUISITES

Foundation skills, such as attention and loose leash walking, should be perfected before beginning this exercise.

If the dog is fearful of other dogs, he should first be counter conditioned. (*See* **COUNTER CONDITIONING FEAR OR AGGRESSION** *page* 130.) This is no small issue and counter conditioning can take quite a while to accomplish.

PREPARATION

Have a pouch of yummy treats, and a hungry dog on leash.

PROCESS

Choose a place with some space so you can walk in the same direction side by side. Leave some room between you, perhaps by placing the handlers between the dogs to create a "barrier". Let the dogs' bodies tell you what they can tolerate.

Continuously observe the dogs to make sure they are comfortable. If they appear uncomfortable, increase the barrier and distance to help them relax. If either dog becomes over stimulated, you are progressing too fast.

As you walk, notice how the dogs begin to accept each other as being no threat. In fact, this non-confrontational position allows them to become interested in each other. As the dogs relax, move one handler to the outside, leaving only one handler between the dogs. If the dogs are comfortable, move both handlers to the outside, with the dogs in the middle. If the dogs are still relaxed, decrease the distance between them. If all goes well, at the end of the walk you can separate a short distance and then meet and walk around each other in a curving or arcing pattern allowing the dogs to meet as they naturally prefer.

SIT

Sit is a good alternative behavior to many undesired behaviors. For example: sit instead of jumping up, or sit instead of chasing.

PREPARATION

Have a dish or pouch of yummy treats, and a hungry dog.

Have dog on drag line so if he tries to walk away you can stand on the drag line and wait for him to return. Don't chase him. Let him return to you, reward his return, and continue the exercise.

PROCESS

Step 1: Get the dog's attention by standing (for a large dog) or kneeling (for a small dog or puppy) in front of him. Hold food directly in front of the dog's nose and move it back over the dog's head. This "lure" will cause the dog's head to bend upward and back, so that the dog's rear has to move downward. Don't raise food way above the dog's head, or he might try to stand or jump to reach it. Let him nibble at your hand if you need to. As he begins to sit, click and give the dog the treat. Walk over to a dish with treats and reward again or toss a treat to get the dog to stand in preparation for another sit.

Start again reinforcing for a little higher criteria of the sit position, such as bottom closer to the ground. Repeat 5-10 times. Stop luring after the first few times. Instead, wait for any movement the dog offers toward sitting and mark and reward that behavior. The dog will learn faster and be more eager to train if you allow him to autonomously offer the behavior that makes you click.

Step 2: Once the dog is offering sits if you were kneeling, stand up. If you were standing, change your position in relation to the dog. Wait for sit. Standing in a different position changes the picture for the dog, so he may not understand he should offer a sit. If he doesn't offer a sit, lure one and reinforce it with a click and treat. Don't hesitate to lower the criteria whenever you change any part of the behavior shaping. If the dog seems confused, click and treat any movement toward your goal and gradually build toward the full sit again.

Step 3: Once the dog is performing the sit fluently even when you change position in relation to him, add the cue "sit". Say "sit" as the dog is doing the behavior. This ensures the dog always performs the behavior on cue, and is reinforced, so begins to associate the cue with the rewarded behavior. Repeat 20-30 times over several training sessions. Then begin to give the cue "sit" before the behavior begins. If the dog doesn't sit immediately, give him a chance to think. If he still doesn't offer a sit, he is not ready to learn the cue. Reward him (it's your error, not his) and return to cueing as the "sit" behavior is happening.

Step 4: Change where you practice sits. Begin to use variable reinforcement by clicking and treating for one sit, then three, then one, then two, then four, then three, gradually increasing the number of sits for one treat, but keeping it variable. Occasionally, reach out and hold the dog's collar before you click and treat, to teach the dog not to pull away when you reach for his collar. Lengthen the time between the sit and the click. Jackpot particularly quick sits.

SIT FOR GREETING

The "sit for greeting" exercise teaches the dog socially acceptable behavior when meeting and greeting people.

PREREQUISITES

Before beginning this exercise, teach the dog the "sit" exercise.

PREPARATION

Have a pouch of yummy treats, and a hungry dog on leash. Recruit a helper.

PROCESS

Step 1:   Hold the leash tightly near your waist so the dog can't pull forward and jump up. Have the helper approach the dog. If the dog jumps up toward helper, they should step back to prevent any contact. The helper should move forward whenever the dog is settled and step back whenever the dog doesn't stay settled. Once the helper can move close to dog without the dog jumping up, ask the dog to sit and have the helper lure the dog into a sit. When the dog sits, click and the helper treats dog and walks past. Repeat this many times with different helpers coming from different directions.

Step 2:   Repeat this exercise at the front door. Have a helper knock or ring the bell and enter one at a time, using food to lure a sit. Have the helper go out the back door and come around again to repeat the sequence. For an excitable dog, use a drag line. Before you open the door step on the leash so the dog is unable to jump.

Step 3:   On walks ask the dog to sit as strangers approach. Click and treat the sit as the stragers pass.

STAY USING THE BODY BLOCK

This exercise teaches the dog to wait and hold his position.

PREREQUISITES

Before beginning this exercise, you need to have trained a good sit.

PREPARATION

Have a pouch of yummy treats, and a hungry dog on leash.

PROCESS

Step 1:   Have the dog on leash, leaving about 6"of slack. Have a big treat (about ¾ inch in diameter) in your hand. Stand facing the dog with a chair (or, for a little dog, a footstool or upturned box) placed slightly behind you.

Step 2:   Take the treat and place it on the chair seat or footstool. Show the dog what you are doing but stay between the dog and the treat. Be balanced and mentally prepared to body block the dog if he thinks about going for the treat. You will not allow him to get the treat. You may need to move back and forth if he tries to duck around you. If he does get by you use the leash to prevent him from getting the food. If you allow him to get the treat you, have reinforced him for breaking the stay. As soon as the dog stops trying to get the food, even for a brief pause, ask him to sit. When the dog sits, pick up the treat and give it to him.

Step 3:   Repeat the exercise. Gradually increase the criteria until the dog is giving you eye contact (taking his eyes off the treat) and sitting before you release and reward him.

Step 4:   Once the dog sits and waits dependably when you put the treat on the chair, move the chair a little further away. Walk out, place the treat and walk back. If the dog moves out of the sit, use a body block to prevent the dog from getting the treat. You may only need to lean toward the dog or raise your hand, palm facing the dog, to block. If the dog stays sitting, pick up the treat and give it to him.

Step 5:   Gradually stop using the chair. Give the "stay" cue and walk away from the dog. Only go as far as the dog can tolerate without moving and then return. Reinforce when you are standing next to the dog. Be interesting and variable. Sometimes use petting as a reward, sometimes praise only, sometimes treats and praise, sometimes go back to putting treats on the chair. Always be ready to block any attempt to move with your body by moving, leaning forward or using your hand.

Step 6:   Give the "stay" cue and walk out in different directions and return. When the dog is staying dependably in a quiet area, begin to add distractions such as other pets, children, doorbells, toys and anything else you can think of. When you introduce distractions, use higher-level reinforcements and reduce your distance from the dog. In other words, keep the exercise successful so the dog can be reinforced for staying in position. Watch the dog's body language so you can identify when you are too far away for him to hold position before he breaks. Train to succeed, not to fail. If the dog moves, you probably didn't watch carefully enough.

Step 7:   Once you have given the "stay" cue 20 or more times, then you can start asking for "stay" and move around. If the dog gets up, help it get back in 'stay' position with a hand signal into the sit position. You always go back to the dog and give the treat at this point and you are no longer tossing a treat out!

TAKING TREATS POLITELY

This exercise is a variation on "Airplane and Hanger", the game played with infants during feeding time. This exercise teaches patience and self-control.

PREPARATION

Have a pouch of yummy treats, and a hungry dog.

Train in an area where there are no distractions, such as in a quiet house with no other people, dogs, cats, etc. around.

PROCESS

Begin with the dog sitting in front of you. Hold a treat above the dog's head and bring it down slowly to his mouth. If the dog attempts to strain by stretching or reaching up to grab the food from your hand, or if he opens his mouth, immediately pull your hand back up over his head.

The analogy is that the airplane is trying to land and then taxi into the hanger but notices that there are people walking around on the ground close to the landing field and hanger so the pilot must pull up quickly. To land the plane (give the dog the treat) the pilot is waiting for the door to close (dog's mouth must be closed) and the dog's position is relaxed and not moving forward.

The goal of the game is to teach the dog that patience is the only way to get the airplane to land (the treat in his mouth). The quick movement of your hand moving away when the dog moves for the food will teach him to close his mouth and wait rather than lunge for the treat. As the dog becomes proficient, you can then bring your hand to the dog from different angles and at different speeds.

In addition to the airplane and hanger game, teach the dog to take food gently from your hand. To do this, place a treat in your fist and let the dog smell your fist. Present your fist with the treat in front of the dog's nose. If he starts to bite and mouth your hand, say "OUCH!" and freeze your hand movement with your fist still closed. When the dog removes his mouth or licks your hand, say "Good. Take it." and slowly open your hand with your palm facing up so the dog can take the treat. Repeat this procedure until the dog stops biting and nibbling your hand. Repeat this at least 20 times a day for at least 2 weeks.

PRACTICAL TIPS

If the dog is over-excited, use lower-value treats.

Politeness around food is terrifically important safety training. If you are consistent and do not allow the dog to get treats unless they are taken in a polite manner, you will be well on your way to having a dog who will not hurt a child with food all over his face or a cookie in his hand.

TEACHING TOY MOTIVATION

For dogs that are crazy for treats but unmotivated by toys, teach toy motivation by combining toy play with food.

Take an old athletic sock and fill the toe with a fist-sized piece of Rollover, baked liver, prime rib, or the dog's favorite treats. Put a rubber band around the opening and attach a 3-6 foot lightweight rope.

Entice the dog into playing tug with the food-sock by making it the most exciting toy the dog has ever seen. If the dog is still uninterested, put the food-sock where the dog can see it but can't have it, such as on top of a shelf or hung from the ceiling. At the time of the day when the dog is most likely to be excited to see you such as when you first get up in the morning, at dinner time, when you come home from work, make a huge commotion while getting the sock from its resting place. I use "I'm going to get it" and sort of sneak over to it, then I grab it and RUN...

Play with it yourself for a while. Give it a name, like "special" (a la John Rogerson, the great English dog behaviorist and originator of this toy game) and make goo-goo eyes and sounds over it. Be animated. Toss it in the air. Make it dance like a small animal around your shoulders. Make it jump around your legs. Drag it around and tease the dog with the attached rope. Let the dog see it and become interested in it, but don't let him have it.

After a few days of keep-away, the dog should be spending an inordinate amount of time mooning over the sock's hideaway location, staring at it for hours, praying you'll come and get it down to tease him with it. Once in a while, as you pass the sock's hideout, point it out to the dog, saying "do you want special?" but do not get it out. Expect claw marks on furniture and walls if you put it just out of his reach. This means you are succeeding!

After you've hit the desired pitch of frenzy, occasionally let the dog catch hold of the toy. When he does, play a wild tug game.

In the beginning, don't control the play too much. Trick him to get it out of his mouth. Swap it for a treat, or point to the floor and say "what's that?" When he looks away and loosens his grip, take the toy away and say "I got it!" I know this is sneaky but it will drive him crazy for the toy and that's just what we want!

Then start the keep-away game again. Ask him where "special" is in that tone of voice that makes him go wild.

Let him get a taste of the "innards" once in a while by making a huge deal over opening the sock and letting him try to gnaw off a small hunk of the food while you hold the sock open, or palm a treat of the same variety as inside (give him the good stuff, no tricks at this point!).

When the dog will play with it madly at home, take the food-sock outside, then down the street, then to the park, and so on. After he will play elsewhere away from home, practice and use it like a ball, for a game of fetch and tug.

Work on introducing the food-sock after attention games and when going to new places.

Hide the food-sock behind your back, and have a friend take it without the dog seeing where it went. Then magically produce it at the end of your training session. Hide it in different places on your body: Under your arm, down your trousers, inside your own sock. Let it magically fall out at various times during training exercises. Be interesting and creative with this toy. For example, let the dog chase it down and "kill it" (give it a shake) or trot off with it as a prize.

I love using this toy to create wait, sit and stay self-control skills while I hide it.

Renew the food stuffing often so it won't spoil, or take the food out and store it in the refrigerator when not in use. If you are doing a good job, you will need to ask all your friends for their old socks, as the dog will begin to destroy food-socks in his enthusiastic play.

TUG GAMES

Tug is a great energy burner and a really motivating play reward. It is good exercise for both dog and handler.

Tug games don't make the dog a predator: He already is one. Tug is an outlet for his natural skills. It makes him feel good. Tug of war isn't a battle, it's a game of cooperation that takes two to play. Because it is cooperative and because it has rules that teach self-control, tug is a game that builds a strong play bond between dog and handler.

Any rough game playing must be played by clear rules. Because many dogs strongly desire a game of tug, it is a great reinforcer for learning amazing self-control. Dogs will work hard for what they want!

Tug provides the handler an opportunity to create an "on-off switch". The dog can rev up to the point of absolute frenzy complete with growling. Then, with one word, the handler can stop the dog in his tracks. The more the dog wants tug as the reinforcer, the faster you can teach the self-control behavior that allows the dog to get the game of tug he desires.

RULES

Tug is only played with a special toy that the handler provides. The dog never successfully initiates the tug game.

The dog waits for the tug while the handler holds it. A cue such as "ready" can be taught for the dog to watch the tug and maintain stillness and self-control. The handler should be able to carry the toy at the dog's eye level and never have the dog snatch it out of their hand.

The dog only touches the toy on a verbal cue, such as "get it".

Any touch of a tooth on skin or clothes ends the game instantly. No accidents are allowed. The dog is never excused because "he was too excited".

Never chase the dog to get the tug. Let the dog keep it. No release word, just immediate cessation of participation by the handler.

The game ends with a release word, such as "give". Once that word is spoken, the game ends whether or not the dog releases the toy. Again, immediate cessation of participation by the handler.

Teach the dog the rules through consistency and timing. If the dog releases the toy within the specific time frame of the "release" cue (up to 30 seconds at the beginning, gradually shortened to two seconds), he is guaranteed a delicious morsel and a new game of tug begins. If the dog doesn't release the toy, the handler lets go and leaves the room. It is impossible to play tug if no one will tug against you.

If you have one of those dogs who won't let go of the toy, be prepared with a yummy treat. While you both still have hold of the toy, let him smell the food. He will have to let go to eat. When he lets go, give him the morsel and praise him. Then say "get it" to start another game of tug. Play tug for a few seconds. Repeat (offer a treat, then play tug again).

By the fourth or fifth time, the dog will automatically let go of the tug in anticipation of the treat. Now, as you offer the food treat, attach the release word "give". Soon you will be able to say "give" before showing the food. Eventually, you will be able to say "give" without having to offer food. Make this transition slowly to ensure success.

Once the dog learns the rules of tug, the game can be used as a motivator. This type of reinforcement is so powerful it will help you gain split-second control of those hysterically prey-driven dogs without the necessity of correction. The dog is free to choose. If the dog wants the tug motivator more than anything else, and he can only get it by figuring out what behavior produces the tug. You can bet you will have a dog doing a lot of thinking.

VOLUNTARY (UNCUED) LOOK BACK

Dogs will bark, chase and bite things for entirely natural reasons. Some of those reasons are based in play/prey (learning to hunt) and some are fear based (feeling threatened by other dogs, people and situations). The voluntary look back teaches the dog to look to you on his own. With your leadership, the dog can develop the self-control to thoughtfully observe his environment, and look to you if he is uncertain how to react.

For the dog trained to look back, the default behavior when other dogs, children or scary things are present becomes looking at the handler instead of barking, growling or pulling on the lead.

This exercise teaches the dog to become a thoughtful observer instead of a barking reactor to new or scary situations, and to automatically look to you for leadership and reassurance.

Have a pouch of yummy treats and a hungry dog on lead.

If the dog's problem is dog-to-dog aggression, the training situation should be carefully set up. The unfamiliar dog (the "stimulus") must have a non-reactive temperament, be on lead, and be handled by a helper working under your instruction so you can maintain an acceptable distance between the dogs. Never stimulate a fearful dog into practicing fearful or aggressive behavior.

Set up the training so you arouse the dog only enough to give you the chance to reinforce the alternate behavior of looking toward you and away from the trigger stimulus.

Choose a calm, non-reactive dog (we call this a "stooge dog"). You must be 100% certain that the stooge dog will never become aroused or excited by the over reactive dog. Work the stooge dog with lots of other dogs before you ever work him with a reactive dog.

PROCESS

This example uses a helper and helper dog as the scary situation for the dog in training.

Stand at a distance from the helper. Have a handful of treats ready. The helper and dog should begin to move around, but should stay at a pre-planned distance. When the helper gets close enough to give the dog about 4 feet of play in the lead, wait for the dog to look back at you. Don't let the trigger stimulus get so close that the dog chooses to lunge or bark. The dog is likely to look back at you, if only to see why you aren't moving. The instant the dog checks in, mark with a click or the word "yes" and reinforce by hand feeding 15 tiny bits of treats, one at a time. If the dog is able to catch the treats, toss them gently to him. This keeps him focused on you so he won't miss catching a treat. If you feed from your hand, do so with the treat in your palm, palm open, so the dog licks at the treat instead of grabbing at your fingers.

While feeding, have a happy praise conversation with the dog for 10-15 seconds. Use your face and your voice, as well as the food, to keep the dog's attention on you and away from the trigger stimulus.

While you are feeding, the helper should quietly retreat.

Your goal is to see the dog look back at you, and to be able to stay focused on you for increasing duration, whether or not there are distractions. The dog will learn that self-control pays.

Once the dog is consistently checking in at the current distance, and is exercising self-control (he can watch but doesn't lunge, growl, or bark), you can begin to raise the level of distraction. Gradually decrease the distance, or change the location, of the trigger stimulus in relation to the dog. Create new situations, and reward the dog for looking back to you.

PRACTICAL TIPS

▶   Always set up the dog for success, not failure; never push beyond the dog's ability to choose you over the stimulus.

▶   Managing the dog so you are always present when the trigger stimulus is in sight is the most critical part of your training plan. You have to be there (physically and mentally), and the trigger stimulus must be under your control. For example, if the dog is obsessed with the cat, the dog must never have access to the cat unless you are there and prepared to reward for alternative behavior. When you are there training the dog to ignore the cat, the cat must be in a safe area. For example: have the cat in the arms of a helper or have a baby gate between the dog and the cat.

▶   For dogs with very high prey behavior or fear aggression, management and training is a lifelong pursuit. Reinforce the look back with food until the dog is fluent in the look back behavior. Over time, you can begin to use alternative types of reinforcement, such as a play or praise.

▶ You are training a behavior substitution. You will get improvement early, but it will be gradual. Be persistent and patient. Counter conditioning fear is a marathon, not a sprint. Do not expect permanent change for at least three to six months, perhaps longer.

▶ Good leaders are proactive. You must continuously anticipate what might trigger a reaction from the dog and intervene before the dog becomes over stimulated. This means you have the food and the energy to reinforce every act of self-control. Whenever you are with the dog, you always have part of your awareness focused on him, constantly reading changes in his posture that may indicate arousal.

This exercise was derived from Suzanne Clothier's 'Teaching the Auto-Check-in'.

WAIT AT DOORWAYS

This exercise teaches the dog to wait at the door before entering or exiting houses, kennels, cars, etc.

"Wait" means stop your forward progress and hold your current position until I release you to continue moving forward. You can use "wait" to have the dog wait politely while you go through doorways first. "Wait" is also a useful behavior in off-leash control. "Wait" is your invisible leash that lets you halt the dog for any safety reason. Wait teaches the dog that you go first. It is part of learning self-control.

I live on a dirt road in a rural area. The house is only 15 feet from a straight stretch of road, so cars tend to speed up as they pass. For safety, I have taught my dogs that they must sit and wait until I release them. I release them, one at a time, to go into or out of the house or car. This skill has been a lifesaver.

PREREQUISITES

Before beginning this exercise, teach the dog the "sit" and the "body block" exercises.

PREPARATION

Have a pouch of yummy treats, and a hungry dog on leash.

PROCESS

Step 1: Start by a closed door with the leash shortened up in your hand. Be prepared to step in front of the dog if he goes to move forward. Reach for the doorknob. If the dog moves toward the door, use a body block movement (step in front of him). When he stops, ask him to sit. If he doesn't sit when asked, step toward him again to move him back. When he either moves away or sits, say "yes" and reward him.

Step 2: Repeat the exercise. If the dog moves forward, say "back" and use the body block. Mark and reward the correct response. The dog should begin to learn to stay still or better yet, move away from the door.

Step 3:   Once the dog is sitting and waiting while you open the door completely, walk through the door and invite the dog out by turning your body sideways to him (so you are no longer blocking his path) and asking him to join you. Once he has learned to wait, the reward for waiting will be your release for him to go out.

Step 4:   For extra pushy dogs, have them go through the door in front of you and then ask for an attentive turn back to look at you and sit.

WAIT FOR PERMISSION GAMES

SIT/STAY OR DOWN/STAY OR STAND/STAY

How wonderful to have our dog believe that calmly "staying in position" is how to make the human give him what he wants (food, toy, play, or just going out the door)! In other words our job as trainers is to teach that holding position – not moving - is how to get the goodie gumball to drop into their paw.

PREREQUISITES

The dog in training must have an understanding of sit and stay and down and stay.

PROCESS

Cue the dog to sit, stand or down and hold a treat about 2 feet away from him. Position yourself so you are standing sideways with one shoulder pointing toward your dog. If your left shoulder is closest to the dog, hold the treat in the hand furthest from your dog-your right hand. Begin to slowly lower the treat straight down to the floor. If the dog moves or gets up as you lower the treat, you should say very matter-of-factly "TOO BAD" or "OOPS" (your No Reward Marker) and at the same time, move the treat away and out of the dog's reach.

Cue the dog to sit again and reposition yourself so that you are standing sideways. If the dog maintains position, then give the dog the treat - while he is in position. Bend down again and lower the treat and pull back with the treat until you can place the treat on the ground about 2 feet from the dog and the dog holds position.
(*See Food bowl game page 149*)
You want the dog to hold position AND to make eye contact before you lift the treat and move to your dog to give it him. Remember, we want the dog to realize that to get us to give them the treat they must:
▶ Hold position and
▶Look at us (not the food or toy)
When you have progressed to where you can put the treat on the ground, you are ready to start moving away from the dog in small steps while the treat is on the ground. Of course, you have to be ready to pick it up if the dog moves. This exercise develops duration of the holding position behavior. You can try this with a ball or toy too. Keep it fun, laugh at your dog when he tries to cheat, reinforce for good efforts.

PERMISSION TO MOVE GAME

Play this game in many places over the course of a week.

1. Stand facing your dog.
2. Hold the leash fairly tightly.
3. Take out 3 treats.
4. Give a treat saying "Take It."
5. Repeat again.
6. Now, saying nothing, toss the remaining treat right past your dog's ear to a spot on the floor behind him. If the dog moves to get it, take a step away saying, " OOPS! " Leave the treat and make sure your dog can't get to it.

Go back to the standing in front of your dog position, and take out 3 more treats.
Repeat 4-6. You are waiting for your dog to figure out that sitting and looking at you is how to get released. IF the dog holds the sit, you may then say "OK, Get IT"!
Continue to find ways and places to challenge your dog's duration and distraction skills.

WAIT OFF LEASH

This exercise teaches the dog to stop moving forward when asked to "wait", and hold position until you give a release cue. This exercise is useful for safe and socially acceptable behavior outdoors, off leash. For off leash work, this skill is trained differently from the doorway wait.

PREPARATION

Have a pouch of yummy treats, and a hungry dog on a drag line.

PROCESS

Step 1: Allow the dog to be loose, dragging the drag line, in a safe and non-distracting environment. Make sure the drag line stays within your reach throughout the exercise. When the dog is a fair distance from you, say "wait" and step on the drag line.

Step 2: Click the dog immediately when he stops his forward motion and turns to look at you. Allow the dog to hold the "wait" position by going to him to give him his reward, rather than encouraging him to come to you. Repeat the exercise 5-8 times.

Step 3: Once the dog is stopping immediately when you say "wait", test the cue. Don't step on the leash right away, wait to see if the dog will pause and look back. If he doesn't look back or stop, step on the leash. Mark and treat each pause.

WALKING PAST OTHER DOGS

Face to face meeting is rude for dogs, and is especially difficult for insecure dogs. Instead of meeting face to face, join other dog handlers and walk together side by side. Side by side walking allows the dogs to give each other as little attention as they are comfortable with.

This exercise teaches the dog the skill of walking calmly alongside another dog on leash.

PREREQUISITES

"Side by Side Walking" should be perfected before beginning this exercise.

If the dog is fearful of other dogs, he should first be counter conditioned. (*See* **COUNTER CONDITIONING FEAR OR AGGRESSION**, *page* 130.) This is no small issue and can take quite a while to accomplish.

PREPARATION

Have a pouch of yummy treats, and a hungry dog on leash.

PROCESS

Once the dog is comfortable walking next to another dog, practice other walking approaches. Set yourselves up as though you are going to duel, each dog/handler pair facing the other about 20 feet apart. The dogs should be either both on left sides, or on right sides, of the handlers. When the handlers pass each other, they should be on the inside, nearest each other, with the dogs on the outside. As the handlers move forward, they should continuously pop yummy treats into their dog's mouth, distracting the dogs so they do not look at one another.

As the handlers walk toward each other, they should click and treat their dog for looking up at them, for looking at other dog, and for any behavior that is non-reactive. The Bar is open (meaning lots of good things happen) while the dogs walk toward another dog. The Bar closes once the dog has gone past. This way, the dog will learn the association "walking toward another dog = yummy treats".

Once the dogs are comfortable walking toward each other, the handlers can stop as they near each other, sitting the dogs beside and a bit behind them. The handlers can greet each other briefly, then carry on walking past.

Once dogs are comfortable with the handlers greeting, the handlers can walk directly toward one another, clicking and treating the dog for looking at the handler, or for looking at other dog without reacting. When they are about 6 feet apart, each handler brings their dog from heel to front position, so each dog is facing his handler. Each handler then puts a treat in front of his dog's nose and walk backward to where he started. This exercise helps the dog learn that walking toward another dog is okay because pressure will be relieved at some point. If needed, the handlers can lure the whole sequence the first few times.

Appendix B

References
and
Resources

BOOKS

Brenda Aloff   *"Aggression in Dogs: Practical Management, Prevention & Behavior Modification"*, Dogwise Publishing

Brenda Aloff   *"Canine Body Language" A Photographic Guide*, Dogwise Publishing

Brenda Aloff   *"Get Connected With Your Dog"*, Dogwise Publishing

Bruce Fogle, DVM, MRCVS *"The Dog's Mind, Understanding Your Dog's Behavior"*, Howell Book House,

Dr. Michael W. Fox   *"Superdog: Raising the Perfect Canine Companion"*, Howell Books,

Gary Wilkes   *"Behavior Sampler"*, Sunshine Books

Gwen Bailey   *"The Perfect Puppy: How to Raise a Well-Behaved Dog"*, Readers Digest

James O'Heare   *"Aggression Workbook"*, DogPsych Publishing

James O'Heare   *"Separation Anxiety"*, DogPsych Publishing

Jean Donaldson   *"Dogs are from Neptune"*, Lasar Multimedia Productions

Jean Donaldson   *"Mine: A Practical Guide to Resource Guarding"*, The San Francisco SPCA

Jean Donaldson   *"The Culture Clash"*, James & Kenneth Publishers

Karen Pryor   *"Don't Shoot the Dog"*, Bantam Publishers

Kay Laurence   *"Clicker Dances with Dogs"* Learning About Dogs Ltd.

Kay Laurence   *"Clicker Foundation Training"* Learning About Dogs Ltd.

Kay Laurence   *"Clicker Novice Training"* Learning About Dogs Ltd.

Kay Laurence   *"Clicker Intermediate Training"* Learning About Dogs Ltd.

Kay Laurence   *"Walk With Me"* Learning About Dogs Ltd.

Leslie McDevitt   *"Control Unleashed"* Clean Run Productions, LLC

Linda Tellington-Jones   *"Getting in TTouch with Your Dog"*, Trafalgar Square Publishing,

Murray Sidman   *"Coercion and its Fallout"*, Authors Cooperative

Pamela J. Reid Ph.D   *"Excel-Erated Learning: Explaining in Plain English How Dogs Learn and How Best to Teach Them"*, James & Kenneth Publishers

Pat Miller   *"The Power of Positive Dog Training"*, Howell Book House,

Patricia B. McConnell Ph.D *"Feisty Fido"*, Dog's Best Friend, Ltd.

Patricia B. McConnell Ph.D *"The Cautious Canine, How to Help Dogs Conquer Their Fears"*, Dog's Best Friend, Ltd.

Patricia McConnell   *"The Other End of the Leash"*, Ballantine Books

Peggy Tillman   *"Clicking With Your Dog"*, Sunshine Books

Pia Silvani & Lynn Echardt *"Raising Puppies & Kids Together"* TFH Publishers

Roger Abrantes Ph.D   *"Dog Language, An Encyclopaedia of Canine Behavior"*, Dogwise Publishing

Roger Abrantes Ph.D   *"The Evolution of Canine Social Behavior"*, Dogwise Publishing

Roy Hunter   *"Fun & Games with Dogs"*, Howln Moon Press

Roy Hunter   *"Fun Nose Work for Dogs"*, Howln Moon Press

Sheila Booth and Dildei Gottfried, *"Schutzhund Obedience: Training in Drive"*, Podium Publications

Sheila Booth   *"Purely Positive Training: Companion to Competition"*, Podium Publications

Suzanne Clothier   *"Bones Would Rain from the Sky"*, Grand Central Publishing

Suzanne Hetts Ph.D   *"Pet Behavior Protocols, What to Say, What to Do, When to Refer"*, American Animal Hospital Assn.

Temple Grandin   *"Animals in Translation"*, Scribner

Turid Rugaas   *"On Talking Terms with Dogs: Calming Signals"*, Legacy By Mail Inc.

Terry Ryan   *"Coaching Peopleto Train Their Dogs"* , Legacy Canine Behavior and Training, Inc.

VIDEOS

Linda Tellington-Jones	"Tellington TTouch, For Happier, Healthier Dog", ASIN 091628915X
Dr. Ian Dunbar	"Dog Aggression: Biting", Ark Features, ASIN B0001LQL9C
Dr. Ian Dunbar	"Dog Aggression: Fighting", Ark Features, ASIN B0001LQL9M
Gary Wilkes	"The Click and Treat Training Kit", "On Target" and "Doggie Repair Kit", Click! & Treat Products
Karen Pryor	"Clicker Magic", Sunshine Books, ASIN 1890948012
Kay Laurence	"Friends for Life", www.learningaboutdogs.com

Suzanne Hetts Ph.D. and Daniel Q. Estep, Ph.D, "Canine Behavior- Body Postures: The Behavioral Healthy Dog" (video sets), Animal Care Training

OTHER PUBLICATIONS

"The Clicker Journal"   A bi-monthly publication for and by trainers using positive reinforcement", 20146 Gleedsville Rd., Leesburg, VA 20175, e-mail cburmaster@aol.com

"Teaching Dogs" Magazine. A bi-monthly publication for all types of training. www.learningaboutdogs.com. Po Box 13, Chipping Campden, Glos. GL55 6WX

INTERNET RESOURCES

Alexandra Kurland	www.clickercenter.com
Gary Wilkes	www.clickandtreat.com
James O'Heare	www.cynologycollege.com
Karen Pryor	www.clickertraining.com
Kay Laurence	www.learningaboutdogs.com
Suzanne Clothier	www.flyingdogpress.com
Susan Garrett	www.clickerdogs.com

Also search for active clicker groups on yahoo.com

EQUIPMENT RESOURCES

Books: www.dogwise.com

Head Halters and Harnesses: www.premier.com

SPECIAL ACKNOWLEDGEMENT

Ted Turner	#1 *"The ABC's of Behavior Shaping and Fundamentals of Training"*
	#2 *"Extinguishing Aggression: Problem Behavior and Proactive Behavior Management"*
Leslie Nelson	Illustrates enlightened techniques for instructing pet obedience classes, behaviour, consultation, problems solving and for instructing the human half of the team.
Patty Ruzzo	Demonstration of training competition obedience using behaviour shaping. Specific focus, attention, heeling, retrieving & handler's ring presentation.

Practical Answers Ted Turner, Leslie Nelson & Patty Ruzzo respond to commonly asked questions.

Appendix C

Forms

YOUR DOG'S HISTORY

Please answer the following questions in detail. If you need more room use additional pages.

Your Name: _____ Phone: Day: _____ Eve: _____ Cell: _____

Address: _____

email: _____

Dog's name: _____ Age: _____ Sex (n/s): _____

Breed/Type: _____

What do you feed your dog? _____

How much and how often do you feed your dog? _____

How long have you owned your dog? _____

Will your dog let you reach for its food bowl or for loose food on the floor? (If not, what does your dog do?)

_____

Can you pat your dog while he is eating? _____

Does your dog play with toys? (Does he play with you or with other dogs or by himself?) _____

_____

Will your dog easily give up a toy? _____

Does your dog play tug of war? _____

Where does your dog sleep? _____

(If he sleeps on your bed or couch, can you get him off without him growling?) _____

If your dog is sleeping or lying in your way, can you ask him to move and he will do it? _____

Does your dog ask to go out and ask to come back, then ask to go out again and ask to come in again - each time without having to urinate or defacate? _____

What kinds of activities do you do with your dog? _____

_____

How much exercise does your dog get daily? _____

_____

How many people live in your home? (Please indicate ages.) _____

_____

_____

_____

Does your dog have problems with only some of the household? _____

_____

Describe the behavioral problem(s) that your dog has:
(Explain fully - include how often the behavior happens and what you think causes it to happen.)

_____

_____

_____

_____

_____

_____

_____

_____

How have you tried to solve your dog's behavioral problems in the past?

_____

_____

**Changing behavior is a slow process.
It will need the consistent support of everyone in your household.**

DOG'S PERSONALITY PROFILE

Date of consultation: _____

Clients Name: _____ Phone: Day: _____ Eve: _____ Cell: _____

Address: _____

email: _____

Dog's name: _____ Age: _____ Sex (n/s): _____

Breed/Type: _____

GENERAL INFORMATION

How did you hear about us? _____

How long have you owned your dog? _____

Where did you get your dog? _____

If adopted, do you have knowledge of your dog's past history? If yes, describe.

_____

_____

Number of people in your household:

Adult males _____ Adult females _____

Male children/ages _____ Female children/ages _____

Does your dog like children? _____

Describe how your dog behaves around children: _____

_____

_____

Is your dog spayed/neutered? _ _ _ _ _ _ _ _   If yes, what age was this done?   _ _ _ _ _ _ _ _ _ _ _

List other animals in your household:

Species	Breed	Neutered	Age	Sex

Describe how your dog gets along with other animals in your household:

_ _

_ _

HEALTH AND GROOMING

Does your dog have a problem with fleas? _

Does your dog have hip dysplasia? _ _ _ _ _

   If yes, what restrictions need to be placed on your dog's activities or movements? _ _ _ _ _ _ _ _ _ _ _ _ _ _

   _

Does your dog have allergies? _

Does your dog like to be brushed? _ _ _ _ _ _ _

   If not, what have you tried to make brushing more enjoyable? _

How often do you brush or comb your dog's coat? _

What kind of brush and/or comb do you use? _

How does your dog react to having his/her nails clipped? _

Does your dog have any sensitive areas on his/her body? _

Where are your dog's favorite petting spots? _

BEHAVIOR

Do visitors bring their dog(s) to your home? _

If yes, how does your dog react? _____

How does your dog react to a stranger coming into your home or yard? _____

_____

Does your dog ever bark or growl at anyone passing outside your home or yard? _____

_____

Are there any kinds of PEOPLE your dog automatically fears or dislikes? _____

Are there any types of DOGS your dog automatically fears or dislikes? _____

How does your dog react to puppies? _____

What does your dog do when you are not at home? _____

How does your dog act when you get home at the end of the day? _____

What does your dog do to show he/she is happy? _____

How does your dog react to other dogs approaching it when you are out on a walk? _____

A. On lead   _____ B. Off lead _____

_____   _____

EXERCISE

How many times per week is your dog walked outside? _____

How long are your walks? _____

Has your dog ever jumped on someone? _____

What were the circumstances? _____

Has your dog ever growled at someone? _____

What were the circumstances? _____

Has your dog ever bitten someone? _____

What were the circumstances? _____

Has your dog ever climbed or jumped over a fence? _

    How high was it? _

Does your dog have any problems in the following areas? If yes, describe:

    Mouthiness _

    Housetraining _

    Barking _

    Digging _

    Ignoring commands _

Is your dog frightened by any noises? _

Is your dog frightened or nervous around anything else? _

Has your dog ever growled or snapped at anyone taking food or toys away? _ _ _ _ _ _ _ _ _ _ _ _ _ _

Has your dog ever shared his/her food or toys with other animals? _ _ _ _ _ _ _ _ _ _ _ _ _ _ _ _ _ _

Does your dog play with any toys? _ _ _ _ _ _

    If yes, what kind of toys does your dog like and what games does he/she play with the toys?

    _

    _

Does your dog play with other dogs? _ _ _ _ _

    What kind of dogs does your dog like to play with? _
_ _

Does your dog prefer to play with male or female dogs? _

What kind of games does your dog play with other dogs? _

What kind of games does your dog play with people? _

TRAINING

Does your dog know any tricks? _____

Has your dog ever been on agility equipment? _____

Has your dog ever had any formal obedience training? _____

    If yes, when and where? _____

What commands does your dog know? _____

_____

_____

Do you walk your dog on your left or right side? _____

What kind of collar do you use when you walk your dog? _____

    Is it effective in keeping him/her under control? _____

Does your dog know any hand commands? _____

Does your dog have a bathroom command? _____

Does your dog have any play commands? _____

Does your dog have a quiet command? _____

What dog food do you use? _____

Other comments or information about your dog that you feel might be helpful:

_____

_____

_____

_____

_____

_____

_____

WAIVER, ASSUMPTION OF RISK,
AND AGREEMENT TO HOLD HARMLESS

I understand that participation in any dog training class is not without risk to myself, members of my family, or guests who may attend, or to my dog, because some of the dogs to which I (we) will be exposed may be difficult to control and may be the cause of injury even when handled with the greatest amount of care.

I hereby waive and release the _____ (Your Name or Business), and any of its employees, trainers, volunteers, owners, and agents from any and all liability of any nature for injury or damage which I or my dog may suffer, including specifically, but not without limitation, any injury or damage which results from the action of any dog, and I expressly assume the risk of any such damage or injury while attending any training class or other function of the _____(Your Name or Business) and its staff or volunteers, or while in the Facility, the grounds of _____(Your Name or Business and/or facility's name) or the surrounding area thereto.

In consideration of and as inducement to the acceptance of my application for training membership in this dog training class, I hereby agree to indemnify and hold harmless the _____ (Your Name or Business and/or the facility's Name) and any of its employees, trainers, volunteers, owners, and agents from any and all claims or claims by any member of my family or any other person accompanying me to any training session or function, or while in or on the grounds or the surrounding area thereto as a result of any action by any dog, including my own.

Signature of Owner or authorized agent (signer must be 18 years of age or older)

Date: _____

Puppy Socialization Chart

Children seen
- Babies (0-2 years)
- Toddlers (2-6 years)
- School age (6-13 years)
- Teenagers (13-17 years)

Preparation for vets/groomer
- Being lifted on to table
- Gentle restraint on table
- Veterinary examination
- Veterinary product smells
- Flea Spray
- Hair dryer

Surfaces to walk on
- Clean grass
- Lino/tiles/slippery surface
- Steps/stairs
- Carpet
- Gravel/stones/pebbles

Experiences
- Watching passing traffic
- Car/van ride
- Park
- Streets
- Bicycles, motorbikes, buses
- Trains
- Countryside
- Towns
- Crowds
- Tasting a variety of foods

Playing with people
- with: a ball
- a tug toy
- a squeaky toy

Types of people seen
- Young adults
- Middle-aged adults
- Elderly people
- Disabled/infirm people/people in wheelchairs
- Loud, confident people
- Shy, timid people
- People wearing hats/helmets
- People wearing glasses
- Men with beards/facial hair
- People in clothing other than uniform
- Postmen/women

Objects to chew
- Nylabone
- Rawhide chew
- Strong toys (eg. Kongs)
- Smoked bones
- Hard biscuit

Other animals
- Friendly adult dogs (no aggressive dogs)
- Cats
- Rabbits/small pets
- Horses
- Goats/sheep
- Fish in tanks
- Chickens

Housetraining
- Taken onto grass after sleep
- Given rewards for going to toilet outside

Learning to be left alone
- Isolation from littermates

Gentle handling
- Head
- Ears
- Mouth
- Neck area
- Tail
- Paws & legs
- 1 minute groom with soft brush
- Collar
- Lead/Gentle leader
- Gentle restraint until accepted
- Car harness
- Reward-based training

Objects to play with (+ toys)
- Cardboard box
- Bucket
- Treat ball
- Large stuffed toy
- Empty plastic bottle

Smells
- Kitchen/household
- Cats
- Baby
- Other dogs
- Veterinary surgery
- Boarding kennels
- Person
- Horses
- Livestock
- Rabbits

Sounds
- Sound tape played

INDEX

INDEX